" The second edition of *Understanding and Supporting Young Writers from Birth to 8* is a truly important contribution to our understanding of writing in early childhood. The chapter authors couple research-based insights about what young children are learning about writing with innovative ideas for supporting young children's joyful participation as writers."

Deborah Wells-Rowe, *Carolyn M. Evertson Professor in Teacher Education, Vanderbilt University, USA*

"This book is a must-read for anyone interested in teaching writing. Grounded in deep and informed understanding of what it means to become a writer, this book situates writing within the context of diverse communities and diverse writing modes, and explores writing development from birth through to middle primary school."

Debra Myhill, *Professor Emerita of Language and Literacy Education, University of Exeter, UK*

"Specialists in early years literacy education bring extensive and varied knowledge and experience to the wide-ranging chapters in this new edition, successfully melding research and practice. The resource is both scholarly and accessible; it contains valuable insights for practitioners and others supporting the development in young writers of this most complex act."

Judy Parr, *Professor Emerita, University of Auckland, New Zealand*

"*Understanding and Supporting Young Writers from Birth to 8* provides us with a comprehensive account of how to best foster children's written expression, accompanied by sage advice to guide our efforts in doing so. I cannot recommend it too highly!"

Peter Afflerbach, *Professor Emeritus, University of Maryland, USA*

T0384856

Understanding and Supporting Young Writers from Birth to 8

Understanding and Supporting Young Writers from Birth to 8 provides practitioners with the knowledge and skills they need to support young children as they learn to write. This fully updated second edition offers new guidance on all aspects of writing, from building children's vocabulary and creating multimodal texts to providing support for children who find writing particularly challenging. All chapters have been revised and updated with increased emphasis on engaging with families and catering for children from diverse communities. A new chapter focuses on the *Draw, Talk, Write, Share* (DTWS) pedagogical approach to teaching writing.

The book discusses the role of oral language in early mark-making and writing in detail and explores the key relationships between "drawing and talking," "drawing and writing," and "drawing, talking, and writing." Each chapter also features practical strategies and samples of writing and/or drawing to illustrate key points, as well as reflective questions to help the reader apply the ideas to their own setting. Further topics covered include:

- progressions in children's writing
- writing in the pre-school years
- developing authorial skills
- developing phonological awareness, phonics, and spelling
- handwriting and keyboarding skills
- teaching writing to plurilingual learners
- assessing writing

Understanding and Supporting Young Writers from Birth to 8 is a contemporary and unique resource that will help early childhood educators, early years schoolteachers, specialist practitioners working with very young children, and students enrolled in Early Childhood or Primary Studies courses to boost their confidence in teaching young learners as they become writers.

Noella M. Mackenzie is an Associate Professor (adjunct) at Charles Sturt University, Australia. She is an experienced literacy educator and researcher. Noella's research, which is largely focused on the learning and teaching of writing, is informed by her ongoing work with classroom teachers and early childhood educators.

Janet Scull is an Associate Professor at Monash University, Australia. She is an experienced tertiary literacy educator with a rich background in practitioner research. Janet's research explores language and literacy acquisition processes and practices that support the continuity of children's learning across early childhood settings and the early years of schooling.

Understanding and Supporting Young Writers from Birth to 8

Second Edition

Edited by Noella M. Mackenzie
and Janet Scull

Routledge
Taylor & Francis Group

LONDON AND NEW YORK

Second edition published 2025
by Routledge
4 Park Square, Milton Park, Abingdon, Oxon, OX14 4RN

and by Routledge
605 Third Avenue, New York, NY 10158

Routledge is an imprint of the Taylor & Francis Group, an informa business

First edition published by Routledge 2018

British Library Cataloguing-in-Publication Data
A catalogue record for this book is available from the British Library

ISBN: 978-1-032-57421-9 (hbk)
ISBN: 978-1-032-57418-9 (pbk)
ISBN: 978-1-003-43926-4 (ebk)

DOI: 10.4324/9781003439264

Typeset in Optima
by SPi Technologies India Pvt Ltd (Straive)

This book is for our youngest mark-makers and writers, and the early childhood educators, teachers and families, who support their learning.

Contents

Foreword

I was delighted to be invited to write the foreword to the 2nd edition of this wonderful resource. This is a significantly revised version of the earlier book, with all chapters updated including the chapters by the two amazing educators and literacy thought leaders; Noella M. Mackenzie and Janet Scull.

I have studied their work and that of many of the other chapter authors for several years and am honored to know and have worked with them in my own research on oral language development. They share their well-researched theories and concepts to inform our understanding of the writing of young children. Since the first edition, much has happened, including COVID, that has significantly impacted literacy learning of which writing is a critical element. As Mackenzie and Scull note, the field has evolved greatly over the last five years and now includes even more multimodal and digital forms of communication. Their unique voices deliver guidance to educators that will truly support them as they work to improve instructional practice. The ideas they suggest range from the need for careful observation of young children, to data gathering and analysis that informs instruction. It is a powerful book that provides clear and very helpful guidance for educators and researchers. They have also included suggestions for working with families in several chapters in this new edition.

In the first chapter, Mackenzie and Scull provide an overview of the research and organization of the book. In discussing the goals of the book, they state: "The first focus is on early writing as a process that integrates children's language experiences and rich contexts for learning" (Mackenzie & Scull, Chapter 1).

As I read the messages shared by Mackenzie and Scull and the other authors, I kept thinking about how young children use language in various forms to communicate. One place they go deeper with this work is in the 2nd chapter, which absorbed the former 5th chapter, and expanded the very helpful case study examples. A big shift is seen in the new 3rd chapter by Keary and McFarland focusing deeply on development from birth to age 2. In Chapter 4, Raban expands on the learning in the preschool context. Reading the different chapters, I was reminded of the early literacy research of Marie Clay:

> When we speak or when we listen to speech, we are constructing and composing. When we write down a phrase, message or story, we are constructing and composing. When we read what someone else has written, we are constructing and composing. These three activities draw upon language knowledge in similar ways.
>
> (2016, pp. 78–79)

Throughout the early chapters a strong case is made for the recognition of mark-making and drawing as an important symbolic meaning-making process, along with encouragement for teaching children to continue to draw long after they have started to write using conventional written text forms. This sets the scene for Chapter 10 by Mackenzie which is totally new; the focus on Draw, Talk, Write and Share (DTWS) deepens the concept of the depth and breadth of what writing is, develops the second focus on the complexity of the writing process, and addresses the array of interrelated skills that are associated with learning to write. This alone is a significant discussion and will be very helpful to teachers as they consider the implications of the many overlaps in the overall process of early writing. In Chapter 11, Kervin and Mantei expand the notion of multimodality and the sharing of stories in digital spaces in the home and school.

Later chapters examine the writing process and how pedagogy must connect oral language and writing instruction. This related to my own work over the last decade in academic language and the interrelationship of language and writing. In another key chapter, Scull discusses assessment in early writing from the perspective of what supportive practices are possible. Scull reiterates other work she has done with Mackenzie, and says, "it is important not to read milestone achievements as a staged, sequenced approach to learning" (Scull, 2018, Chapter 8 in this volume). In Chapter 6, Daffern explores the complexities of English spelling and provides practical support for teachers around orthography, phonology, and morphology while Mackenzie and Spokes clarify some of the contemporary issues associated with transcription skills and writing in Chapter 7.

The authors develop a third area of focus in the book: the recognition of the need for explicit teaching and systematic interventions to address the achievement gap in writing. This is a new way of looking at interventions and is critically important. In Chapter 12, Molyneux expands our understanding of how to support plurilingualism in young writers, and in Chapter 13, Thompson and Scull focus on how, when learning to write, children need to learn to plan, compose, and record their ideas. They make the point that each aspect of the process requires deliberate attention and draws across discrete skill sets.

Once again, a number of the chapters were contributed by key voices in the field. Mackenzie and Scull have brought together the most current thinking and research and then applied these theories to classroom practice. This work will inform literacy instruction for a long time to come and contribute to changing the understanding of writing instruction within Early Childhood and Early Years settings.

This book is focused not only on what happens as children are learning to draw and write, and how to support children, but also how we, as educators, learn in the midst of curriculum requirements, pedagogical shifts, and the realities of school in our various systems across the globe. The authors have highlighted the importance of transfer and the need for educators to understand *"the why,"* or the theory of learning, in order to implement *"the how"* of effective practice, and then *"the what"* of curricular resources.

Written by researchers and educators who are practitioners working in schools and with teachers in professional learning communities, as well as families, this book provides many ways to understand and support learning with young children. Children are always at the heart of the authors' work and the focus on our youngest learners will enable children to make remarkable gains in writing and ways to communicate their thinking. I am so pleased that Mackenzie, Scull, and all the other authors came together to share their work in this valuable book.

by Adria F. Klein Ph.D., Professor Emerita
California State University San Bernardino

Reference

Clay, M.M. (2016). *Literacy lessons designed for individuals* (2nd ed.). Heinemann.

Acknowledgements

We recognise and acknowledge the efforts of the many early childhood educators and teachers, who despite working tirelessly for the betterment of the children they teach, found time to contribute to the many research projects that informed this book. Thank you for making us welcome in your preschools and schools, and for sharing your stories, and your ways of thinking about early drawing and writing. We thank the children, and their families, who allowed us into their homes, challenged our understanding of how different children learn to draw and write, and shared the many ways drawing and writing are supported in the home. We also acknowledge and thank the children, early childhood educators, and early years teachers who generously shared their photos, drawings, and writing samples, and allowed us to use these. The book is richer for their inclusion.

About the editors

Noella M. Mackenzie is an experienced literacy educator and researcher. Her career began in schools teaching children from 5 to 12 years. Noella spent 13 years as a literacy specialist working with teachers in literacy early intervention and special education before moving to Charles Sturt university, where she taught undergraduate and postgraduate students. Noella's research has largely focused on teachers and the learning and teaching of writing and is informed by her ongoing work with classroom teachers. She has co-edited 3 books, and authored 26 book chapters, 31 refereed research papers, and 9 professional articles. Noella is currently an Associate Professor (adjunct) at Charles Sturt University, NSW, Australia.

Janet Scull is an experienced tertiary literacy educator with a rich background in practitioner research. Her research focuses on language acquisition, literacy teaching and assessment, and teaching practices that support the continuity of children learning across early childhood settings and the early years of schooling. Janet has also contributed to the design, implementation and evaluation of approaches to early literacy teaching, for students from a range of culturally and linguistically diverse backgrounds. She is currently an Associate Professor at Monash University, coordinating language and literacy subjects in teacher education undergraduate and postgraduate degree programs.

About the contributors

Tessa Daffern (PhD) is an Adjunct Associate Professor at the LaTrobe University, Australia. She has contributed to education in various capacities for more than 20 years: as a classroom teacher, teaching and learning specialist, academic, literacy education consultant, and curriculum advisor. Tessa's award-winning research focusses on written language conventions, with a specific focus on spelling, and has disseminated her work through journals, books, conferences, and multimedia platforms. Tessa regularly works with teachers across Australia and overseas for professional development in spelling, writing, and reading.

Anne Keary is an Associate Professor with the Faculty of Education, Monash University. She is an experienced educator who has taught across the early childhood, school, and higher education sectors. Anne's research, teaching and engagement work enhances the provision of socially just education in diverse linguistic and cultural educational settings. She has a particular interest in language and play and intergenerational family practices.

Lisa Kervin is Professor in Education in the Faculty of the Arts, Social Sciences and Humanities at the University of Wollongong, where she is also Director of Early Start Research. Lisa has been researching in literacy education, play theory, and digital technologies using qualitative and mixed methods for more than 20 years. She has published more than 70 papers in peer-reviewed journals and 40 book chapters in areas of education, social sciences, and technology. In 2020 Lisa was a successful Chief Investigator in the seven-year ARC Centre of Excellence for the Digital Child, where she co-leads the national "Educated Child" program of research and leads the UOW Children's Technology Play Space.

Jessica Mantei is Associate Professor in Language and Literacy in the Faculty of the Arts, Humanities and Social Sciences at the University of Wollongong. Jessica is a researcher in UOW's Early Start facility and an Associate Investigator in the ARC Centre of Excellence for the Digital Child. Jessica's research interests include flexible literacy learning environments, pedagogies for literacy learning, teacher professional identity, and the development of young children's language and literacy proficiencies within and beyond school.

Laura McFarland is a Research Fellow at the Research in Effective Education in Early Childhood Centre (REEaCh) at The University of Melbourne. Laura has worked in the early childhood education field for more than 20 years in a variety of roles including early childhood teaching, family support, consulting, and university teaching and research. Laura's research focuses on supporting quality relationships amongst children, families, and educators, in order to provide the best outcomes for children. Laura's research also recognises the importance of high-quality early childhood education settings and educator-child interactions in contributing to children's learning and development.

Paul Molyneux is an Honorary Senior Fellow in the Faculty of Education at The University of Melbourne. He has taught and coordinated subjects across a suite of postgraduate and pre-service courses particularly in primary school languages and literacy education. In addition, his research output and supervision centres on the transformative potential of plurilingual pedagogies and place-based education for immigrant, refugee-background, and marginalised learners. A former primary school teacher himself, he led a longitudinal research project that evaluated innovative bilingual teaching and learning in the Karen language alongside English.

Marian Nicolazzo is currently a Lecturer in Language and Literacy Education in the Melbourne Graduate School of Education, University of Melbourne. She is a highly experienced language and literacy teacher and teacher educator. As a consultant and literacy coach, Marian has worked with teachers, literacy leaders, and school principals in both primary and secondary schools across government, Catholic, and independent sectors in Australia. She is particularly interested in using functional grammar to teach writing.

Bridie Raban is Honorary Professor of Education at the University of Melbourne Faculty of Education. Her teaching and research has focussed on early years language and literacy development, and Bridie continues to publish in that area extensively. More recently she was Professor of Early Childhood at Hong Kong Baptist University and was awarded an Honorary University Fellowship in 2021.

Rebecca Spokes is an occupational therapist who worked as a private therapist and business owner within the private paediatric setting. Rebecca primarily worked within the education setting supporting children with handwriting difficulties, specific learning difficulties, executive dysfunction, and physical disability. Whilst supporting students,

Rebecca also worked collaboratively with educators across early education, schools and with Charles Sturt University to bring together the knowledge from occupational therapy and education in the areas of handwriting and written expressions.

Natalie Thompson is a Lecturer in Education in the Faculty of Arts and Education at Charles Sturt University. Her teaching and research interests lie in the areas of literacies, inclusive education, and critical pedagogies. She is currently researching and writing about inclusive writing pedagogies, sociomaterial accounts of literacies, and the changing nature of teacher education, amid complex and competing educational quandaries.

Introduction to *Understanding and Supporting Young Writers from Birth to 8*

Noella M. Mackenzie and Janet Scull

A great deal has happened in the world since the first edition of this book was published in 2018. COVID-19, which was identified in late 2019, quickly spread across the globe, and impacted people's lives in numerous ways. For preschool children, early learning and care was disrupted; for some this was cancelled, for others learning moved online, with parents and caregivers mediating and facilitating children's education at home. Similarly, for school-aged children, *in person school routines* were replaced with *remotely delivered online or hybrid instruction* for months at a time, over a two-year period. While the short-term impacts of the pandemic on school-aged children were considerable, Giorgio Di et al. (2020) have also predicted long-term negative consequences. Reimers (2021) suggests that the pandemic limited student opportunity for interactions with peers and teachers and for individualized attention—decreasing student engagement, participation, and learning—while augmenting the amount of at-home work which, combined with greater responsibilities and disruptions, diminished learning time while increasing stress and anxiety, and for some students, aggravated mental health challenges. Skar et al. (2022) examined the learning of grade 1 students in Norway, "comparing the quality of writing, handwriting fluency, and attitude toward writing" (p. 1553) during the pandemic with those of children from the same schools the year before. They found that scores were lower for children attending grade 1 during the pandemic (Skar et al., 2022, p. 1553). Graham et al. (2023) examined the teaching of writing in middle and high school classrooms in the United States during the pandemic and found that teachers devoted very little time to writing when designing their online and hybrid lessons.

Literacy, of which writing is a critical element, along with numeracy and socio-emotional skills, is listed by UNICEF as fundamental to "all other learning, knowledge and higher-order skills that children and youth need to attain" (UNICEF, 2023, p. 1). Becoming literate is a child's right and expectation, although the process is enacted to different degrees and in different ways in different parts of the world. While oral

DOI: 10.4324/9781003439264-1

language provides the basis of all literacy learning, for many young children, early drawing and writing experiences are symbolic of commencing their journey towards becoming literate. The first texts they create build their awareness of the ways marks, signs, and symbols communicate messages to others. Children learn how messages are represented and communicated in a literate world, across time, and space, and in a range of forms, including visual images and print, alongside digital and multimodal texts. They see adults in their world communicating in these ways and want to join in, drawing on a range of semiotic codes and resources for text production to create meaning for themselves and to be shared by others. Even for adult writers, "working or living with others who write invites cognizance about other people's writing processes and the conditions in which they write" (Brandt, 2015, p. 15). That means children should see how writing is relevant to their current and future lives (Vygotsky, 1978, p. 118) and as such "must assume a niche in the symbolic repertoire of a particular sociocultural group, including those consisting of children" (Dyson, 2016, p. 5).

Policies and research concerning literacy have largely neglected the role of writing in literacy development, instead focusing almost exclusively on oral language development (Kendeou, van den Broek, White & Lynch, 2009), reading, and resources to support these areas (Hempenstall & Buckingham, 2016; Konza, 2014). The Science of Reading lobby has, in recent times, strengthened the central place of reading and phonics in some school curricula (Compton-Lilly et al., 2020). This emphasis on reading and phonics has recently been demonstrated in the *Improving Outcomes for All: The Report of the Independent Expert Panel's Review to Inform a Better and Fairer Education System* (O'Brien et al., 2023) in Australia. A search of the report finds the word *reading* used 56 times, and *phonics* 65 times, while *writing* appears only 11 times (and on each occasion is linked with reading and/or numeracy), and *oral language* only three times (O'Brien et al., 2023). However, despite this, we continue to argue for a greater focus on writing, including a need to re-imagine what young children are learning about writing with traditional and digital technologies and to examine how educators support children's progressions and continuity in early writing as they develop over the first eight years of their lives.

Central to our understanding of the growing primacy of writing is the work of Brandt (2015, 2019). Writing has always been used, according to Brandt (2015), for work purposes, but writing itself is increasingly becoming "the product that is bought and sold, as it embodies knowledge, information, invention, service, social relations, news – that is, the products of the new economy" (p. 16). What Brandt's work has highlighted is the central role of writing in the current era and an increased need to develop high-level writing skills to actively participate with the new technologies. Brandt (2019) questions why writing remains subordinate to reading in literacy education, given that more people are expected to write "at work, at school and in civil and social spheres" (p. 36). In recent times, Brandt has referred to writing as a craft that "develops in association with vocation, ambition, publicity, guild membership, and, most critically, apprenticeship to a master craftsperson" (2019, p. 37). We would argue that teachers should see themselves as the master craftspeople, who are teaching the world's newest writing apprentices.

Dramatic changes in literacy practices, developing technologies and new economies have "impacted directly on what literacy is seen to be, what can and should be included in literacy curriculum, and how literacy pedagogy should be organized, delivered and assessed" (Lo Bianco, 2016, p. v). Reflected in these contextual realities, literacy is now recognised as a priority learning area in early years curricula and referenced in curriculum frameworks (Australian Government Department of Education, AGDE, 2022). In Australia, Early Childhood (EC) educators are advised to develop children's "capacity, confidence and disposition to use language in all its forms" (AGDE, 2022, p. 57). Specifically with regard to early mark-making and writing, the Early Years Learning Framework (EYLF) states that children should have opportunities to "experiment with ways of expressing ideas and meaning using a range of media and begin to use images and approximations of letters and words to convey meaning" (AGDE, 2022, p. 61). School-based curriculum has also been revised with a renewed emphasis on language and literacy (Australian Curriculum Australian Curriculum, Assessment and Reporting Authority, ACARA, 2023). The teaching of language has a clear focus on expressing and developing ideas while the literacy strand intends to expand students' repertoires of English use, including the creation of written and multimodal texts that entertain, inform, and persuade readers.

Curriculum innovation and professional expectation exerts their own pressures on EC educators' and early years (EY) teachers' engagement with language and writing and leads to a range of pedagogical responses. Recent policy and curriculum reform has legitimised the discussion of literacy in preschools and has challenged EC educators to address the teaching of early writing, embedded within rich and meaningful pedagogies (Raban & Scull, 2023). Similarly, for teachers in primary schools, opportunities exist for teacher learning and professional collaborations that enable teachers to review the teaching of writing, building component skills while emphasising the pleasures of writing as a meaning-making process (Lyons & Scull, 2023; Mantei et al., 2022).

The increasing range "of representational forms that are becoming increasingly significant in the overall communications environment" (New London Group, 2000, p. 9) affords us further opportunities to reconceptualise writing for young learners. Digital media are now part of children's everyday activities (Flewitt & Clark, 2020) with the "repertoire of literacy practices needed to engage with contemporary texts continuing to increase exponentially, transforming reading and other textual engagements" (Laidlaw & Wong, 2016, p. 31). Current and evolving literacies and literate practices require EC educators and EY teachers to be cognisant of the multimodal and digital modes of communication young children use, and to become familiar with new pedagogies for teaching writing.

Our goal was to create a book that would help readers to respond to and engage in the debates and discussions of contemporary issues related to writing and young children. To support this goal, the book is organised around a number of key areas and brings together a range of approaches and pedagogies for writing. In designing this second edition, we took note of reviewers' comments as well as feedback from our readers. Each chapter has been updated, and in one case a new chapter has been added, while two chapters from the previous edition were combined. If you are familiar with the first edition, you will find a stronger reference to diverse communities and families across this edition, with many chapters including a section on families or providing suggestions for working with families at the end of the chapter. Where we thought it would be helpful, we have added a short glossary to the end of some chapters, and carefully considered our use of acronyms.

The first focus of this book is early writing as a process that integrates children's language experiences and rich contexts for learning. Learning about writing occurs before children start school, yet few studies of writing have included very young children and those in preschool (Puranik et al., 2018). Children develop their literacy skills as they construct and interpret meaningful spoken, drawn, painted, written, and multimodal texts. While oral language provides the starting point for literacy development and reading is sometimes seen as providing the scaffold for writing, in this book we switch this relationship around to focus on writing as a support for reading. Brandt (2015) argues that reading is increasingly occurring "within acts of writing" (p. 13), while Turbill and Bean (2006) suggest that reading and writing are both acts of composing (p. 14). To read is to interpret the words (and perhaps images) that have been created by an author (writer) for a particular purpose. A reader will always interpret the text through their own eyes and experiences, creating their own meanings as they engage with the text. Some of those meanings may have been intended by the author while others may be personal to the reader and quite idiosyncratic. The authors of Chapters 2, 3, and 4 examine children's early mark-making and writing, and address the continuity in children's learning to ensure a clear articulation of practices as children transition from home to preschool and to school. In Chapter 2, Mackenzie illustrates the drawing and writing journey of young children with illustrations of the progression from *sign creation* (drawing) to *sign use* (conventional written text). There is no suggestion that the process is a linear, step-by-step process that will be experienced by all children in the same ways. A strong case for the recognition of drawing as an important symbolic meaning-making process is made, with encouragement for teaching children to continue to draw long after they have started to write using conventional written text forms. Mackenzie also discusses two overlapping transitions; one is the transition from preschool to school, and the second is the transition from drawing to conventional written language. Consideration is given to the impact these transitions may have on diverse learners with different needs. Questions are raised about the 4–6-year-old group that are shared by preschools and schools in Australia. An appendix that provides drawing and writing milestones has been included in Chapter 2. Keary and McFarland open up the *writing* conversation to include children from birth to age 2 in Chapter 3. Illustrations of very young children's exploration of mark-making provide evidence of children's eagerness to engage with written meaning-making, as they develop trusting relationships with adults and engage in symbolic representations through drawing and play. In Chapter 4, Raban takes us into the preschool setting, sharing evidence of children's experimentation and educators' methods for supporting early writing to help children experience the permanency and purpose of writing.

The second focus area of the book examines the complexity of the writing process and addresses the array of interrelated skills that are associated with learning to write. To write is to create a text for a particular purpose, for example, a list of words, a poem, a sentence, a paragraph, a recipe, report, narrative, a book, or a multimodal electronic story. Usually, a text is written for one or more readers. Writing is also associated with "thinking," as to write we must sort our thoughts and ideas into a shape that may be understood by others, although reflective writing is sometimes intended for an audience of one – the writer. A writer reads as they write, going back and forth across their text as well as re-visiting the text as they draft and re-draft. The number of times an author will re-read and re-draft a text will depend upon the purpose and audience. For example, a letter to a friend may be a single draft and the author may not read the letter before sending it, but a letter to a politician or an important client may be read and re-read as it is drafted and re-drafted, to remove potential ambiguities. Throughout the book, the key principle for practice is to teach the component skills of writing *as children write*, avoiding isolated skill development.

The process of constructing texts is elaborated in Chapters 5–7. Each of these chapters explores aspects of the writing process and illustrates the progressions in children's learning as they produce more complex texts for a wide range of purposes and audiences. Writing as an expressive language skill with its basis in oral language is the focus of Chapter 5. In this chapter, Scull and Mackenzie explore the authorial aspect of writing and illustrate how children's early writing develops from a familiarity with the functions, forms, and features of oral language. The authors suggest the need for an early years literacy pedagogy that integrates oral language and writing instruction, with opportunities for children to master the more intricate forms of language commensurate with the complexity of written discourse (Myhill 2009). This presents a challenge for EC educators and EY teachers as it requires a deep knowledge of language acquisition and developmental processes but also knowledge of how oral language skills are importantly yet differentially related to written text forms (Derewianka, 2022; Spencer & Petersen, 2018).

Secretarial, or transcription, skills are also examined as critical to the process of constructing texts. In Chapter 6, Daffern's focus is on how young children learn to use phonological, morphological, and orthographic knowledge when spelling (Daffern & Fleet, 2021). Children's approximations towards conventional spelling are discussed in the context of text construction. The need for children to have the skills to efficiently record their messages on paper using handwriting tools, or a screen using computer keyboards, is discussed by Mackenzie and Spokes in Chapter 7. A case is made for the explicit teaching of both handwriting and keyboarding skills, preparing children to be *hybrid writers* (Malpique et al., 2023) who can choose the appropriate tools for the purpose and audience of a text. It is also argued that these skills should be taught within the context of writing authentic texts.

In Chapters 8, 9, 10, and 11, practices for assessing and teaching writing are shared and explained. In Chapter 8, Scull explores writing assessment through the application of an analysis tool designed to recognise both the authorial and secretarial/editorial dimensions of writing. The tool, which was an outcome of a research project that examined children's writing samples (Mackenzie, Scull & Munsie, 2013), has been used to explore the shifts in children's writing over time (Mackenzie, Scull & Bowles, 2015) and has proven to be a useful tool for teachers (Mackenzie & Scull, 2016). Scull applies the tool in ways that help to identify what writers already know about writing and what they would benefit from learning next. In Chapter 9, Nicolazzo and Mackenzie focus on pedagogical approaches to the teaching of writing in the early years of school. They pay particular attention to the *Shifting Levels of Support Cycle, Interactive Writing* and *Mentor Texts* as powerful strategies for teachers. Examples are provided as a means to illustrate the teaching strategies. In Chapter 10, Mackenzie introduces the reader to a pedagogical approach that she has called *Draw, Talk, Write and Share* (DTWS) (Mackenzie, 2022). DTWS is supported by research that has explored the relationship between talking, drawing, and early writing conducted by the author (Mackenzie, 2011; Mackenzie & Veresov, 2013). In Chapter 11, Kervin and Mantei explore the opportunities digital technologies offer to children as they create multimodal stories in their home, school, and digital spaces. Using examples from research, they discuss ways that children can be supported to create and share written texts created using digital technologies.

The third area of focus for the book is the recognition of the need for explicit and systematic teaching to meet the diverse learning needs of students. Chapter 12 explores writing practices shaped in response to the needs of plurilingual children. In this chapter, Molyneux makes clear that when students' existing literacy and cultural resources are understood, affirmed, and extended, they provide a foundation upon which English language and literacy skills can be developed. In Chapter 13, Thompson and Scull review the many different reasons why some children find learning to write more challenging with an acknowledgement that the fresh start may first require a teacher to take a *renewed look* at what a child can already do in terms of writing. The importance of teacher observations to supplement assessment data is highlighted in the chapter. The authors also consider aspects of the writing process as the structure for a discussion of how to provide additional support for children experiencing difficulties.

Dyson (2016) suggests that writing is "a window to societies' ways of socialising children into literacy through schooling" (p. 4), arguing that as a symbolic tool, writing provides potential insights into experienced childhoods. The chapters that follow are all informed by research conducted by their authors and are based on close observations of children and understandings of the experiences of young writers. There are 13 chapters in the book; each is designed to stand alone, although they are also complementary of one another. Each chapter includes a number of reflection prompts designed as opportunities for a reader to step outside a chapter and reflect on their own context or experiences before continuing to read. A number of recommended readings are provided at the end of each chapter, followed by a list of references that pertain to the particular chapter. Some chapters have appendices and most have glossaries for further clarity. In all, this volume is designed to help early childhood educators and early years teachers to reflect on their practice and provide positive opportunities for children learning to write.

References

Australian Curriculum, Assessment and Reporting Authority (ACARA) (2023). English Curriculum: version 9.0. https://v9.australiancurriculum.edu.au

Australian Government Department of Education [AGDE] (2022). *Belonging, Being and Becoming: The Early Years Learning Framework for Australia (V2.0)*. https://www.acecqa.gov.au/sites/default/files/2023-01/Belonging_Being_And_Becoming_V2.0.pdf

Brandt, D. (2015). *The Rise of Writing: Redefining Mass Literacy*. Cambridge, UK: Cambridge University Press.

Brandt, D. (2019). The problem of writing in mass education. *Utbildning och demokrati, 28*(2), 37–53. https://doi.org/10.48059/uod.v28i2.1120

Compton-Lilly, C. F., Mitra, A., Guay, M., & Spence, L. K. (2020). A confluence of complexity: Intersections among reading theory, neuroscience, and observations of young readers. *Reading Research Quarterly, 55*, S185–S195.

Daffern, T., & Fleet, R. (2021). Investigating the efficacy of using error analysis data to inform explicit teaching of spelling. *Australian Journal of Learning Difficulties, 26*(1), 67–88. https://doi.org/10.1080/19404158.2021.1881574

Derewianka, B. (2022). *A New Grammar Companion for Teachers* (3rd. ed). Marrickville, NSW: Primary English Teaching Association.

Dyson, A. H. (2016). *Child Cultures, Schooling, and Literacy: Global Perspectives on Composing Unique Lives*. New York: Taylor & Francis.

Flewitt, R., & Clark, A. (2020). Porous boundaries: Reconceptualising the home literacy environment as a digitally networked space for 0–3 year olds. *Journal of Early Childhood Literacy, 20*(3), 447–471. https://doi.org/10.1177/1468798420938116

Giorgio Di, P., Biagi, F., Costa, P., Karpinski, Z., & Mazza, J. (2020). *The likely impact of COVID-19 on education: Reflections based on the existing literature and recent international datasets*. Federal Reserve Bank of St Louis.

Graham, S., Huebner, A., Skar, G. B., Azani, J., & Weinberg, P. (2023). Teaching writing during the COVID-19 pandemic in the 2021–2022 school year. *Reading & Writing*. https://doi.org/10.1007/s11145-023-10457-9

Hempenstall, K., & Buckingham J. (Ed.). (2016). *Read About It: Scientific Evidence for the Effective Teaching of Reading, CIS Research Report 11*. St. Leonards, NSW: Centre for Independent Studies.

Kendeou, P., van den Broek, P., White, M. J., & Lynch, J. S. (2009). Predicting reading comprehension in early elementary school: The independent contributions of oral language and decoding skills. *Journal of Educational Psychology*, *101*(4), 765–778.

Konza, D. (2014). Teaching reading: Why the 'Fab Five' should be the 'Big Six'. *Australian Journal of Teacher Education*, *39*(12), 153–169.

Laidlaw, L., & Wong, S. S. (2016). Literacy and complexity: On using technology within emergent learning structures with young learners. *Complicity: An International Journal of Complexity and Education*, *13*(1), 30–42.

Lo Bianco, J. (2016). Understanding growing up literate. In J. Scull & B. Raban (Eds.), *Growing up Literate: Australian Early Literacy Research* (pp. iii–vi). Prahran, VIC: Eleanor Curtain Publishing.

Lyons, D., & Scull, J. (2023). Narrative inquiry: Critiquing narrative inquiry's epistemological pillars within a large-scale study into the teaching of phonics. *International Journal of Research & Method in Education*. https://doi.org/10.1080/1743727X.2023.2196066

Mackenzie, N. M. (2011). From drawing to writing: What happens when you shift teaching priorities in the first six months of school? *Australian Journal of Language and Literacy*, *34*(3), 322–340.

Mackenzie, N. M., & Scull, J. (2016). Writing analysis: Using the electronic analysis tool. *Practical Literacy: The Early and Primary Years*, *20*(2), 35–38.

Mackenzie, N. M. (2022). Multimodal text creation from day 1 with Draw, Talk, Write, *Share. The California Reader (TCR)* 55(1), 9–14.

Mackenzie, N. M., Scull J., & Bowles, T. (2015). Writing over time: An analysis of texts created by Year One students. *Australian Educational Researcher*, *42*(5), 568–593. doi.org/10.1007/s13384-015-0189-9

Mackenzie, N. M., Scull, J., & Munsie, L. (2013). Analysing writing: The development of a tool for use in the early years of schooling. *Issues in Educational Research*, *23*(3), 375–391.

Mackenzie, N. M., & Veresov, N. (2013). How drawing can support writing acquisition: text construction in early writing from a Vygotskian perspective. *Australasian Journal of Early Childhood*, *38*(4), 22–29.

Malpique, A. A., Valcan, D., Pino-Pasternak, D., Ledger, S., & Kelso-Marsh, B. (2023). Shaping young children's handwriting and keyboarding performance: Individual and contextual-level factors. *Issues in Educational Research*, *33*(4), 1441–1460.

Mantei, J., Kervin, L., & Jones, P. (2022). Examining pedagogies for teaching phonics: lessons from early childhood classrooms. *The Australian Educational Researcher*, *49*(4), 743–760. https://doi.org/10.1007/s13384-021-00454-8

Myhill, D. (2009). Becoming a designer. In R. Beard, D. Myhill, J. Riley & M. Nystrand (Eds.), *The sage handbook of writing development* (pp. 402–414). Los Angeles: SAGE.

New London Group. (2000). A pedagogy of multiliteracies designing social futures. In B. Cope & M. Kalantzis (Eds.), *Multiliteracies: Literacy Learning and the Design of Social Futures* (pp. 9–38). London: Routledge.

O'Brien, L., Paul, L., Anderson, D., Hunter, J., Lamb, S., & Sahlberg, P. (2023). *Improving Outcomes for All: The Report of the Independent Expert Panel's Review to Inform a Better and Fairer Education System*. The Education Department.

Puranik, C. S., Phillips, B. M., Lonigan, C. J., & Gibson, E. (2018). Home literacy practices and preschool children's emergent writing skills: An initial investigation. *Early Childhood Research Quarterly*, *42*, 228–238. https://doi.org/10.1016/j.ecresq.2017.10.004

Raban, B., & Scull, J. (2023). Literacy. In D. Pendergast & S. Garvis (Eds.), *Teaching Early Years: Curriculum, Pedagogy and Assessment* (2nd ed., pp. 35–48). London: Routledge.

Reimers, F. M. (2021). Learning from a Pandemic. The Impact of COVID-19 on Education Around the World. In F. M. Reimers (Ed.), *Primary and secondary education during covid-19: Disruptions to educational opportunity during a pandemic.* (pp. 1–37). Springer International Publishing, AG. https://doi.org/10.1007/978-3-030-81500-4_1

Skar, G. B. U., Graham, S., & Huebner, A. (2022). Learning Loss During the COVID-19 Pandemic and the Impact of Emergency Remote Instruction on First Grade Students' Writing: A Natural Experiment. *Journal of Educational Psychology, 114*(7), 1553–1566. https://doi.org/10.1037/edu0000701

Spencer, T. D., & Petersen, D. B. (2018). Bridging oral and written language: An oral narrative language intervention study with writing outcomes. *Language, speech & hearing services in schools, 49*(3), 569–581. https://doi.org/10.1044/2018_LSHSS-17-0030

Turbill, J., & Bean, W. (2006). *Writing Instruction K-6: Understanding Process, Purpose, Audience.* Katonah, NY: Richard C. Owen Publishers.

UNICEF, (2023). Tracking progress on foundational learning 2023. https://www.unicef.org/media/144156/file/Tracking%20progress%20on%20foundational%20learning%202023.pdf

Vygotsky, L. S. (1978). *Mind in Society: The Development of Higher Psychological Processes.* Cambridge, MA: Harvard University Press.

2 Drawing and writing

Journeys, transitions, and milestones

Noella M. Mackenzie

Introduction

In this chapter, I explore children's drawing and writing journeys, discuss some of the transitions experienced by children as they learn to draw and write, and touch on some of the milestones that demonstrate their learning. In Section 1, I begin with children's first scribbles marks, early drawings, and tentative explorations of written language, and finish with exemplars from young writers in the early years of school. One child's journey from age 3 to 7 is used as a case study, although samples from other children are also included to illustrate children's learning progressions. Milestones help illustrate the journeys experienced by children as they explore mark-making. In Section 2 I move on to a discussion of transitions. The term *transition* is often associated with children starting school, although humans experience transitions every day across their lifetime. A change of career may create a snowball effect leading to a number of transitions – for example, new job, new location, new colleagues, and so forth. However, in this chapter I restrict my focus to the overlapping transitions of *starting school* and *learning to write*. Prompts, to aid reflection, are included throughout the chapter, and suggestions for families follow the conclusion. An appendix, summarising children's text creation milestones, completes the chapter.

Section 1: Drawing and writing journeys

Some people look for a linear explanation of learning to write, where children begin with scribbles and then move to role-play writing and invented spelling followed by conventional use of written language. However, experience and research provide

DOI: 10.4324/9781003439264-2

evidence of writing developing spontaneously and simultaneously at many levels, with print only one of a repertoire of symbolic representations explored along the way (Genishi & Dyson, 2009). However, possible milestones or events can suggest advancement in knowledge or evidence of a new way a child engages with the writing process (Mackenzie & Scull, 2015). No two children are expected to travel the same writing journey or necessarily experience all the milestones in the order described in the appendix. Proficient writing (and reading) can be achieved by following different paths to common outcomes (Clay, 2014).

I'm watching you

Learning about writing and text creation starts well before children start preschool or school as they notice what is going on around them. They see people with pens and paper as well as electronic devices. They watch as messages are created, received, and interpreted. They are keen to copy. In Figure 2.1, we can see a young child, just 6 months old, sitting in his walker. We can see how alert he is, and can only imagine how much he is taking in.

In Figure 2.2, the same child is 15 months old. While he rides his bike he plays with an old "hands free" phone. He regularly engages in telephone conversations, copying his parents. Similarly, if we want children to want to write, they need to see the adults and older children in their world engaged in writing, and we must provide them with resources and encouragement to join in.

Figure 2.1   Watching and learning

Figure 2.2   Copying behaviour

Reflection prompt

How do you model writing behaviour to the young children in your context?

This looks like fun

Between 1 and 2 years of age, most children enjoy using a range of writing implements (e.g., pens, pencils, crayons) as well as electronic devices (e.g., phones and tablets) if they are accessible. They may also improvise using tools not designed for writing (e.g., lipstick) in ways that may not be appropriate (e.g., drawing on walls). While many adults will see this early experimentation as a signal to provide opportunities for supervised experimentation, others remove the tools from the child's reach. How the child moves forward at this point is in the hands of the adults in their world, unless they have access to tools belonging to older siblings or writing materials at childcare.

Learning to talk

Talk is important for learning to write, as talking promotes control over the grammatical structures of spoken language and vocabulary development, both of which are predictors of success with early writing (Mackenzie & Hemmings, 2014). When children begin to talk, we see evidence of their learning in approximations of standard forms of expression. For example, they approximate pronunciation, overgeneralise or confuse tenses, use incorrect or immature grammar, and sometimes make inappropriate word choices. The adults or more experienced language users in their world usually value children's attempts, respond to their intended meanings and often model the correct forms. Adults are often excited by children's close attempts, rather than worried about their mistakes. Consider the following "conversation":

Baby: da da da da da

Father: Did "baby" just say dad? Wow, "baby" can say "dad" – did you hear that? Isn't he clever?

Baby: da da da da da

Father: Clever "baby" – dad dad dad dad

The father provides a response to the child that indicates that he "understands" what the baby is saying and he engages the baby in a "conversation." With this kind of supportive interaction, the *da da da da* will in time be replaced by *dad dad dad* and "baby" may soon realise the connection between the sounds he is making and this person who is so special to him. The father does not correct the baby, but rather he provides a model for how to say the word he thinks he is trying to say.

Here is another example with two conversations. In the first conversation the child is 18 months old.

Child: Dink? Dink?

Mother: Would you like a *drink* darling? Of course, you can have a *drink* (accentuated pronunciation of drink). [The child is given a drink.]

Imagine if the same child asks in the same way when she is 2½–3 years of age. The mother responds quite differently.

Child: Dink? Dink?

Mother: I beg your pardon? You know how to ask for a drink properly. What do you say?

Child: Me have a drink? Pleeeeease?

Mother: Of course you may have a drink, darling. Thank you for asking so nicely.

Reflection prompts

Why has the mother's response changed in the second example? What can we learn from this, in terms of how we respond to children's early writing attempts?

Meet Charlie

Charlie is the eldest of two boys with parents who are not educators but are very interested in, and supportive of their children's learning. He is well supported with experiences and resources to encourage his literacy learning. Charlie was read to from when he was a baby and his home is full of books. He is also a keen soccer player and loves to jump on the trampoline and play with his younger brother, friends, and the family dogs. He is 4 years of age in this photo, but his writing journey started when he was much younger. We will follow Charlie as he learns to draw and write throughout this chapter, understanding that while we can learn from Charlie's journey, other children's writing trajectories may be quite different (see Figure 2.3).

Figure 2.3   Charlie

I can draw too

Children love to draw if they are encouraged to do so. They also love it when adults draw with them. The discussion of children's drawings in this chapter is in terms of how they "relate to text construction and early writing, not as a manifestation of children's fantasies or artistic capabilities" (Mackenzie & Veresov, 2013, p. 22). Drawing and writing are both purposeful, expressive acts that depend on the same cognitive abilities and require some of the same psychomotor skills. (See also Chapter 10 for a discussion of the relationship between drawing, talking, and writing in preschool and the early years of school.)

In Figure 2.4, you can see one of Charlie's early drawings. While we often assume that young children need large paper and child-friendly pens or crayons, many of his early drawings were created on small "sticky note" pages using pens found by Charlie in his grandmother's desk drawer. This early sample (Figure 2.4) is quite typical of children at this age.

At age 3, Charlie was fascinated by the underwater sea creatures in his parents' *Field Guide to Marine Fishes of Tropical Australia and South-East Australia* (Allen, 2009) and started to draw jellyfish and other underwater sea creatures. Figure 2.5 shows the sea creatures but also includes an early attempt at writing his name at the top of the page. You can see how his attempts to write are already quite different to his drawings.

Sea creatures were his favourite topic for quite some time, and in Figure 2.6 you can see him drawing octopuses. Charlie was 3½ when this drawing was created. Drawing

Figure 2.4   Early drawing behaviour

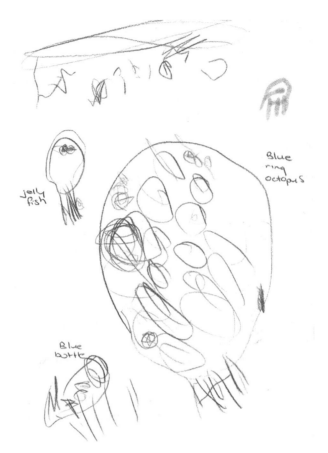

Figure 2.5   Jellyfish, octopus, and blue bottle drawing

Figure 2.6   Charlie and the underwater sea creatures drawing

with this amount of detail requires imagination and concentration and helps with fine motor development. He was fortunate to have parents who encouraged him to draw, provided the tools that he needed, and sometimes drew with him. Young children's compositions often involve multiple forms of representative media, including play and drawing (Dyson, 2001), long before they have control over the alphabetic principles and conventions of print.

Early writing experimentation

When children first begin to explore writing, they often demonstrate some of the more universal characteristics of writing (e.g., lines, units, and spaces), and these representations are clearly abstract, in contrast to their drawings (Puranik & Lonigan, 2009). In Figure 2.7 we can see a letter written by a young child to his aunt and uncle when he was 3½ years old. This is quite typical of this process of experimentation with squiggles, symbols, or letter like shapes.

There is evidence that the young writer understands the linear representation of text and how words are made from symbols. He recited his letter as he "wrote," combining two different modes of meaning-making: early writing and talking. It is clear that he was

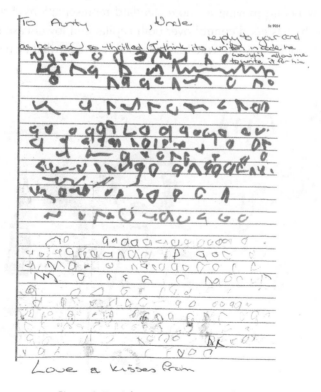

Figure 2.7   A letter to my aunt and uncle

not trying to draw a picture. Sometimes experimentation with letter-like behaviours and early drawing behaviours occurs simultaneously, but other times children show an understanding of these two modes, using them separately.

I can write my name

Learning to write their name is an important rite of passage for all young children. It is this important word that often encourages children to attend to the details in letters and words. In Figure 2.5 we saw how the child was experimenting with this process at 3½. As they learn to write their name, children discover what it is that makes their name a unique word.

Krisha was at preschool when she created the drawing you can see in Figure 2.8. She proudly added her name at the top. She wrote it the way her mother taught her – in capital letters (KRISHA). Many parents teach their children how to write their names in capital letters, knowing instinctively that it is easier, or because they are unsure of the script used by their local school.

It is not uncommon for children starting school in Australia to be faced with their name carefully printed on their desk and the hook where they should place their bag in a form that they do not recognise. It may be helpful for teachers who are working with new entrants to ask the family how the child has been taught to write their name and use that form initially before moving to more standard representations. Krisha is a good example. When she has good control over both capital and lower-case letters she can easily be taught "another way" to write her name (Krisha). She will then have "two ways"

Figure 2.8   Name writing

(KRISHA and Krisha) that she can write and read her name. In the interim she can confidently read and write her name in capital letters. To take that away would be a shame for Krisha and her family, who may feel that they have done something wrong. Interestingly in Finland, all preschool children are taught how to write their names in upper-case letters, progressing to lower case when appropriate.

Children's names are also rich resources for meaningful early engagement with writing. It is common for children to use the letters from their name to experiment with writing. At 4½ Charlie was combining drawing and writing. If you look closely at Figure 2.9, you will see that all the letters he used came from his name, with the addition of 'T'

Figure 2.9   Drawing plus experimentation with written text

which was the first letter of his cousin's name. This was a shared drawing, with his father providing the outline of the flying fox and Charlie doing the rest.

Children show more interest and control over their name than they do over other words (Both-de Vries & Bus, 2009). Both-de Vries and Bus also claim that children's phonetic sensitivity skills start with the first letter of their name and suggest that "young children are successful in recognizing this letter in spoken words before any other letter" (2009, p. 13). They also argue that "the way grown-ups react to name writing (for instance, recognizing the name and reading it aloud) may stimulate the shifts in children's procedural knowledge of writing" (p.13). Other research has shown a link between children's ability to write their names in preschool and emergent literacy skills development (Diamond & Baroody, 2013, p. 20) (see Milestone 6, Appendix at the end of this chapter and Chapter 4).

Reflection prompts

Who usually teaches children how to write their name? How could you facilitate the process? Why are children's names such an important writing resource?

More complex text creation

If given an audience and purpose for their writing, children will begin to create texts that include a number of ideas, using simple clauses (noun, verb, and adverb), using everyday vocabulary and possibly some topic-specific words. Their spelling attempts become more plausible, although they are not necessarily correct (See Chapter 6). They may use known common words correctly, control early print conventions (e.g., left to right with return sweep, spacing between words), but sometimes lapse in their application. They may still confuse upper-case and lower-case letter use and may still be experimenting with punctuation. Their letter formations may be correct or still developing. (See Milestones 8 and 9 in the Appendix for this chapter, also see Chapter 7.)

Understanding how texts are used for specific purposes

As children become more aware of how texts are used for different purposes, they begin to create texts that demonstrate an understanding of text type or genre. Children experiment with different text structures for different purposes (e.g., letters, narratives, recounts) as well as different sentence structures (simple, compound, and complex). They may use pronouns correctly, and their vocabulary may demonstrate variety and a careful choice of words for specific purposes (e.g., description or emotion). They may be experimenting with punctuation beyond capital letters, full stops, and question marks. Most words will be spelled correctly, and children will be applying more complex spelling rules and patterns, although not always correctly. Their handwriting may be well positioned and spaced with most letters well formed. While some children will demonstrate all of these writing features at the same time, others may be strong in some and have less control over others. For example, a child may have poor handwriting and spelling but be showing mature control over text structure, sentence structure, and ideas, and be making sophisticated vocabulary choices. Further, their profile of skill development may vary from text to text (see Milestones 10 and 11, Appendix, this chapter). In Chapter 8, you will be able to read about the analysis of writing samples.

Summary

In this first section of the chapter, I have given you an introduction to some of the indicators of children's journeys from *sign creation* to *sign use*. Charlie's journey was illustrative of the journeys children may take. The Appendix, at the end of the chapter, provides descriptions of possible milestones, although there is no suggestion that all children will move through all milestones in the order that they are listed. You will notice that the age range for some milestones is up to two years and some milestones may overlap (e.g., Milestones 4, 5, 6, and 7 are demonstrated by children between the ages of 3 and 5 years). I will now move to Section 2 of the chapter, which will focus on the transitions children may demonstrate as they move from *sign creation* to *sign use*.

Section 2: Transition – sign creation to sign use and preschool to school

The transition from *sign creation* to *sign use* is a transition from creative, non–rule driven forms of written communication (e.g., drawing only) to rule driven, conventional forms of written communication (e.g., written English). Most children experience this transition as they move from preschool into school, although for a small number of children this transition may occur before they begin school. Starting school is a complex time for many children as they deal with *shifts in critical learning contexts* at the same time as they move from *non–rule driven ways of meaning-making (e.g., drawing) to rule driven forms (writing)*. Whatever the timing, the transitions will be unique to each child and the process will require the support of the educators in the context in which they are situated.

The preschool-to-school transition

Effective transition programs are designed to support continuity in children's learning. However, in a study conducted in Victoria in 2015, preschool and school teachers reported that transition programs often run with little or no consultation with preschools despite the preschool educators having extensive knowledge of the children that have attended their preschool (Mackenzie & Petriwskyj, 2017). They also reported minimal communication between the preschool and the school, with educators from preschools uncertain of what is expected of children when they start school. Likewise, the school-teachers in the study reported limited understanding of the pedagogical approaches utilised by their local preschools (Mackenzie & Petriwskyj, 2017).

While there is evidence to indicate that there are pockets where successful initiatives have led to shared understandings and seamless transitions for children starting school (Scull & Garvis, 2015), there is still work to be done in this area (Mackenzie & Petriwskyj, 2017). No matter which side of this learning divide you are currently on, your ability to support children in a "safe crossing" from *preschool to school* and *sign creation to sign use* will be influenced by your awareness and understanding of what happens in the two learning spaces involved, rather than just the space you work in.

Reflection prompt

If you are a preschool teacher, how much do you know about what happens in the Foundation year (first year of formalised schooling)? How much do you know about the way the nearest school is organised? Have you been to visit in recent times?

If you are a Foundation year teacher, how much do you know about what happens in the local preschool? Have you been to visit recently?

Preschools and schools: Differences and common ground

Australia, Austria, Italy, Iceland, Belgium, Denmark, Norway, and Spain are examples of countries that have 6 years of age as the compulsory school starting age. This contrasts with the starting ages of 4 years in Northern Ireland, 5 years in England, Scotland, Wales, and the United States, and 7 years in Finland, Sweden, Poland, and Serbia. Although traditionally most children in Australia start school close to their fifth birthday, they may start as young as 4 years and 6 months. A trend of not starting boys at school until they are older now sees more 6-year-old children in preschools. This means that children can vary in age by more than 18 months (from 4½ to 6 years) in the last year of preschool and the first year of school in Australia.

Time spent at preschool and school

In Australia, all 4-year-old children are funded by the government for 15 hours of preschool per week in the year before they start school. This may be offered over two days or two-and-a-half days across the week. Some states also fund 3-year-old preschool. Preschools operate in the same weeks as schools, unless they are embedded within private childcare settings that are open during school holidays. Learning and play spaces are combined and organised both inside and outside. Children at preschool can usually choose when to be inside and when to be outside, although there may be times of the day when they are all inside or outside for particular activities. Educators will often be outside playing with children or observing them as they play. There may be multiple drawing, painting, and other creative activities for children to choose from. There may or may not be a writing area.

Schools in Australia operate for five days per week. The day usually starts close to 9:00 a.m. and finishes somewhere around 3:00 or 3.30 p.m. Teachers usually work to a structure that is organised around one recess (approximately 20 minutes) and one lunch break (approximately 50 minutes) although the timing of these varies from school to school. Programs of instruction offer a range of opportunities for children to engage in writing in different forms and for a variety of purposes (see Chapters 9 and 10), although lessons are often structured and teacher directed. Drawing, painting, and other creative activities are also structured and timetabled at particular times across the week. There is little free choice in most Foundation classrooms (also called Prep, Reception, and Kindergarten in different states). Children at school spend most of the day inside their classroom. Outside time is usually restricted to play times linked to recess and lunch, along with timetabled physical education lessons or sport. Outside play is usually conducted in large playgrounds that may include children from Foundation to Year Six in the same area. They are supervised by teachers on playground or yard duty. During the week there will be other timetabled activities (e.g., school assemblies, library lessons, physical education lessons, and perhaps sport). Consider the starting school experiences of Cruz and Charlotte in the following scenarios.

Scenario 1 (Cruz; 4 years and 8 months when he started school)

Cruz (not his real name) had not attended preschool. When he started school, he wasn't sure which hand he should use to hold his pencil, nor could he write his name. He was often tired and would put his head down on the table. Other times he would leave his desk and wander around the classroom until he was asked to return to his seat. Sometimes he slid under the table and disrupted other children. He would sometimes draw when he was supposed to be writing. His teacher did not think she had the time to allow him to draw at school and felt that it was important that he caught up with the rest of the class as quickly as possible. She gave him extra homework sheets to practise at home.

(You may find Chapters 10 and 13 helpful for children like Cruz.)

Scenario 2 (Charlotte, started school at 5 years and 9 months)

Charlotte (not her real name) had attended preschool for three days per week for two years. She had also attended childcare for two days per week in the year before she started school. Charlotte was an only child but spent time with older cousins and had been exposed to writing tools (pencils and felt-tip pens) from when she was quite young and enjoyed drawing pictures. Charlotte had been read to every day from birth. In the six months prior to starting school, Charlotte had learned to write her name, "mum" and "dad" and knew much of the alphabet. She was excited about starting school and learning to read and write. Her transition to school was smooth in every way. She had visited the school as part of the transition to school program and knew her way around. Her teacher had been part of the transition program and was therefore a familiar figure before school started. The school day was actually shorter than the days she had been accustomed to at preschool and childcare. Charlotte thrived at school from day one.

Cruz's and Charlotte's preschool to school transitions are in direct contrast and yet they could be in the same classroom at the same school. They were 13 months apart in age when they started school. Prior-to-school experiences and learning needs were very different for these two children despite both being in the first year of school.

Reflection prompt

Compare the prior-to-school experiences of Cruz and Charlotte. Where would you start with Cruz and Charlotte in terms of writing?

Curricula and pedagogy

Contrasting curricular and pedagogical expectations may create an unnecessary break in children's learning. The Early Years Learning Framework (EYLF) suggests that literacy includes music, movement, dance, storytelling, visual arts, media, and drama as well as talking, listening, viewing, reading, and writing, but the emphasis is on communicating. A play-based curriculum is common in Australian preschools, and children usually spend much of the day in unstructured play with friends. Opportunities are provided for children to experiment with letters using magnetic letters, letters that are made from sandpaper, and so forth. In some preschools children are provided with their names for copying and if they ask for help, they are shown how to write their names. Preschool educators often add text to children's pictures and some children may start to copy this process or ask for assistance with adding words to their pictures and paintings. They progress from scribble and drawing to a combination of drawing and signs, symbols, and idiosyncratic letter shapes, and may begin to combine drawings with conventional written text if given the support and encouragement.

Australian schools work within the guidelines of the Australian Curriculum, although states and territories interpret the curriculum in different ways. There are three strands to literacy identified within the Australian Curriculum: Language, Learning and Literacy

(ACARA, vs 9, 2023). Schools then break these down into further sub-strands for instructional purposes: reading, writing, listening, speaking, viewing, representing, spelling, handwriting (and possibly keyboard skills), grammar, phonics, and phonemic awareness. Different teaching and learning strategies are utilised by classroom teachers to teach children how to write (see Chapters 9 and 10). Although classroom talk has been prioritised and encouraged in school classrooms for some time (see for example, Edwards-Groves, 2014), classroom talk is controlled by the teacher in a way that is quite different to the way talk flows freely in preschool settings. Much of the teacher talk is directed at the class, rather than the individual. Many of the tasks are "for the teacher" rather than "for the child."

Children at preschool usually have more freedom and choice than those at school. The play-based approach offered by most preschools, with opportunities for engagement in sign creation (drawing and exploring mark-making in non–rule driven ways), will be perfect for most preschool children, although some may be ready for sign use.

Assessment processes

Processes for assessing children's learning can be quite different across preschools and schools. In preschools, educators often gather data through observations and detailed anecdotal records of children engaged in "real time" experiences. These are turned into transition statements and provided to schools when children transition from preschool to school. While some schools find the transition statements useful, others prefer their own data-gathering systems. Some schools use standard procedures developed by states or systems. Many schools supplement formal testing data with observations of children during transition programs, although not all children attend these.

Supporting children's transition from sign creation to sign use at preschool or school

- There may be children at preschool who are ready to move from sign creation to sign use, who need to be supported as they make this shift;

- There may be children who start school already competent at sign use;

- There may be children in the first year of school who need opportunities to explore sign creation, before they are required to engage in sign use; and

- There may be children in both contexts who want to continue to draw while learning how to add writing to their meaning-making repertoire.

In the scenarios that follow, Sean, Billy, and Tara are all transitioning from sign creation to sign use. While Billy and Tara are in the first year of school, Sean is at preschool. Despite the different learning locations, they are of similar age.

Scenario 1 (Sean; 5 years and 4 months attending Preschool)

Sean (not his real name) had been attending preschool since he was 4 and was still 6 months away from starting school. He had been drawing in detail from a young age and his mother had taught him his name and many of the letters of the alphabet. His preschool teacher thought he should wait until he started school to write so she discouraged him from any attempts at writing.

Scenario 2 (Billy, started school at 5 years and 4 months)

Billy (not his real name) had been drawing for a long time before he started school. His drawings were detailed and he had started using the letters from his name to add "text" to his drawings. His mother said he could happily draw for up to an hour. After a few weeks at school, he told his family that the teacher had told him that there wasn't time to draw at school. His teacher valued colouring-in over drawing, but he found the colouring-in worksheets frustrating.

Scenario 3 (Tara, started school at 5 years and 7 months)

Tara (not her real name) had been writing letters and stories for two years before she started school. She started by drawing pictures and dictating her stories to her mum. By the time she started school she could use pictures combined with simple sentences using invented spelling and known words to create stories. At school, she discovered that this kind of writing was not expected. She compliantly traced over the letter of the week and coloured in the picture on the worksheets given to her by her teacher. Her mum gave Tara reasons to write at home but Tara did not want her teacher to know what she was doing at home because she didn't think her teacher would be pleased. This continued throughout the first year of school.

Reflection prompt

What do these scenarios tell us about children's engagement with drawing and writing and how educators should support their learning?

Sean wanted to learn more about sign use, and his preschool educator should have felt comfortable supporting that learning without feeling that she was "stepping over an imaginary line" or teaching formal lessons. Others who have not had mark-making modelled in the home context or had access to drawing and writing implements may avoid engagement with mark-making altogether unless an educator steps in and provides the necessary scaffolds (see Chapter 10). Tara and Billy needed their teachers to make time to talk with them, and to observe them informally as they created texts, before moving into formalised instruction. That way they may have been able to introduce some flexibility into the implementation of their writing programmes. They may also have discovered more children like Billy and Tara as well as children who may need more time and support with *sign creation* before moving into *sign use* (see Chapter 10).

Conclusion

Learning to write in English offers many challenges to young children and their journeys from creative non–rule driven mark-making to conventional English vary greatly. Children come to preschool and school from different home and community contexts and although there was no space to explore this fully in the chapter, the scenarios should help to illustrate some of these differences. Young children also experience quite different learning-to-write opportunities, based upon whether they are in preschool or school. While that may initially seem as it should be, the fact that both contexts serve children in the same age range (4½ and 6 years) suggests that the decisions about teaching and learning should be based on each individual child and their current learning, rather than whether they are at preschool or school. Preschools do not need to become foundation classrooms, nor do foundation classrooms need to mirror preschools (Mackenzie and Hemmings, 2014), but how educators respond to children's learning should be based upon shared understandings of the writing process and the learning journeys of each child, rather than being based upon location (Mackenzie & Petriwskyj, 2017). In this chapter, I have shared the mark-making journeys of a number of children, through samples and scenarios. To complete the chapter please refer to the milestones provided in the Appendix, suggestions for families, and some recommended readings.

Working with families

Families all want what is best for their children. They want their children to succeed with learning to write and they learn to value what educators value. Ensure that you demonstrate by your comments, and what you share and display, that mark-making at all stages is important. Encourage families to:

1 Provide children with writing demonstrations from birth;
2 Provide children with appropriate resources, encouragement, and support to experiment with drawing and writing from very young;
3 Provide a space that supports drawing and writing without concern for damage to furniture (perhaps a particular table and space in the family room);
4 Encourage children to talk and to use talk in conjunction with drawing and writing;
5 Listen to children as they talk and draw;

6 Draw with your child and teach them to write their name when they show an interest or just before they start school;

7 Encourage children to create and write on cards at Christmas and birthdays;

8 Encourage children to write lists for shopping or at Christmas;

9 Encourage children to draw and write while on holidays or after family celebrations; and

10 Make drawing and writing a regular activity in the home.

Appendix: Text Creation Milestones

Milestone	Approximate age	Observable behaviours
1	0–1 year	Children may begin to notice how others around them are engaging with text creation.
2	1–2 years	Children begin to engage with mark-making using any writing tools that are available to them – pens, pencils, crayons, electronic devices as well as tools that are not necessarily designed as writing tools (e.g., lipstick, food).
3	1–3 years	Children intentionally engage with writing tools in an exploratory way. What they create is often referred to as scribble.
4	3–5 years	Children intentionally create "drawings" that may remain meaningful to them alone, or they may share these with others. They may talk as they draw. With experience drawings may become more recognisable and complex.
5	3–5 years	Children begin to create "text-like" representations; these may include squiggles, symbols or letter like shapes and that look like words, and they may demonstrate an understanding of lines and spaces. Milestones 4 and 5 can occur simultaneously.
6	3–5 years	Children explore writing their name. Often, they are taught to write their name at home, by a parent (often their mother). They often use uppercase letters. This is an important milestone, as they learn that their name is able to be represented in print, and that this visual representation remains largely stable.
7	3–5 years	Children create drawings with text included or added (usually using letters from their name). They often add *words* or *labels* for their drawings. In some cases, children can *read* these words; in other cases they are just happy to have created what to them looks like real writing. They may ask an adult to *read* their text, assuming that they have written something that can be read by those who know how to read.

(continued)

Milestone	Approximate age	Observable behaviours
8	5–6 years	Children create text with purpose and an audience in mind that is not currently present. The text may be interpreted by others. They may use semi-phonetic or phonetic invented spelling and known words. Letters may include a mix of upper- and lower-case letters. They may involve one or more unrelated ideas. They may show an awareness of sentence parts including noun-verb agreement. Some or all of these features may be evident.
9	5–6 years	Children create meaningful texts that may include several ideas, using simple clauses with nouns, verbs, and adverbs and using everyday vocabulary and possibly some topic-specific words. Their spelling attempts will show plausible attempts with most sounds in words represented. This does not suggest correct spelling necessarily (e.g., they may write "kabn" for *cabin*). They may know some 3–4 letter commonly used words (e.g., *the*, *like*). They may be experimenting with capital letters and full stops (correctly or incorrectly). Their letter formation may be mostly correct, yet be poorly spaced, positioned and may be messy. Some or all of these features may be present. Drawings may still play an important role, if this has been encouraged.
10	5–8 years	Children create texts, which demonstrate an understanding of genre or text type (e.g., recount, narrative, letter). They may be experimenting with different sentence structures (simple, compound, and complex). Pronoun reference may be correctly applied to track a character or object over the text. Their vocabulary may demonstrate variety and may or may not include descriptive and emotive language. While most of the spelling will be correct, there may be demonstrations of the incorrect application of irregular spelling patterns. They may be experimenting with a variety of punctuation (correctly and incorrectly). Their handwriting may be well spaced and positioned with correct letter formations. Some or all of these features may be present at this time. A child may be demonstrating quite advanced skills in some areas (e.g., text structure, sentence structure, ideas, and vocabulary choices) but still be struggling with letter formation and spelling. Alternately, writing may appear neat and spelling accurate but sentence structure and vocabulary may be simple and ideas limited.

(continued)

Milestone	Approximate age	Observable behaviours
11	6–10 years	Children create increasingly complex texts, which may show strong evidence of the features of text and/or purpose and audience. They may demonstrate variety in sentence structures and length and use a range of sentence beginnings. Sentences will flow with a logical sequence throughout the text and show a consistent use of tense. Correct use of unique field or technically specific vocabulary will be evident. Spelling will mostly be correct, including multisyllabic and phonetically irregular words. Errors will demonstrate plausible attempts. They will demonstrate control over a range of punctuation and their handwriting will be correct, consistent and legible and appear to be fluent. Many children will demonstrate some of these features before others. The shifts across milestones 10–11 are blurred with children making shifts in control at different times. These shifts will be greatly affected by the emphasis of the class program. For example, children who are in a classroom where the educator emphasises handwriting and punctuation but neglects spelling and vocabulary may make more rapid progress in handwriting and punctuation than spelling and vocabulary.

Adapted from Mackenzie & Scull (2015)

Recommended reading

Mackenzie, N. M. (2020). Writing in the early years. In A. Woods & B. Exley (Eds.), *Literacies in Early Childhood: Foundations for Equity and Quality*. Melbourne, VIC: Oxford University Press.

Mackenzie, N. M., & Petriwskyj, A. (2017). Understanding and supporting young writers: Opening the school gate. *Australasian Journal of Early Childhood, 42*(2), 78–87.

References

Allen, G. R. (2009). *Field Guide to Marine Fishes of Tropical Australia and South-East Australia*. Perth, WA: Western Australian Museum.

Australian Curriculum (vs 9, 2023). https://v9.australiancurriculum.edu.au/teacher-resources/understand-this-general-capability/literacy

Both-de Vries, A. C., & Bus, A. G. (2009). It's All in the Name. In D. Aram & O. Korat (Eds.), *Literacy Development and Enhancement Across Orthographies and Cultures* (pp. 3–15). Springer US. https://doi.org/10.1007/978-1-4419-0834-6_1

Clay, M. M. (2014). *By different paths to common outcomes*. York, Maine: Stenhouse Publishers.

Diamond, K. E., & Baroody, A. E. (2013). Associations among name writing and alphabetic skills in prekindergarten and kindergarten children at risk of school failure. *Journal of Early Intervention, 35*(1), 20–39.

Dyson, A. H. (2001). Writing and children's symbolic repertoires: Development unhinged. In S. B. Neuman & D. K. Dickinson (Eds.), *Handbook of Early Literacy Research* (Vol. 1, pp. 126–141). New York: Guilford Press.

Edwards-Groves, C. (2014). Talk moves: A repertoire of practices for productive classroom dialogue. *PETAA Paper, 195*, 1–12. Marrickville, NSW: Primary English Teaching Association Australia.

Genishi, C., & Dyson, A. H. (2009). *Children, Language and Literacy: Diverse Learners in Diverse Times*. New York: Teachers College Press.

Mackenzie, N. M., & Hemmings, B. (2014). Predictors of success with writing in the first year of school. *Issues in Educational Research, 24(12)*, 41–54.

Mackenzie, N. M., & Petriwskyj, A. (2017). Understanding and supporting young writers: Opening the school gate. *Australasian Journal of Early Childhood, 42(2)*, 78–87.

Mackenzie, N. M., & Scull, J. A. (2015). Literacy: Writing. In S. McLeod & J. McCormack (Eds.), *Introduction to Speech, Language and Literacy* (pp. 398–445). Melbourne, VIC: Oxford University Press.

Mackenzie, N. M., & Veresov, N. (2013). How drawing can support writing acquisition: Text construction in early writing from a Vygotskian perspective. *Australasian Journal of Early Childhood, 38(4)*, 22–29.

Puranik, C. S., & Lonigan, C. J. (2009). From scribbles to Scrabble: Preschool children's developing knowledge of written language. *Read Write*. DOI 10.1007/s11145-009-9220-8

Scull, J., & Garvis, S. (2015). *Transition: A Positive Start to School, for the Department of Education and Training, Victoria*. Melbourne, VIC: Monash University.

Discovering writing birth–2 years

Anne Keary and Laura McFarland

Introduction

Children begin learning the functions and purposes of reading and writing as they hear and see those around them interacting with symbols and written texts of all kinds, in meaningful real-life situations. A brief review of the importance of language development and learning precedes a discussion of the importance of setting up rich and engaging birth–2 play-based learning environments in ways that support mark-making, scribbling and early drawing. The discussion then moves to multimodality and digital technologies for young learners. Finally, processes for observation and documentation which capture children's early mark-making and drawing development are outlined. Throughout the chapter examples of strategies which support and promote children's early mark-making in birth–2 play-based environments are shared and supported with illustrative examples of practice. Reflection prompts are included throughout the chapter and recommended reading provided after the conclusion.

The importance of trusting, responsive relationships

Babies come into the world seeking attachments with their caregivers and depend on their caregivers to respond sensitively to their needs. This responsive caregiving allows a baby to develop a sense of trust in the caregiver and fosters a feeling of safety and security for the child. When a child feels safe, they can explore their environment, trusting that the caregiver will be there when needed. This building of caring and attentive relationships with others creates an environment for cognitive growth and learning (Australian Government Department of Education, AGDE, 2022).

Through intentional interactions with family and caregivers and during play-based experiences, children are encouraged to be active learners in everyday events that extend and enhance learning. This can be seen in Figure 3.1 as Mariam's father supports her to build a

DOI: 10.4324/9781003439264-3

Figure 3.1   Mariam and her father

tower with plastic blocks. You can imagine that he will be using language associated with construction, but also words of encouragement and guidance. Successes will have been celebrated, and perhaps near misses or collapses laughed about. Early socialisation experiences and young children's active engagement in these interactions shape relationship building (Irving & Carter, 2018), with a young child's social world often extending beyond the family to include educators, the community, and other young children.

The foundations for a positive attitude towards literacy learning generally, and writing specifically, are built in and through these early interactions and trusting relationships (AGDE, 2022). When children have trust in their caregivers and educators, they feel safe to explore the environment and engage in a variety of experiences in their world. Children observe and experience what is happening around them at home, the homes of their extended families and friends, the shops, childcare, perhaps their older siblings' preschool, school, or sporting events, and sometimes their parents' workplaces. For some young children, a parent may work from home and engage in multiple literate activities from home. They hear and see people interacting with each other face-to-face as well as with physical and digital symbols and objects, and they may begin to learn the purposes of these and their roles in interaction. They discover that people can communicate messages orally, with hand actions and gestures, by writing with a pen on a pad or piece of paper, by writing messages on a phone that may include photos or videos and typing emails on a computer. They may also discover that some people use all hand gestures (signing) to communicate. As they get closer to 2 years old, they might learn that an anecdotal recount of an event, or telling of a story, provides enjoyment and positive emotions from shared interpersonal connections. Through these observations and interactions, children learn the purposes of communication and of literacy practices.

As children explore mark-making and engage in a range of literacy activities, the adults in their world should be available and responsive and encourage the efforts of the young child.

Encounters such as the one illustrated in Figure 3.1 provide opportunities for conversation and vocabulary development as well as learning the rules of turn-taking, eye contact, and listening. The adult is available and responsive and can encourage the efforts of the young child. When young children (birth–2) have trust in their caregivers and educators, they feel safe to explore the environment and engage in a variety of experiences. This same kind of interaction can revolve around shared drawing and mark-making, where an adult and child/ren draw and talk together. If provided with the tools (paper, crayons, pencils, chalk), spaces (a table and chair that is the right size for them) and encouragement, young children will eagerly engage with mark-making, scribbling, and drawing if this is valued by the adults that they trust (see also Chapter 2).

Language development and learning

From birth, young children communicate with significant others in a range of ways. Language in its various forms is central to communication and it is important for educators and carers to understand language development. For many carers and educators, learning to speak, read, and write are viewed as a developmental process with phases represented as a trajectory that can be used as a guide to plan for learning (see for example, Australian Education Research Organisation, AERO, 2023). However, it is important to remember the different experiences, opportunities, and abilities of young children of a similar age as illustrated by the milestones provided in Chapter 2. These text creation milestones sometimes overlap, and in some cases are observed in children who may range in age by 2 years. For example, Milestone 2 may be observed any time between ages 1 and 2, while Milestone 3 may be observed any time between ages 1 and 3.

Children's diverse linguistic and cultural backgrounds, and their social contexts, influence the way they learn language and their conceptual development. Intergenerational transmission of home languages facilitates meaningful communication between the extended family, such as parents and grandparents, fostering the growth of children's cultural identities and encouraging bi/multilingualism (ACTA, 2023). It is important that home languages, including Aboriginal and Torres Strait Islander languages, and all community and family languages, are maintained and strengthened. Caregivers and educators can enhance young children's sense of belonging by valuing their language(s) and their ways of interacting and communicating (AGDE, 2022). Supporting young children's learning of home languages also leads to effective learning of English as an additional language and/or dialect (ACTA, 2023). Initial literacy developed in home languages supports more effective acquisition of early writing skills in English and other languages and dialects (UNESCO, 2020).

Reflection prompt

List the various home languages of the children in your care. How do you encourage parents/caregivers to maintain and strengthen children's home languages and what opportunities do you provide for children to use home languages?

Knowledge of spoken or signed language underpins the foundations for reading and writing in the early years. From the earliest stages children need to *learn* language, learn *through* language, and learn *about* language (Halliday, 2004). A "communication-rich" home and community environment works best for learning language. Young children who are proficient in using language for communication have a stepping off point for learning to write. Yet, as discussed in Chapter 5, oral language varies from written language. Oral language is dependent on the context of the "here and now," while written language provides additional information to the reader as it is detached from the context (Raban & Scull 2023). Also, many conventions of written language are not present in everyday talk, for example, in everyday interactions we often do not need to respond to a question by producing a full sentence; a word or two will be enough, and speaking and writing involve different styles of expression.

Incidental reading like reading the labels on packaging or signs in the landscape along with the reading of books for enjoyment or information are also literacy practices that young children observe adults and older children engaging with. Through these observations our youngest children begin to discover the purposes of oral and written communication. Being read aloud books from birth has been shown to support children's language development, vocabulary, and understanding of story and to promote positive academic outcomes in grades 5 and 8 (Brown, Wang & McLeod, 2022). There is also considerable research to support a strong relationship between talking, drawing, and early writing (see for example, Neumann, 2023; Pinto & Incognito, 2022).

Reflection prompt

Think about the different kinds of reading and interpreting symbols that you engage with in a single day. These might include reading labels, text messages, emails, social media posts, maps, street signs or other signs, or interpreting the symbols in vehicles or public transport.

What everyday literacy tasks do the children in your care see you engaging with?

Early mark-making, scribble, and drawing

Just how do young children develop writing skills? Research examining young children's drawings and early mark-making suggests that children under 3 years of age "have the capacity to use graphic marks in highly intentional and reasoned ways" (Lancaster, 2007, p. 149). It appears that children draw upon not only conventional symbolic systems, but also on a variety of personal, social, and bodily experiences in order to construct signs and texts. These findings from Lancaster's (2007) small study of young children challenge the commonly held perception that children under the age of 3 engage only in drawing, to the exclusion of *writing*. In fact, evidence suggests that children under the age of 3 are beginning to use "some of the syntactic principles that underlie writing systems earlier than might have been thought" (Lancaster, 2007, p. 149). More recently, based on a second small study of young children, Lancaster (2014), found that rather than being a predictable developmental sequence, representational principles of drawing and writing are more likely to develop concurrently. Lancaster suggests children also "appear to start to use and investigate symbolic principles from the outset, through the construction of meaningful signs, often using macro, 'generic' frameworks of their own devising" (2014, p. 44). There is clear evidence of mark-making exploration in the Milestones included in Chapter 2, although these Milestones demonstrate that the age and order that children explore and demonstrate certain mark-making processes can vary by up to two years. Chapter 2 also discusses children's mark-making journey through the case study of Charlie.

In Figure 3.2, you can see an example of 2-year-old Olive's drawing with crayons. According to the developmental perspective of writing and drawing, Olive's drawing demonstrates that she is in the scribbling stage of drawing, as she creates random circular marks on the page.

Figure 3.2   Olive's drawing

The emergence of early writing is a complex process influenced by a variety of factors, with the development of literacy skills collectively influenced by child-based,
home-based factors, and early educational settings (Puranik et al., 2018). Rowe and
Neitzel (2010) found that young children's participation in early writing was related to
their "interests." Interests not only included preferences for "particular kinds of action
potentials inherent in social activities and materials" (p. 193), but also broader interest
orientations expressed in their play. Early writing is complex and multi-faceted as children exert agency in their participation and learning in the area of writing (Rowe &
Neitzel, 2010). Becoming aware of written language supports an understanding that
written language conveys meaning.

Other research suggests that early mark-making can be supported by more knowledgeable adults or older children. According to Vygotsky, children's development and
learning can be effectively supported through a zone of proximal development, which
includes what the child can do without any assistance to what the child can do with
assistance (Vygotsky, 1978). More knowledgeable others can support children through
this zone of proximal development through the use of scaffolding, whereby the child is
given guidance and instruction. Indeed, some research suggests that scaffolding from a
more knowledgeable other can assist children to be more successful in all literacy tasks
(Neumann, 2020). However, it is important to keep in mind that all children develop
differently, and children should not be pressured to learn how to write before they are
ready (Berk & Meyers, 2015). It is clear that early exposure to a rich environment full of
opportunities to scribble, draw, and write is important for children in the first few years
of life. These first few scribbles or lines all help to prepare children to learn to write with
birth–2 educational settings particularly important environments to support early mark-
making and writing.

Reflection prompt

*What are some age-appropriate ways you could facilitate young (6 months to 2
years) children's drawing and mark-making?*

Language, communication, and early mark-making

Communication with others begins from birth "using eye contact, whole body movement, gestures, sounds, language, digital and assisted communication" (AGDE, 2022,
p. 57). Young children can communicate through a range of tools and media such as
music, dance, and drama as a means of expression and to interact and connect with
others. Fostering language through communication in responsive and reciprocal relationships is therefore an essential first step for encouraging a positive attitude towards
written language and written texts.

Educators can engage babies and toddlers in dialogue during daily play and caregiving routines. For example, educators can describe what is happening as it occurs, and provide the spoken words for a child's actions. Even if a child is not speaking yet, they can be viewed as an active participant in the "conversation." In the excerpt below, notice how, rather than simply picking the child up and changing her nappy, the educator takes the time to expose the child to language and turn it into a learning experience:

Educator: Hi, Katie, it looks like you have a wet nappy. Let's go change you into a dry nappy. I'm going to pick you up and take you to the change table.

In many cultures adults use a special style of speaking with babies and young children, known as infant-directed or child-directed speech, or baby talk (and formerly, motherese). In these styles adults use, for example, more variation in the pitch of their speech, providing an exaggerated up and down tune, longer vowel sounds, repetition of words and phrases, and "baby" words, for instance "doggy" for "dog". These styles have been comprehensively shown to be positive for children's language development (e.g., Golinkoff et al., 2015).

Social activities, both with other children and with educators, can also provide young children opportunities to engage in conversation and learn language. A variety of experiences and materials in the environment can support language development. It is important to remember that the outdoor environment offers opportunities for language as well. For example, taking children on outings, talking about where you are going, naming objects and talking about their experiences can expand their vocabulary and foster conversation skills. Simple, everyday experiences like this are powerful opportunities to support children's emerging language.

For young children, becoming literate involves the capacity and disposition to engage in and use language meaningfully in its various forms such as written, oral, signed, visual, and auditory. Caregivers and educators can provide children with a range of texts for enjoyment and to facilitate learning, including electronic and print-based media with adult modelling of reading, writing, and speaking an important strategy to support children's language and early literacy skills development. Telling stories, reading age-appropriate books, encouraging older toddlers to talk about their experiences, and singing and using rhyming games, including hand or body actions foster language development (Gonzalez-Mena & Widmeyer Eyer, 2015). Reading aloud to babies and toddlers helps them to develop many of the competencies they will need to become skilled readers (Kinsner & Parlakian, 2021) but also to understand the way written language differs from spoken language.

Early experiences with the symbolic nature of print can also be fostered when writing children's names on their artwork, with educators naming the letters as they write them. "'S' 'A' 'M,' that spells Sam." Importantly, babies and toddlers should be offered opportunities to actively participate in mark-making and drawing activities. Exerting their agency will allow young children to co-construct their knowledge of writing, rather than being passive recipients of the transmission of knowledge (Makin, 2006). If the activities are enjoyable and satisfying, children will more likely want to participate. Educators can also link early writing and drawing activities with events in the child's life, as well as communicate with families to find out what has been happening at home, in order to build on the child's interests. If there is something a child wants to tell their parents about their day, the educator can transcribe their words on a piece of paper or other communication tool, which they would later deliver and "read" to their family. However, this type of activity should be used cautiously, as not all 2-year-olds will be ready for this.

Play-based environments

Play is highly valued in early childhood education, with the importance of play for young children's healthy development and learning well documented and researched (Robinson et al., 2018). The United Nations Convention on the Rights of the Child recognises children's right to play (See United Nations, Article 31, adopted in 1989). Caregivers and educators play an important role in extending and enriching children's learning through play (Peterson & Friedrich, 2022).

Young children learn a great deal about themselves, others, and the world around them through play. During play, young children communicate with sounds, gestures, actions, and non-verbal means even before they talk. Play also provides a social context for exposure to language in its many forms, laying the foundations for literacy development, including mark-making, scribbling, drawing, and eventually writing. Play also provides a purpose for communication such as negotiating, informing, problem-solving, requesting, and asking questions (Robinson et al., 2018). Young children can be provided with opportunities to play with language and literacy through various modes of communication including the arts, music and drama, dance, storytelling, and literacy-type activities (AGDE, 2022).

Drawing, mark-making, and painting may be thought of as playing with crayons, pencils, and paint. During play young children may explore the meaning of symbols and texts through watching, listening, touching, and handling objects, scribbling, painting, and drawing. These play experiences encourage socialisation into literacy and provide a context for the development of writing in meaningful real-life contexts (O'Grady, Scull & Lyons, 2024). In a play-based setting, appropriate for children from 0 to 2, inferring meaning from symbols and texts takes place everywhere from book reading activities to sandpit and pretend play activities and playing with words and sounds. The main point is to have fun with language and mark-making through play.

In addition to encouraging social interactions and language development, opportunities for fine motor development in a play-based environment are important for the development of early writing as children gradually learn to grasp writing tools. For very young babies, allowing them time to move around on the floor, hold toys within their reach, providing them with different surfaces to crawl on and providing different textures for them to explore are ways to support fine motor development. For toddlers who can grip writing tools, a variety of art and sensory activities can support mark-making. With supervision, finger paint, modelling materials, paint on easels, felt tip pens, crayons, chalk, coloured pencils, stickers, and sand are all meaningful ways to support the fine motor skills needed for mark-making. Introducing scissors and glue for those almost 3 would require careful supervision.

Reflection prompt

What are some ways you could incorporate drawing and early mark-making into children's play?

Multimodality and text creation

Multimodality is described by Pahl and Rowsell as a "concept of communication that subsumes the written, the visual, the gestural, and the tactile into one entity" (2005, p. 26), while Mackenzie (2022a) defines a multimodal text as a text that simply includes more than one mode. Therefore, a text created by drawing and talking can be understood as a multimodal text, as is a text that includes a mix of drawing and letter like symbols. According to Mackenzie, "to become truly literate, children need to learn to create, comprehend and use single mode (written, visual or spoken) and multimodal texts" (2022a, p. 9). Multimodality does not necessarily involve technology, although digital texts are usually multimodal. Multimodal texts may also include:

- Paper-based multimodal texts such as picture books and posters;
- Live multimodal texts such as dancing and oral storytelling which convey meaning through a combination of a range of modes including gesture, spatial, audio, and oral language;
- Digital multimodal texts such as film, animations, digital stories, and webpages.
                    (Department of Education and Training Victoria, 2020)

In the birth-to-2-year age range, children enjoy engaging with a range of texts, including digital texts and print-based media and are often immersed in these new communication technologies from a young age. Young children are introduced to still and moving images from birth and begin to engage with signs and symbols to make sense of their world. The effect of a multimodal environment is significant as "the tools of new media become a part of childhood's everyday objects and materials of play" (Laidlaw & Wong, 2016,

p. 30). Yet as discussed above, play and learning are deeply relational and young children begin to explore, question, problem-solve, represent, and experiment with contemporary text forms in secure and safe environments in interactions with others.

Digital texts and young children

Children growing up in "contemporary homes in post-industrial countries use digital media as part of everyday activities" (Flewitt & Clark, 2020, p. 447), and valuable early learning opportunities with digital technologies can be incorporated into everyday activities with caregiver and/or educator support (O'Grady, Scull & Lyons, in press). Figure 3.3 shows Olive and her γιαγιά (grandmother) viewing family photos on a mobile/cell phone. The photos are powerful in their own right, but supported by conversation between the adult and child, the text becomes multimodal and interactional. Creating personalised texts using a phone can be very powerful for our young learners (0–2) who recognise themselves, family, or friends in familiar contexts. The support of conversation adds extra complexity and support. Simple but meaningful multimodal texts comprising photos or videos and supported by talk can be created using digital devices at home and in care or education settings.

Reading, writing, seeing, viewing, hearing, listening, and other sensory experiences are all aspects of early literacy development. New technologies and multiliteracies surround young children in their educational play environments. Yet, children make choices about the content and activities they want to engage with, selecting and initiating content. Young children's exposure to and engagement with screen-based technologies requires careful consideration by caregivers and teachers (Hughes, 2018).

Figure 3.3 Olive and her γιαγιά (grandmother)

Reflection prompt

Think about the different kinds of modalities, symbols, and texts you encounter and use in a single day. Do you notice people communicating using their hands, bodies, eyes, or facial expressions? What opportunities do you provide for young children to communicate using various modes and technologies?

Observations and documentation of early mark-making: Why and how?

Pedagogical documentation is an important observation and monitoring process in birth–2 education settings, which can be used to capture children's early mark-making and drawing attempts (AGDE, 2022). This involves gathering information about children from a range of contexts and sources and collaborating with families about children's learning (Tayler et al., 2023). To be meaningful and authentic, pedagogical documentation of young children's learning should be embedded in children's daily experiences, rather than done in isolation (Siraj-Blatchford & Clarke, 2000). See Chapter 2 for Charlie's drawing and mark-making journey, and the text creation milestones.

There are many pedagogical documentation strategies that birth–2 educators can use to capture young children's rich experiences in early mark-making and drawing. Anecdotally recording observations is a strategy for collecting and recording information. It is important when documenting young children's early literacy experiences that the approaches to documentation are holistic, consider the child's strengths, and provide insights into the child's interests and learning processes (Tayler et al., 2023). A strength-based approach to documentation positions young children as competent and capable, and shows what they can do, rather than what they cannot do (Dahlberg, Moss & Pence, 2007). Documentation can then be shared with families and interpreted with their assistance. Perspectives from families on young children's early literacy skills development can also help the early childhood educator plan further activities to build on children's interests and abilities.

Work samples collected over time can show how the writing process develops over time. Work samples can include anything created by the child to represent early communication, such as drawings, paintings, and collages. It is also helpful to add descriptive notes, jottings or a brief anecdotal record to the work samples in order to provide some additional context (Arthur et al., 2015). For example, are there any insights into what the child was thinking when producing the artefact? Were there any conversations that were occurring at the time? Children who are verbal can be asked to contribute their own ideas to this context.

Photographs of a work sample can be taken and later used in the child's portfolio, particularly if the child wants to keep the original painting or drawing. Photographs can also be used to capture the child's engagement in an experience, particularly as they interact with other children. Again, documentation of the context of the photograph can be included to better understand the child's learning processes in relation to mark-making. Photos, either digital or in hard copy, can also be shared with families via a daily communication book. In this way, families can see the day-to-day learning experiences in which their young children engage.

Learning stories are a narrative form of documentation that focus on children's strengths, involves children's everyday lived experiences, and makes visible and values young children's learning (Carr & Lee, 2019). Learning stories aim to document children's growth and interests, helping to make children's competencies more "explicit and transparent" (Hatherly, 2006, p. 33). Learning stories typically involve educators in a process of noticing, recognizing, and responding to children's learning using photographs and work samples, either digital or hard copy, while also revisiting and reviewing conversations with children (Carr & Lee, 2019).

> The Early Years Planning Cycle Resource (VCAA, 2020, p. 36) gives an example of a 23-month-old showing her understanding of spatial terms (such as "in") as she matches her bodily gestures with the words of a song she is singing. At a later stage she was observed playing in the sandpit, pointing to a bowl, and telling another young child to add more sand to the bowl by saying "in, in here." This observational information of the young child's music experience and play in the sandpit was observed and recorded. This provided evidence of how the young child used bodily gestures to match actions with a spatial term in a song and in her sandpit play and giving instructions to her peer using the same spatial term.

In relation to early literacy, Hatherly (2006) suggests that learning stories may help families to see the literacy practices that are embedded in everyday experiences in the early childhood education setting. This is particularly important in birth–2 settings, where early literacy skills may not be obvious. Families may not always recognise that children's early marks on paper, scribbles, and free exploration with drawing and writing tools are important writing experiences. Educators can make this more visible by carefully documenting and interpreting children's early drawing and early writing experiences in a format that can be accessed by children and families and give children voice.

See also Chapter 10 for a discussion of the Draw, Talk, Write, and Share Observational Protocol (Mackenzie, 2022b) which is used by many EC educators to help document children's mark-making journeys.

Reflection prompt

In what ways are families given opportunities to contribute to children's learning stories and portfolios in your setting?

Conclusion

Engagement with written language and early writing opportunities for children under 3 has received little attention in research (Puranik et al., 2018). However, the youngest children can be supported in learning the functions of reading and writing in a variety of ways within the home and in birth–2 educational settings. And while early childhood educators' pedagogical beliefs and practices related to early writing will vary, the EYLF V2.0 supports the provision of language-rich writing and literacy experiences in a range of ways (AGDE, 2022). Throughout this chapter, we have discussed the importance of:

- Promoting oral and/or signed language and early literacy experiences in a context of responsive, respectful relationships within the birth–2 educational setting.
- Creating a rich and engaging birth–2 early childhood education environment to support oral language development.
- Providing opportunities for written language awareness and early reading and writing experiences in a play-based environment.
- Promoting early mark-making by building on children's interests and agency.
- Recognising that multimodality and digital technologies are important modes for encouraging early text creation processes.
- Engaging with a variety of pedagogical documentation strategies to communicate and collaborate with families in relation to children's early mark-making journeys.

Acknowledgement

We would like to acknowledge Associate Professor Carmel O'Shannessy (Australian National University) for her valuable feedback on this chapter.

Recommended reading and resources

Lindstrand, S. H., & Willen, P. B. (2016). 'When you give them a pencil they often say they're writing': Preschool teachers' categorisation of written language work with toddlers. *Australasian Journal of Early Childhood*, 41(1), 90–99. https://doi.org/10.1177/183693911604100112

O'Grady, K., Scull, J., & Lyons, D. (in press). Exploring the early writing experiences of young children within the home through autoethnographic reflections. *Issues in Educational Research*.

Wilson-Ali, N., & Early Childhood Australia (2021). *Promoting Infant-Toddler Cognitive Learning and Development*. https://www.earlychildhoodaustralia.org.au/our-publications/research-practice-series/research-practice-series-index/2021-issues/promoting-infant-toddler-cognitive-learning-and-development/

Wright, T. S., Cabell, S. Q., Duke, N. K., & Souto-Manning, M. (2022). *Literacy Learning for Infants, Toddlers, and Preschoolers: Key Practices for Educators*. National Association for the Education of Young Children.

References

ACTA [Australian Council of TESOL Associations] (2023). ACTA principles for early childhood education. https://tesol.org.au/wp-content/uploads/2022/09/ACTA-ECE-Principles.pdf

AERO [Australian Education Research Organisation] (2023). Language and communication – Early childhood learning trajectory. https://www.edresearch.edu.au/resources/language-and-communication-early-childhood-learning-trajectory

Arthur, L., Beecher, B., Death, E., Dockett, S., & Farmer, S. (2015). *Programming and Planning in Early Childhood Settings* (6th ed.). South Melbourne, VIC: Cengage Learning.

Australian Government Department of Education [AGDE] (2022). Belonging, being and becoming: The early years learning framework for Australia (V2.0). https://www.acecqa.gov.au/sites/default/files/2023-01/Belonging_Being_And_Becoming_V2.0.pdf

Berk, L., & Meyers, A. (2015). *Infants, Children and Adolescents* (8th ed.). Boston, MA: Pearson.

Brown, M. I., Wang, C., & McLeod, S. (2022). Reading with 1–2 year olds impacts academic achievement at 8–11 years. *Early Childhood Research Quarterly, 58*(1st quarter), 198–207. https://doi.org/10.1016/j.ecresq.2021.09.008

Carr, M., & Lee, W. (2019). *Learning Stories in Practice*. London: SAGE Publications Ltd.

Dahlberg, G., Moss, P., & Pence, A. (2007). *Beyond Quality in Early Childhood Education and Care: Postmodern Perspectives*. London: Falmer Press.

Department of Education and Training (2020). Overview of multimodal literacy. https://www.education.vic.gov.au/school/teachers/teachingresources/discipline/english/literacy/multimodal/Pages/multimodaloverview.aspx

Flewitt, R., & Clark, A. (2020). Porous boundaries: Reconceptualising the home literacy environment as a digitally networked space for 0–3 year olds. *Journal of Early Childhood Literacy, 20*(3), 447–471. https://doi.org/10.1177/1468798420938116

Golinkoff, R. M., Can, D. D., Soderstrom, M., & Hirsh-Pasek, K. (2015). (Baby) talk to me: The social context of infant-directed speech and its effects on early language acquisition. *Current Directions in Psychological Science*. 24(5), 339–344.

Gonzalez-Mena, J., & Widmeyer Eyer, D. (2015). *Infants, Toddlers and Caregivers: A Curriculum of Respectful, Responsive, Relationship-based Care and Education* (10th ed.). New York: McGraw-Hill.

Halliday, M. A. K. (2004). *The Language of Early Childhood: Volume 4* (1 ed.). London: Bloomsbury Publishing.

Hatherly, A. (2006). The stories we share: Using narratives to build communities of literacy participants in early childhood centres. *Australian Journal of Early Childhood, 31*(1), 27–34. https://doi.org/10.1177/183693910603100105

Hughes, M. (2018). Language, literacy and children's literature. In E. Irving & C. Carter (Eds.). *The Child in Focus: Learning and Teaching in Early Childhood Education* (pp. 190–222). South Melbourne, Victoria, Australia: Oxford University Press Australia & New Zealand.

Irving, E. C., & Carter, C. (2018). *The Child in Focus: Learning and Teaching in Early Childhood Education*. South Melbourne, Victoria, Melbourne: Oxford University Press.

Kinsner, K., & Parlakian, R. (2021). Reading aloud with infants and toddlers. *YC Young Children*, *76*(3), 90–93.

Laidlaw, L., & Wong, S. S. (2016). Literacy and complexity: On using technology within emergent learning structures with young learners. *Complicity: An International Journal of Complexity and Education*, *13*(1). 30–42.

Lancaster, L. (2007). Representing the ways of the world: How children under 3 start to use syntax in graphic signs. *Journal of Early Childhood Literacy*, *7*(2), 123–154.

Lancaster, L. (2014). The emergence of symbolic principles: The distribution of mind in early sign making. *Biosemiotics*, *7*(1), 29–47. https://doi.org/10.1007/s12304-013-9195-3

Mackenzie, N. (2022a). Multimodal text creation from day 1 with draw, talk, write, share. *The California Reader 55*(1), 9–14.

Mackenzie, N. M. (2022b). Finding out what they know and can do with DTWS. *Practical Literacy: the early and primary years*, *27*(1), 23–24.

Makin, L. (2006). Literacy 8–12 months: what are babies learning? *Early Years*, *26*(3), 267–277. https://doi.org/10.1080/09575140600898449

Neumann, M. M. (2020). Teacher scaffolding of preschoolers' shared reading with a Storybook App and a printed book. *Journal of Research in Childhood Education*, *34*(3), 367–384. https://doi.org/10.1080/02568543.2019.1705447

Neumann, M. M. (2023). Drawing and writing together: Using iPads to support children's language, literacy, and social learning. *YC Young Children*, *78*(1), 78–83.

O'Grady, K., Scull, J., & Lyons, D. (2024). *Exploring the Early Writing Experiences of Young Children within the Home through Autoethnographic Reflections*. Issues in Educational Research, 34(1), 145–162.

Pahl, K., & Rowsell, J. (2005). *Literacy and Education: Understanding the New Literacy Studies in the Classroom*. London: Sage.

Peterson. S. S., & Friedrich. N. (2022). Introduction: Playce-based language literacy learning in early childhood. In S. Stagg-Peterson & N. Friedrich (Eds.), *Roles of Place and Play in Young Children's Oral and Written Language* (pp. 3–16). Toronto, Canada: University of Toronto Press.

Pinto, G., & Incognito, O. (2022). The relationship between emergent drawing, emergent writing, and visual-motor integration in preschool children. *Infant and Child Development*, *31*(2). https://doi.org/10.1002/icd.2284

Puranik, C. S., Phillips, B. M., Lonigan, C. J., & Gibson, E. (2018). Home literacy practices and preschool children's emergent writing skills: An initial investigation. *Early Childhood Research Quarterly*, *42*, 228–238. https://doi.org/10.1016/j.ecresq.2017.10.004

Raban, B., & Scull, J. (2023). Literacy. In D. Pendergast & S. Garvis (Eds.), *Teaching Early Years: Curriculum, Pedagogy and Assessment* (2nd ed., pp. 35–48). Routledge.

Robinson, C. E., Treasure, T., O'Connor, D., Neylon, G., Harrison, C., & Wynne, S. (2018). *Learning through Play: Creating a Play-Based Approach Within Early Childhood Contexts*. South Melbourne, Victoria, Australia: Oxford University Press.

Rowe, D. W., & Neitzel, C. (2010). Interest and agency in 2- and 3-year-olds' participation in emergent writing. *Reading Research Quarterly*, *45*(2), 169–195. https://doi.org/10.1598/RRQ.45.2.2

Siraj-Blatchford, I., & Clarke, P. (2000). *Supporting Identity, Diversity and Language in the Early Years*. Buckingham, UK: Open University Press.

Tayler, C., Ishimine, K., & Page, J. (2023). Assessment. In D. Pendergast & S. Garvis, (Eds.) *Teaching Early Years: Rethinking Curriculum, Pedagogy and Assessment* (2nd ed.). Sydney: Allen & Unwin.

UNESCO (2020). Mother tongue and early childhood care and education: synergies and challenges. https://unesdoc.unesco.org/ark:/48223/pf0000374419

United Nations (1989). *The United Nations Convention on the Rights of the Child.* https://downloads.unicef.org.uk/wp-content/uploads/2010/05/UNCRC_PRESS200910web.pdf?_ga=2.78590034.795419542.1582474737-1972578648.1582474737

VCAA [Victorian Curriculum and Assessment Authority] (2020). *Early Years Planning Cycle Resource for the Victorian Early Years Learning and Development Framework.* Melbourne Australia: VCAA.

Vygotsky, L. S. (1978). *Mind in Society: The Development of Higher Psychological Processes.* Cambridge, MA: Harvard University Press.

Writing in the preschool years

Bridie Raban

Introduction

Early writing happens easily if young children are given appropriate support and resources. Indeed, they want to write before they can read. Initially, they are more fascinated by their own marks than those made by others and use drawings and paintings to capture their worlds and imaginations. This chapter focuses on the learning and development that takes place before children begin formal schooling. There is much they need to experience and understand about writing before they produce recognisable words. Telling stories and composing, typically through their drawings, helps children experience the permanency and purpose of writing. In particular, a significant contribution to their perception and developing skill is their growing interest in writing their own name. Educators draw on a range of resources and activities to support young children during these early years, and this chapter provides a starting point for exploring the numerous opportunities that are available in their programs (see also Chapters 2, 3, and 10).

Early writing in practice

Children don't wait until they start school to learn how to write; young children, once they know it is physically and culturally possible, leave "messages" and "stories" in a mix of marks, scribbles, and drawings. This is because, for many young children, writing things down is part of family life (Axelsson, Lundqvist & Sandberg, 2020; Heath & Thomas, 2020; Puranik, Phillips. et al., 2018). For instance, they will be included in writing shopping lists, emailing family members, sending cards, leaving notes and Sticky

DOI: 10.4324/9781003439264-4

notes on the fridge door. However, as Mackenzie (2022) has pointed out, the combined complexities of knowing what to write (composing) and knowing how to write (concepts about print, written language as opposed to spoken forms and handwriting) can be overwhelming obstacles for some children. What we now know is that writing develops through constant invention and reinvention, including not only the development of language, but the development of cognition and understanding, as well as the development of fine motor skills (Chandler, et al., 2021).

Educators and family members can provide many and diverse opportunities for young children to explore writing in all its forms at different points in time as they gain control over their writing (Krijnen, et al., 2020). Consideration needs to be given to the awareness and development of decontextualized language necessary for successful writing down the track (Raban & Scull, 2023). Children's attention needs to be drawn to the different concepts about print, including how letters are formed, directionality, spaces between words, and the like, and they need to be given many opportunities to "write" for themselves in different play settings (Scrafton & Whitington, 2015). Nutbrown (2020) stresses that adults writing for and with children will be an important supportive activity throughout the preschool years.

Before being able to write conventionally, children attempt to convey messages through various forms of mark-making. In a study of young children aged 2–4 years (Levin & Bus, 2003), it was found that those children unable to convey their messages by writing spontaneously used drawing-like devices, again indicating the primacy of drawing as a representational-communicative system. In time, children come to use scribbles to convey their messages, using dots, circles, lines, and shapes that may or may not be arranged linearly.

Cocker (2013) identifies the substantial challenges involved in young children's writing development, particularly the confluence of skills and knowledge necessary to write words. These challenges facing young children, as they move from mark-making to scribble and on to letters and words, include:

- Understanding that writing is used to communicate,

- Unlocking the conventions and concepts about printed language, and

- Discovering that letters of the alphabet are used to represent speech sounds, and need to be formed appropriately.

Nevertheless, in spite of this complexity, learning about writing and how to write starts long before children enter formal school and much can be done to support this early development and understanding both at home and in early childhood settings (Guo, Puranik, Kelcey et al., 2021; Nutbrown, 2020).

Reflection prompt

In what ways do you encourage and value children's mark-making?
How do you engage families in supporting their children's desire to send messages?

Name-writing

Campbell and colleagues (2019) argue that young children's various representations of their name provide a valuable indicator of their growing understanding and awareness of print. Clay (2016) points out that through the activity of writing their name, young children come to understand that letters in words need to be in the same order on each occasion and that capital letters are placed at the beginning of significant and important words like their name. Researchers have found that the progression from scribble to recognizable writing appears to be task-dependent. The young children observed in one study (Ferreiro & Teberosky, 1982) used advanced writing features for easier writing tasks (like writing their name), but resorted to more basic features like scribble or drawing when the writing task proved more of a challenge, for instance, when asked to write about their holiday. These researchers also pointed out that young children's knowledge regarding their names is more advanced than their other writing, probably because it resonates more personally and they write it more frequently.

Because the printed name is synonymous with identity, children's names are often their first stable written form with meaning, and this represents an important benchmark in young children's early literacy understandings and development (Bradford & Wyse, 2022). In addition, Riverlland (2020) points out that focussing on a child's name provides both a culturally and socially relevant activity connecting both home and preschool. Name-writing serves an ongoing role, helping children make connections to letters, words, sounds, and reading and writing concepts (Guo, Dynia & Lai, 2021).

In an earlier study of 4-year-olds writing their name (Welsch et al., 2003), many children (33 per cent) could make marks, not distinguishable as letters, but 15 percent could write their name correctly. This range of name-writing ability across this sample correlated positively with these young children's other developing knowledge about literacy. Those who could write their name correctly and separate it from a picture of themselves, also achieved higher scores relating to rhyme and beginning sounds of words, alphabet knowledge, concept of a word, and print knowledge generally. However, later work by Drouin and Harman (2009) cautions that name-writing should not be the only indicator of children's conceptual knowledge about literacy.

Figures 4.1–4.3 show different examples of children writing their name. Geordie (Figure 4.1) is unsure of either the purpose or the relevance of this activity and makes random marks on the page. Peter (Figure 4.2) is copying from a name card and is in the early stages of learning to make marks. In Figure 4.3 Stevie shows a clear understanding of what is required and is well on the way to writing his name for himself.

Figure 4.1   Geordie

Figure 4.2   Peter

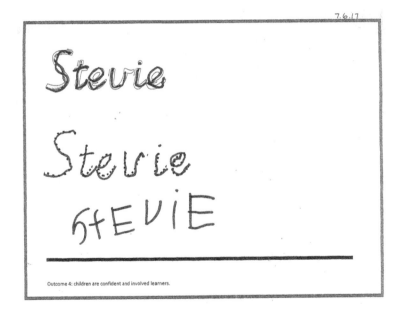

Figure 4.3   Stevie

Language development

Hill (2021) points out that spoken language and written language are quite distinct, and young children need to understand and learn about these differences. In everyday conversation, children might say, "over there" while pointing to a set of drawers when asked where their toys are, for instance. However, with writing, the language is required to be much more explicit. If you are helping children leave instructions for a friend who is visiting, they need to learn that the "reader" (a friend, in this case) knows nothing about where the toys are kept and, because of this, will require more explicit information. In this case, "over there" may well become "I put the toys away in the top drawer of the cupboard by the back door."

Written language, therefore, is decontextualized language; without an evident context, it needs to be more explicit than spoken language. With spoken language, posture, tone of voice, emphasis on particular words and facial expression all provide a context for the listener and contribute to the interpretation or understanding of the meaning of the message. All these clues are missing for the reader of a written message, as the message is transported through time and space.

How, then, can early childhood educators support young children into using more explicit ways of expressing themselves? An important means of introducing children to more explicit language necessary for later writing is, of course, to read stories from an early age. Stories are rarely about the "here and now"; they are more typically about "Once upon a time …" and so more context needs to be provided, and this requires more language. Encouraging children to retell stories, with prompts, helps them to keep the details embellished as necessary, and discussions of activities not shared by all the children will also help them to use more explicit language for themselves. Engaging children in talk when something new and interesting happens provides opportunities for the use of detail and explanation. During these occasions, educators can act as "purposely ignorant" by not always following what a child is explaining and asking questions for clarification, thus "pressing" for more information and more explicit language, to clarify the message.

In one setting, a further opportunity for developing more explicit language from the children was found during their response to finding that the fox had eaten their chickens during the Easter break. The children were full of ideas about stopping this happening again and made drawings of this to illustrate their solutions. Their educator captured this by scribing their instructions beside their drawings.

One boy said,

> "Our chooks died by a chook! No I mean a fox! He dug a hole and attacked them. Then he runned off so this is how we should build their new home. We should put a big spider web at the door. He will get stuck."

The educator has scribed exactly what this boy said/dictated. She is right to do this as when he reads back his "story," he will say it exactly the same way again. But when the educator responded to his story she said, "When the fox ran off, where do you think he went?" She modelled correct form. However, what is impressive here is that at the beginning of Term 2, this incident around losing their chooks prompted a greater volume of and more explicit language than where these children had left off in Term 1

"Our chooks died by a chook.. no. 1 He dug a hole and attaked them. Then he runned off. So this is how we should build their new house. We should put a big spider web at the door. He will get stuck."

Lev,

10-4-2016

Figure 4.4   Chooks

(see Fig 4.4). It is also significant to point out here that these children were more likely to write about the "here and now" (see Fig 4.5) and were less interested in "Once upon a time …"

Roskos, Tabors, and Lenhart (2009) point out that to achieve literacy, young children need writing to help them learn about reading, reading to help them learn about writing, and they need oral language to help them learn about both. These researchers and others (e.g., Brodin & Renblad, 2020) identify activities that can be used to help young children use, explore, learn about, and develop oral language in the preschool. These activities include:

I like to go shopping
with mum

Alice

Figure 4.5   Alice

Reflection prompt

List different ways you can engage with children to make their spoken language more explicit.

Invite family members to sometimes "not know" what the child is referring to in a shared conversation, to prompt the child to provide the necessary details and a more elaborated response.

- shared book reading;

- songs, rhymes, and word play;

- storytelling;

- time for discussion and sharing; and

- pretend play.

Shared book reading

After sharing a book, it can be placed somewhere easily accessible for the children so they can return to the book and talk about the pictures, introducing characters, sequencing events and bringing the story to a close. Tabors (2001) shows that there can be many different ways of reading a book together and in her research, she explores this further – how shared book reading can range from a straight reading of the text from cover to cover, or talking about the illustrations, or telling the story from the pictures (not reading), and reading punctuated with extensive interactions with the children. These interactions can involve explanations required of the text or illustrations, engaging the children to make inferences about what might happen next, and exploring the motivations of different characters – asking why they behaved in certain ways and how the story might conclude differently (see Stevens, Raban & Nolan, 2014).

Clemens and Kegel (2021) point out that reading to and with young children positively impacts their language and vocabulary development, both their receptive language and expressive language. Through listening to books read aloud to them, children hear words that are not familiar to them in everyday conversations. In addition, they learn vocabulary associated with experiences unfamiliar to them. They hear sentences constructed differently and texts that are sequentially ordered with beginnings, events, and endings. This is especially important for children, who may be more interested in following instruction books for making things or finding out how they work. By prompting children to talk about texts, through questioning what certain words mean, asking what motives could cause certain outcomes, and anticipating alternative outcomes, children will be supported in continuing their language development journey towards the extended and more explicit language required for writing.

It is interesting to note that when Aram and Biron (2004) compared two group interventions with 3-to-5-year-old children, it was found that the group receiving a shared storybook reading set of activities did not make as much progress with early literacy as the group who experienced shared additional writing activities. This finding underlines the significance of early writing opportunities and activities both within the preschool program and at home (Rowe, Shimizu & Davis, 2022).

Song, rhymes, and play with language

Being able to play with words is the beginning of a more sophisticated understanding of how language works. Through songs and rhyming stories (like those written by Dr. Seuss, for instance), children's attention can be drawn to the patterning of words that sound similar (Critten et al., 2021). This starts with an awareness of rhyming words /toll/ /roll/, moving on to words that end the same way /jumping/flying/ and onto words that start with the same sounds /stand/ /stop/. Eventually, children will be able to segment the syllables of a word /catch - ing/ and clap to the syllables of their name. What is clear here, however, is that children move from larger units to smaller ones as they gain confidence through games and other activities (Block, 2020; Palmer, Bayley & Raban, 2014) while receiving continuing support and feedback from their educators.

Raban (2014) and Holmes et al. (2022) talk about the need to "play" with language in order to reach an understanding that language is apart from what it refers to. Bilingual and multilingual children reach this understanding earlier than monolingual children as they already have access to different words relating to the same object or experience (Gampa, Wermelinger & Daum, 2019). Activities that create opportunities to experience and learn about language, apart from what it refers to, include defining words, making words up, thinking of another word that means the same, playing rhyming word games, and later "I Spy," which draws attention to how words begin and share beginning sounds.

Reflection prompt

List activities that you would use with children to help them understand that a word is apart from what it stands for. What kinds of similar activities can you share with families?

Storytelling

Storytelling gives children opportunities to listen to and engage with the educator, developing a storyline and explaining how and why some things happen (Holmes, Kohm, et al., 2022; Stevens, Raban & Nolan, 2014). Roskos, Tabors, and Lenhart (2009) identify different protocols for storytelling, moving from the educator modelling storytelling to the educator supporting the child(ren) by providing ideas for topics and stories. Through these activities, successful listening skills will be demonstrated, positive attitudes and encouragement will be experienced by the storyteller, and the educator will be continuously making time for discussion and sharing ideas (Lenhart, Lenhard, Vaahtoranta, et al., 2020).

Time for discussion and sharing

Casbergue et al. (2008) address issues around high-quality early childhood literacy environments with respect to language and early literacy development. In particular, they discuss how educators spend their time during children's free play activities. Some educators move round the room, joining different groups and posing questions related to the activities taking place, while others choose to spend the whole time with a particular group or individual. How educators use their time is less important than the nature of the interactions they employ. For instance, child-chosen play experiences provide opportunities for the educator to use "rare" words which may be unfamiliar to the child, to use extended discourse around a particular activity, to listen carefully to each child's explanations and build on these (Purdon, 2016). This provides opportunities for undivided attention that can lead to a better understanding of each child's language development.

Pretend play

Pretend play, sometimes referred to as "dramatic play," benefits children both socially and cognitively (Francis & Gibson, 2023). However, and equally as important, pretend play gives opportunities for the generation of sophisticated language use and interaction. This is because children have to explain themselves to each other, their roles and their plans for action. To achieve this successfully, children will need the support of their educators who can extend their play with encouragement, challenge, appropriate language, and resources.

> ## Reflection prompt
>
> *Think of the different ways you can resource pretend play that will lead to children composing a story.*
> *Check with family members if there are opportunities for pretend play at home.*

Understanding the purpose of writing

Cognitive strategies involved in learning about writing and being able to write for oneself include, broadly, understanding that language can be captured and retained for further review and reflection. Growing up in a literate society (Scull & Raban, 2016) will give young children many opportunities to see print in the environment and begin to understand that it carries meaning. They come to know where the road crossing is, which is the shop "open" that sells takeaway food, and where we get our petrol, along with other real-life experiences. Educators build on this understanding and have print around their room, directing children to different play areas and including them in what to write for their notice board (Prior & Gerard, 2004; Vukelich & Christie, 2009). They will involve children in selecting texts for their portfolios, as a record of the children's achievements and activities. Educators, like family members, draw children's attention to print, while reading a story, or out walking, or on screen. Yaden et al. (2000) have investigated how children learn to understand that their own spoken words can be held in this way for future reference, they can compose, and they can become "authors" themselves (Hall, 2019).

Children need to understand how writing is used to communicate, to whom and for what purposes. However, children do not wait until they can formally write to achieve communication strategies. Mackenzie and Scull (2015) have pointed out that mark-making and drawing, in particular, perform an early step in children's written communication development. As mentioned earlier in this chapter, Levin and Bus (2003) also identified the primacy of drawing as a representational-communicative system for children who are yet to master conventional writing.

While writing is a "closed" system, defined by rules and a finite alphabet, drawing is an "open" system and offers endless opportunities for children to "tell their story" in whatever way they choose. Drawing might be considered by some as an arbitrary time-filler or merely as "play." Nevertheless, drawing can be seen as an outcome of impressive neuro-logical activity and development (Sheridan, 2002, 2012). Indeed, drawing for composi-tional purposes is a powerful form of communication (Mackenzie & Veresov, 2013), particularly during the early stages of writing development, both before and during the early years of school. In addition, children develop concepts about print (Clay, 2019) including words, letters, print displays, along with directionality and spacing.

Having to compose and grapple with a writing instrument and the necessary *concepts about print* all at the same time can see many children feeling defeatist about their writing. Focusing on the composition alone through drawing can relieve the tension and enable children to share their stories from a much earlier age. In discussion with educa-tors and family members, children can talk about their drawing. In response, the educa-tor can write what they say and display the writing with the drawing for others to view as a complete composition (Mackenzie, 2011).

Through these experiences, children come to understand that what they think about and what they say can be transported over time and conveyed to others (Rowe & Neitzel, 2010). In addition, because their spoken words have been re-presented (written down for them), they can "read" them and share their composition with others (Love, Burns & Buell, 2007).

Figure 4.6 shows a child "writing" his story to share with others, showing what will happen if they eat too much:

Figure 4.6   Monster

It's a scary monster!! It's trying to steal toys because he ate too much chocolate and hot chocolate and marshmallows

---

Reflection prompt

What other play opportunities could be resourced to generate integrated writing activities?

Conventions and concepts about printed language

Justice et al. (2009) point out that providing children with many experiences of both reading and writing in early childhood years provides a robust foundation for literacy development, including knowledge of the alphabet, an awareness of sound and letter correspondences in written language, and an understanding of the structures of print, referred to as "concepts about print" (Clay, 2019). Many of these concepts will be learned from the children's experiences of reading, like directionality, individual words, and some punctuation. However, the spaces between words may be less well understood (Jackson, 2014), and this will become apparent as they begin to make their own marks and scribbles.

In English, children have to learn 40 distinct letter shapes with some upper-case letters similar to their lower-case component (e.g., S and s) and others not so similar (R and r). In addition, there are two ways children learn about letters: by naming letters or using letter sounds. Studies show evidence of the role letter name knowledge plays in the development of word knowledge, before children grasp the alphabetic principle (Albuquerque & Martins, 2021). Some letters, like B and F and Z, have names that give clues to their sounds while others do not (W and H, for instance). Piasta et al. (2010) have indicated that the sounds of letters with clues from their names will be learned more easily.

Through a range of activities, children can be shown the directional aspects of print, by finger pointing, tracking left to right, from top to bottom of the page. When educators write important notices for the day together with the children, for instance, they point out the need to "write" one letter at a time. They can engage children in thinking about what letter might come next and think of words that sound like the one they want to write. In one study (Puranik & Lonigan, 2011) it was revealed that print knowledge and alphabet knowledge made unique contributions to children's ability to write/form letters.

Children need many and varied opportunities for experimenting with writing in order to try out and improve their developing capabilities (Loyola, Grimberg & Colomer, 2020). Support, through the use of prompts, cues, modelling, and feedback, facilitates early skill development, especially for children experiencing difficulties (Bus & Out,

2009). Importantly, children learn best when the words of a sentence are prompted and modelled within the context of a real event, where the writing is seen as part of the whole activity (Mackenzie & Scull, 2015).

Fine motor development

Holding a pen or pencil and controlling the fine motor movements required of handwriting takes time to develop, with some children still finding this difficult when they start formal school. Handwriting in the early years, therefore, is encouraged through the development of large muscle movements of the arms and hands, leading to finger painting and other mark-making (Clere & Raban, 2017; Simpson, et al., 2019). It has been stressed that children need to participate in a variety of activities intentionally designed to promote fine motor control (Huffman & Fortenbury, 2011). Fine motor skills are difficult for preschoolers to master because the skills depend on muscular control, patience, judgement, and brain co-ordination. Whole arm, whole hand, and pincher and pincer movements need to be explored and built on via a range of different activities.

Young children need to participate in a variety of activities intentionally designed to promote fine motor control. Caletti et al. (2012) have used tracing as a technique for preschool children to help with letter formation. Using the letters of their name, children were supported by being shown where to start tracing each letter and being told which way to go, with this support being systematically "faded" as the child required less and less support. However, activities like this require the child to be writing recognisable letters and many may not be at that point of fine motor development, experiencing difficulty holding a pencil or felt-tip pen. Pencil grip can be strengthened by using scissors, using a plastic dropper (with a squeezy top) to paint a picture or pattern with a paintbrush, doing up buttons, and the like.

One study used whole body activities as well as directional games and letter-play activities all of which improved the children's handwriting beyond a control group who did not receive the intervention (Lust & Donica, 2011). Activities outlined by Huffman and Fortenbury (2011) help to develop the upper body and strengthen arm muscles. These activities include making large circular movements with arms, hand and finger games as well as using utensils to interact with other objects, like using tweezers to pick up small objects.

Figure 4.7 shows a different stage of mark-making. This child is mark-making in an orderly fashion (although possibly from right to left). Children need many opportunities to write and having their own "writing" book where they try out words and letter strings will be helpful. Providing a writing table with a range of different paper and pens, pencils, crayons and felt tip pens, coupons, raffle tickets, for instance, will invite children to explore writing in their own time and in their own way.

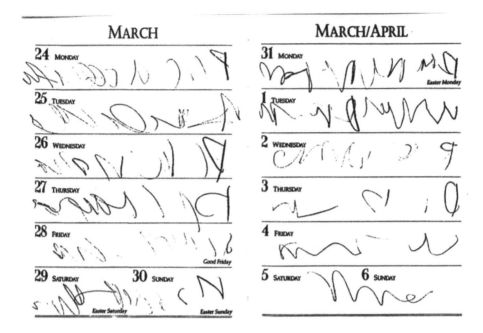

Figure 4.7   Diary

Children move towards control of letter-forms, both capitals and lower case, through many opportunities to write for a variety of purposes. See also Chapter 7 in this text for further discussion of the skills necessary for handwriting.

Reflection prompt

Make a list of the different resources that support writing development – (a) in a room you visit, and (b) consider how you might add to these.

Supporting early writing development in the preschool

Educators can provide many and diverse opportunities for young children to explore writing in all its forms at different times in children's learning and development. Consideration needs to be given to the awareness and development of explicit language necessary for successful writing down the track. Children's attention needs to be drawn to the different concepts about print, including letters, directionality, spaces between words and the like, and they need to be given many opportunities to "write" for themselves in different play settings. Educators writing for and with the children will be an important supportive activity throughout the preschool years.

With the increasing use of digital technology, in both the home and the preschool and school, it is tempting to explore possible ways in which young children's writing can be stimulated and concepts about print better understood. Families may be involving their young children in the composition of emails to distant family members and friends, constructing and adding comments to saved photographs on a family member's smartphone, for instance. However, when Quinn and Bliss (2021) report on their comprehensive exploration and examination of more than 470 early writing apps, they found the choice of apps used to be critical. They found that many apps were of low quality and of limited use in developing young children's writing ability beyond tracing letters.

Writing is a complex activity made up of a variety of aspects which progress at different rates depending on purpose and opportunity. A helpful progression that young children move through is outlined in the following table. It outlines the trajectories that children may take as their understandings of the purpose and function of writing develops (Table 4.1).

Table 4.1 Supporting Early Writing Development in the Preschool Years

Writing Components	Suggested Activities
Writing as composition	Looking at writing around the community or around the room and talking about this. How is information conveyed and why? Children make marks to stand for objects and ideas. Children will use drawings to convey their ideas. Children "read" their drawings and these can be scribed for them. "What shall we draw about today?" encourages children to think about their own stories or pieces of information to "write" about with adult scribing.
Written language v. spoken language	Written language is more "dense," more precise than spoken language. e.g., "dog" "That's my dog.' "This is my dog and he has long fluffy hair." "My dog has long fluffy hair and he likes to go for walks." "My dog loves his bones but sometimes he buries them in the yard and Dad gets really cross." Young children must learn that writing is about more than the "here and now". Opportunities to talk about things in the past or future require the language to be more detailed and explicit. "Pretending" not to understand what a child says can provide opportunities for explanations and requests with more explicit language.

(continued)

Writing Components	Suggested Activities
Concepts about print	Pointing to words as you read what is scribed.
	Understanding that the squiggles on the page tell the story, not the picture.
	Getting the idea of directionality, top of page, moving left to right.
	Children's individual marks can resemble whole words or a phrase.
	Random squiggles that do not resemble letters.
	Some letter-like forms, usually letters from their own name, some upside down and backwards.
	Leaving spaces between marks and letters.
	Writing their name gives children the idea of capital and lower-case letters, letters in a specific order, spaces between words.
Handwriting	Large muscle movements from the shoulder, like throwing a ball into a container.
	Using arm and elbow movements in time to music.
	Using finger movements to pick up and sort buttons or marbles.
	Using felt-tip pens to make marks on paper
	Using pincers or tweezers to play a game with moving small objects round a board.
	Patterns on paper:
	/\/\/\/\/\/\ OOOOOOOOOOO
	Using pens and pencils to make capital letters of own name well formed.
	Lower-case letters of own name.

Reflection prompt

Think about how you might assess children's developing knowledge about writing.
See Chapter 8.

Conclusion

There is much that can be done to encourage and support young children's early writing development during the preschool years. As educators, it is important to build on children's interests and provide experiences that support their growing awareness of the many forms and purposes of writing. By providing numerous opportunities for mark-making and valuing a variety of different writing activities, young children will begin to gain confidence and explore more complex possibilities. Remember, it is largely through the ways educators provide for and engage with young children, in a variety of rich contexts, that enable the children to develop an understanding of the concepts that promote literacy learning more generally.

Acknowledgements

Special thanks are expressed here to the staff of Orbost Preschool, Mildura West Kindergarten, Country Way Early Learning, and Pasadena Preschool (Mildura), who contributed to both the thinking and the examples of children's work in this chapter.

Glossary

Terminology: Meaning

Alphabet knowledge: Letter identification, upper- and lowercase

Alphabetic principle: Understanding that words in English are made up of letters, and letters and groups of letters represent sounds

Concepts about print: Understanding how print works – letters, words, directionality, spaces, punctuation

Decontextualised language:

- No assumption about shared experiences or background knowledge, so language is denser and more explicit
- Language is apart from what it refers to
- Language can be removed from the here and now

Directionality: In English, written language is written left to right and top to bottom of the page

Expressive language: Being able to put thoughts into words and sentences in a way that makes sense to a reader or listener

Fine motor skills, control, development, movements: Coordination of small muscle movement in fingers and hands.

Print awareness: Understanding of forms, functions, and conventions of written language

Representational communicative system: Making your message understood through drawing writing and talking

Recommended Reading

Adams, A. M., Soto-Calvo, E., Francis, H. N., Patel, H., Hartley, C., Giofrè, D., & Simmons, F. R. (2021). Characteristics of the preschool home literacy environment which predict writing skills at school. *Reading and Writing 34*, 2203–2222. DOI: 10.1007/s11145-021-10133-w

Puranik, C. S., & Lonigan, C. J. (2012). Name-writing proficiency, not length of name, is associated with preschool children's emergent literacy skills. *Early Childhood Research Quarterly, 27*(2), 284–294. DOI: 10.1016/ecresq.2011.09.003

Zhang, C., & Quinn, M. F. (2020). Preschool children's interest in early writing activities and perceptions of writing experience, *The Elementary School Journal, 121*(1), 52–74.

References

Albuquerque, A., & Martins, M. A. (2021). Invented spelling activities in kindergarten: The role of instructional scaffolding and collaborative learning, *International Journal of Early Years Education, 29*(1), 90–113. DOI: 10.1080/009669760.2020.1760085

Aram, D., & Biron, S. (2004). Joint storybook reading and joint writing interventions among low SES preschoolers: Differential contributions to early literacy. *Early Childhood Research Quarterly, 19*(4), 588–610. DOI: 10.1016/ecresq.2004.10.003

Axelsson, A., Lundqvist, J., & Sandberg, G. (2020). Influential factors on children's reading and writing development: The perspective of parents in a Swedish context. *Early Childhood Development and Care, 190*(16), 2520–2532. DOI: 10.1080/03004430.2019.1590348

Block, M. K. (2020). Invitations to play: Using play to build literacy skills in young learners. *Michigan Reading Journal, 52*(3), Article 11. https://scholarworks.gvsu.edu/mrj/vol52/iss3/11

Bradford, H., & Wyse, D. (2022). Two-year-old and three-year-old children's writing: the contradictions of children's and adults' conceptualisations. *Early Years, 42*(3), 293–309. DOI: 10.1080/09575146.2020.1736519

Brodin, J., & Renblad, K. (2020). Improvement of preschool children's speech and language skills. *Early Child Development and Care, 190*(14), 2205–2213. DOI: 10.1080/03004430.2018.1564917

Bus, A. G., & Out, D. (2009). Unraveling genetic and environmental components of early literacy: a twin study. *Reading and Writing, 22*, 293–306. DOI: 10.1007/s11145-008-9115-0

Caletti, E., McLaughlin, T. F., Derby, K. M., & Rinaldi, L. (2012). The effects of using visual prompts, tracing and consequences to teach two preschool students with disabilities to write their names. *Academic Research International, 2*(3), 265–270.

Campbell, K., Chen, Y.J., Shenoy, S. & Cunningham, A.E. (2019). Preschool children's early writing: Repeated measures reveal growing but variable trajectories. *Reading and Writing 32*(5), 939–961. https://doi.org/10.1007/s11145-018-9893-y

Casbergue, L., McGee, L. M., & Bedford, A. (2008). Characteristics of classroom environments associated with accelerated literacy development. In L. M. Justice, C. Vukelich, & W. H. Teale (Eds.), *Achieving excellence in preschool literacy instruction* (pp. 167–181). New York: Guilford Press.

Chandler, M. C., Herde, G. K., Bowles, R. P., McRoy, K. Z., Pontifix M. P., & Bingham, G. E. (2021). Self-regulation moderates the relationship between fine motor skills and writing in early childhood. *Early Childhood Research Quarter, 57*(4), 239–250.

Clay, M. M. (2016). *Literacy Lessons: Designed for individuals*. Part 2 (2nd ed) North Shore, NZ: Heinemann.

Clay, M. M. (2019). *An observation survey of early literacy achievement* (4th ed.). Auckland, New Zealand: Heinemann.

Clemens, L. F., & Kegel. C. A. T. (2021). Unique contribution of shared book reading on adult-child language interaction. *Journal of Child Language, 48*(2), 373–386. DOI: 10.1017/S0305000920000331

Clere, L., & Raban, B. (2017). *Child-initiated Early Writing; Ideas for engaging children in the writing process*. Blairgowrie: Teaching Solutions.

Cocker, D. (2013). Writing instruction in preschool and kindergarten. In S. Graham, C. A. MaCarther & J. Fitzgerald (Eds.), *Best practices in writing instruction* (2nd ed., pp. 26–47). New York: Guilford Press.

Critten, S., Holliman, A. J., Hughes, D. J., Wood, C., Cunnane, H., Pillinger, C., & Hilton, S. H. (2021). A longitudinal investigation of prosodic sensitivity and emergent literacy. *Reading and Writing, 34*(2), 371–389. DOI: 10.1007/s11145-020-10077-7

Drouin, M., & Harman, J. (2009). Name writing and letter knowledge in preschoolers: Incongruities in skill and the usefulness of name writing as a developmental indicator. *Early Childhood Research Quarterly, 24*(3), 263–270. DOI: 10.1016/ecresq.2009.05.001

Ferreiro, E., & Teberosky, A. (1982). *Literacy before schooling*. Exeter, NH: Heinemann Educational Books.

Francis, G. A., & Gibson, J. L. (2023). A plausible role of imagination in pretend play: Counterfactual reasoning and executive functions. *British Journal of Psychology, 114*. DOI: 10.1111/bjop.12650

Gampa, A., Wermelinger, S., & Daum, M. M. (2019). Bilingual children adapt to the needs of their communication partners, monolinguals do not. *Child Development, 90*(1), 98–107. DOI: 10.1111/cdev.13190

Guo, Y., Dynia, J. M., & Lai, M. H. C. (2021). Early childhood special education teachers' self-efficacy in relation to individual children: Links to children's literacy learning, *Early Childhood Research Quarterly, 54*(1), 153–161. DOI: 10.1016/j.ecresq.2020.09.002

Guo, Y., Puranik, C., Kelcey, B., Sun, J., Dinnesen, M. S., & Breit-Smith, A. (2021). The role of home literacy practices in kindergarten children's early writing development: A one-year longitudinal study, *Early Education and Development, 32*(2), 209–227. DOI: 10.1080/10409289.2020.1746618

Hall, A. H. (2019). *Every Child is a Writer: Understanding the Importance of Writing in Early Childhood*. Institute for Child Success. https://www.instituteforchildsuccess.org/resources/resource/every-child-is-a-writer-understanding-the-importance-of-writing-in-early-childhood-writing/

Heath, S. B., & Thomas, C. (2020). The achievement of preschool literacy for mother and child. In J. R. Hayes, R. E. Young, M. L. Matchett, M. McCaffrey & C. Cochran (Eds.), *Reading empirical research studies: The rhetoric of research* (pp. 180–207). New York: Routledge.

Hill, S. (2021). *Developing early literacy: Assessment and teaching* (3rd ed.). South Yarra, VIC: Eleanor Curtain Publishing.

Holmes, R. M., Kohm, K., Genise, S., Koolidge, L., Mendelson, D., Romeo, I., & Bant, C. (2022). Is there a connection between children's language skills, creativity and play? *Early Child Development and Care, 192*, 1128–1189. DOI: 10.1080/03004430.2020.1853115

Huffman, J. M., & Fortenbury, C. (2011). Helping preschoolers prepare for writing. *Developing fine motor skills. Young Children, 66*(5), 100–103.

Jackson, H. (2014). *Words and Their Meanings* (Chapter 1). London: Routledge.

Justice, L. M., Kaderavek, J., Fan, X., Sofka, A., & Hunt, A. (2009). Accelerating preschoolers' early literacy development through teacher-child storybook reading and explicit print referencing. *Language, Speech, and Hearing Services in Schools, 40*(1), 67–85. DOI: 10.1044/0161-1461(2008/07-0098)

Krijnen, E., van Steensel, R., Meeuwisse, M., Jongerling, J., & Severiens, S. (2020). Exploring a refined model of home literacy activities and associations with children's emergent literacy skills. *Reading and Writing 33*(1), 207–238. DOI: 10.1007/s11145-01909957-4

Lenhart, J., Lenhard, W., Vaahtoranta, E., & Suggate, S. (2020). More than words: Narrator engagement during storytelling increases children's word learning, story comprehension, and on-task behavior. *Early Childhood Research Quarterly, 51*(2), 338–351. DOI: 10.1016/j.ecresq.2019.12.00

Levin, I., & Bus, A. G. (2003). How is emergent writing based on drawing? Analysis of children's products and their sorting by children and mothers. *Developmental Psychology*, *39*(5), 891–905. DOI: 10.1037/0012-1649.36.5.891

Love, A., Burns, M. S., & Buell, M. J. (2007). Writing, empowering literacy. *Young Children*, *62*(4), 12–19.

Loyola, C. C., Grimberg, C. A., & Colomer, Ú. B. (2020). Early childhood teachers making multiliterate learning environments: The emergence of a spatial design thinking process. *Thinking Skills and Creativity*, *36*(2). DOI: 10.1016/j.tsc.2020.100655

Lust, C. A., & Donica, D. K. (2011). Effectiveness of a handwriting readiness program in Head Start: A two-group controlled trial. *The American Journal of Occupational Therapy*, *65*(5), 560–568. DOI: 10.5014/ajot.2011.000612

Mackenzie, N. M. (2011). From drawing to writing: What happens when you shift teaching priorities in the first six months of school? *Australian Journal of Language and Literacy*, (34)3, 322–340.

Mackenzie, N. M. (2022). Finding out what children 'know and can do' with DTWS. *Practical Literacy: The Early and Primary Years*, *27*(1), 23–25. DOI: 10.3316/informit.27965659805042

Mackenzie, N. M., & Veresov, N. (2013). How drawing can support writing acquisition: Text construction in early writing from a Vygotskian perspective. *Australasian Journal of Early Childhood*, *31*(4), 22–29.

Mackenzie, N. M., & Scull, J. (2015). Literacy: Writing. In S. McLeod & J. McCormack (Eds.), *Introduction to speech, language and literacy* (pp. 398–445). Melbourne, VIC: Oxford University Press.

Nutbrown, C. (2020). Writing before school: The role of families in supporting children's early writing development. In H. Chen, D. Myhill & H. Lewis (Eds.), *Growing into writing* (pp. 40–59). London: Routledge.

Palmer, S., Bayley, R., & Raban, B. (2014). *Foundations of early literacy: A balanced approach to language, listening and literacy skills in the early years*. Albert Park, VIC: Teaching Solutions.

Piasta, S. B., Purpura, D. J., & Wagher, R. K. (2010). Fostering alphabet knowledge development: A comparison of two instructional approaches. *Reading and Writing*, *23*(6), 607–626. DOI: 10.1007/s11145-009-9174-x

Prior, J., & Gerard, M. (2004). *Environmental print in the classroom: Meaningful connections for learning to read*. Newark, DE: International Reading Association.

Puranik, C. S., & Lonigan, C. J. (2011). From scribbles to scrabble: Preschool children's developing knowledge of written language. *Reading and Writing*, *24*(5), 567–587. DOI: 10.1007/611145-009-9220-8

Puranik, C. S., Phillips, B. M., Lonigan, C. J., & Gibson, E. (2018). Home literacy practices and preschool children's emergent writing skills: An initial investigation. *Early Childhood Research Quarterly*, *42*(1), 228–238. DOI: 10.1016/j.ecresq.2017.10.004

Purdon, A. (2016). Sustained shared thinking in an early childhood setting: an exploration of practitioners' perspectives. *Education 3–13*, *44*(3), 269–282. DOI: 10.1080/03004279.2014.907819

Quinn, M., & Bliss, M. (2021). Moving beyond tracing: The nature, availability and quality of digital apps to support children's writing. *Journal of Early Childhood Literacy*, *21*(2), 230–258. DOI: 10.1177/146879841983598

Raban, B. (2014). TALK to think, learn and teach. *The Journal of Reading Recovery*, *13*(2), 5–15.

Raban, B., & Scull, J. (2023). Literacy. In D. Pendergast & S. Garvis (Eds.), *Teaching early years: Curriculum, pedagogy and assessment* (2nd ed., pp. 35–48). London: Routledge.

Riverlland, J. (2020). Linking literacy across different contexts. In C. Barratt-Pugh & M. Rohl (Eds.), *Literacy learning in the early years* (Chapter 2). London: Routledge.

Roskos, K. A., Tabors, P. O., & Lenhart, L.A. (2009). *Oral language and early literacy in preschool*. Newark, DE: International Reading Association.

Rowe, D. W., & Neitzel, C. (2010). Interest and agency in 2 and 3 year old's participation in emergent writing. *Reading Research Quarterly*, *45*(2), 169–195. DOI: 10.1598/RRQ.45.2.2

Rowe, D. W., Shimizu, A. Y., & Davis, Z. G. (2022). Essential practices for engaging young children as writers: Lessons from expert early writing teachers. *The Reading Teacher, 75*(4) 485–494. DOI: 10.1002/trtr.2066

Scrafton, E., & Whitington, V. (2015). The accessibility of socio-dramatic play to culturally and linguistically diverse Australian preschoolers. *European Early Childhood Education Research Journal, 23*(2), 213–228. DOI: 10.1080/1350293x.2015.1016806

Scull, J., & Raban, B. (Eds.). (2016). *Growing up literate.* South Yarra, VIC: Eleanor Curtain Publishing.

Sheridan, S. R. (2002). The neurological significance of children's drawings: The Scribble Hypothesis. *Journal of Visual Literacy, 22*(2), 101–128. DOI: 10.1080/23796529.2002.1167458

Sheridan, S. R. (2012). *Saving literacy: A guide for professional caregivers.* Conshohocken, PA: Infinity Publishing. files.eric.ed.gov/fulltext/ED514424.pdf

Simpson, A., Al Ruwaili, R., Kelly, R., Leonard, H., Geeraert, N., & Riggs, K. J. (2019). Fine motor control underlies the association between response inhibition and drawing skill in early development. *Child Development, 90*(3), 911–923. DOI: 10.1111/cdev.12949

Stevens, J., Raban, B., & Nolan, A. (2014). *Storytelling and storymaking in the early years.* Albert Park, VIC: Teaching Solutions.

Tabors, P. O. (2001). Parents and children reading books together. In D. K. Dickinson & P. O. Tabors (Eds.). *Beginning literacy with language* (pp. 31–52). Baltimore, MD: Paul Brookes Publishing Co.

Vukelich, C., & Christie, J. (2009). *Building a foundation for preschool literacy: Effective instruction for children's reading and writing development.* Newark, DE: International Reading Association.

Welsch, J. G., Sullivan, A., & Justice, L. M. (2003). That's my letter: What preschoolers' name writing representations tell us about emergent literacy knowledge. *Journal of Literacy Research, 35*(2), 757–776.

Yaden, Jr. D. B., Tam, A., Madrigal, P., Brassell, D., Massa, J., Altamirano, L. S., & Armendariz, J. (2000). Early literacy for inner-city children: The effects of reading and writing interventions in English and Spanish during the preschool years. *The Reading Teacher, 54*(2), 186–189. http://www.jstor.org/stable/20204894

Developing authorial skills

Child language leading to text construction, sentence construction, and vocabulary development

Janet Scull and Noella M. Mackenzie

Introduction

When composing texts, the three authorial dimensions of writing mark the shift over control in written language: text construction, sentence construction, and vocabulary development. Children need to learn: (1) how to organise their ideas or information into a text that often follows the rules of a particular text type (e.g., letter, narrative); (2) how simple, compound, and complex sentences are constructed and how punctuation supports sentence construction and (3) how to choose words to add precision to their writing. Each authorial dimension will be expanded upon and examples provided. We begin with a short discussion of oral language and identify the connections between oral language and writing. This chapter connects strongly to Chapters 6 and 7, which focus on the secretarial/editorial elements of writing, Chapters 3 and 4, which focus on preparing children for writing (0–2 and 3–5 years), and Chapters 9 and 10, which focus on pedagogical approaches to teaching writing in early years classrooms. We have included prompts to aid reflection, suggestions for how parents may support young children as they learn about the authorial elements of text creation, and recommended readings.

Developing oral language skills

Oral language, and specifically increased control over literate discourse, is critical to children's ability to create texts in the early years of schooling and beyond. Yet the differences between oral and written language become more evident as children progress

DOI: 10.4324/9781003439264-5

through the years of schooling, with teachers needing to understand the patterns of written language that children must master (Christie, 2005; Scull, Mackenzie & Bowles, 2020). Oral language also allows children to share ideas and communicate what they know. Indeed, oral language development is critical to children's ability to think and learn (Raban, 2014) and forms the foundation for all literacy learning (Dickinson et al., 2012; Hoff et al., 2020). In addition, the social nature of language learning provides the necessary contexts for use, with adults as models who are at best responsive and supportive of children's use of language (Emmitt et al., 2014), (See Chapters 2 and 3.) In 2000, Raban argued that:

> Children's curiosity and persistence are supported by those who direct their attention, structure experiences, support learning attempts, and regulate the complexity and difficulty levels of information and share with them the appropriate language through focused conversations.

> (p. 44)

From the very start, children need to be supported by adults who recognise the situated language practices of young children. Language development is greatly influenced by the level, amount, and type of conversations that children are immersed in and their exposure to print texts (through shared books and environmental print) and media (Hoff et al., 2020). The words they learn and use and the ways they use and pronounce words will be directly related to the language they hear. "At every point in development, children differ in the size of the vocabularies they command, the complexity of the structures they produce, and the skill with which they communicate" (Hoff, 2006, p. 56), and we must appreciate the cultural influences on language use and learning (Gee, 2002). The wide variation in children's language use is also reflective of the fluid world of cultural and linguistic diversity and multiplicity of languages and literacies available as resources for meaning-making (New London Group, 2000). Hence, when children are learning to write, their speech can be a prime resource or a major problem, depending upon the latitude and flexibility of the audience (Dyson, 2016). Here we recognise the tension between the acceptance of varied communicative practices and the need for conformity to a range of conventional written discourse patterns recognised as fundamental to early writing competence.

Oral language and authorial skills

As children transition from preschool to the early years of schooling, they develop a deeper appreciation of both oral and written language and acquire a rich network of language skills for learning. With respect to children's diverse preschool experiences, many children start school with early understandings of book language, and written language registers, and this supports them to build the oral language skills needed to progress with learning to write (Teberosky et al., 2020). We note activities such as shared and dialogic book reading that can have a positive impact on aspects of young children's language learning with these effects tied to the interactions between the adult and child (Noble et al., 2019; Riordan et al., 2022). When complemented by quality teaching conversations, children are supported to build effective talk practices and develop the language resources required for literacy achievement (Raban & Scull, 2023).

Over time children need to develop a range of language skills, with oral language skills importantly and differentially related to written text forms. While oral language is learned and generally used in face-to-face interactions, often referring to the surrounding context, writing is more often produced at some distance from an interaction and event, requiring a more structured, planned response, drawing on a range of complex language skills (Christie, 2005). These features of written expression become more marked as children learn to create written and multimodal texts for a range of more abstract audiences and purposes (Derewianka & Jones, 2023; Myhill, 2021). When writing, children are required to use extended discourse forms, to elaborate the context, to select vocabulary and to add detail and interest to their texts, appropriate to the intended audience and purpose. Topic-specific vocabulary to describe events and characters and increasing levels of control over text structures and sentence grammar are necessary for text coherence, cohesion, and connections (Teberosky et al., 2020). Students' knowledge of and developing control over these areas of written language assist students to sequence ideas and create texts with increasing sophistication and precision. In the sections that follow, as the authorial aspects of writing are described, we pay attention to children's oral language and how this is both foundational to and facilitative of children's early writing.

Authorial skills

The three authorial dimensions of writing, in many ways, signal the shift over control in written language: text construction, sentence construction, and vocabulary development. Children need to learn:

1 How to organise their ideas or information into a text that will follow the rules of a particular text type (even the simplest recounts, lists, or letters show evidence of text structures);

2 How to use simple, compound, and complex sentences to convey meaning at the sentence level (being able to choose appropriate sentence length and complexity allows meaning to be clearly expressed); and

3 How to choose words to add precision to their writing (the more choice, the more precise).

While punctuation is in fact a secretarial/editorial skill, it is discussed in this chapter as it provides the conventional framework for sentence structure.

Text structure

There is clear evidence in children's earliest utterances that purpose and audience drive young children's language learning. Young children understand that language is meaningful and an important mechanism for meeting their needs and engaging with others in their world (Emmitt et al., 2014). Recognising the purposeful nature of children's communication efforts, Halliday (1975) charted children's language development in terms of the different functions he found in children's repertoire of use. He identified seven functions of language that enable young children to meet their physical, emotional, and social needs. The first four functions Halliday (1975) refers to are: instrumental (used to satisfy a need), regulatory (used to influence the behaviours of others), interactional (used to develop social relationships), and personal (used to express feelings, opinions, and individual identity). The next three functions are described as helping the child to come to terms with his or her environment: heuristic (when language is used to gain knowledge), imaginative (when language is used to tell stories and jokes, and to create an imaginary environment), and representational (the use of language to convey facts and information). Children learn to use language in different ways and the structure of language enables them to achieve their communicative purposes in social contexts (Christie, 2005).

Text structure and children's writing

Just as in speech, writing is a social activity situated within specific contexts, where the "products are further influenced by the kinds of writing the community values and the audience of interest" (Graham, 2018, p. 263). Learning to write, therefore, requires children to understand the text forms and genres that are socially valued (Frow, 2015). Here we are using *genre* to refer to the ways different social purposes and organisational structures are used to convey meaning (Love, 2010). At school, this involves the use of a commonly identified set of genres or text types. For example, children write to recount events, to give instructions, to provide information, to argue a position, to explain phenomena or narrate a story (Wing Jan & Taylor, 2020).

There is a certain level of predictability pertaining to school-based text types (Wing Jan & Taylor, 2020), and as young children learn to write, they develop an awareness of the way language is structured and patterned for particular purposes. For example, when writing a recount text, to tell what happened or recall events, the text is generally sequenced to include:

- An orientation – providing details of the participants, the time and place;
- A sequence of events – presenting the series of events in order;
- A conclusion – stating a personal comment or opinion.

Similarly, children learn to control the language features of a recount, including the use of temporal connectives to order events (first, then, later), the use of action verbs (went, ate, played), and the use of past tense (Gibbons, 2002). However, we also recognise that "with increasing complexity of purpose comes increasingly complex genres" (Derewianka, 2022, p. 131), and children begin to work outside the conventional structures to craft a range of diverse text forms. Over time, with appropriate teaching and support, children develop control and flexibility over the tools needed for shaping their writing, giving them increased control over the organisational structure of written texts (Christie & Dreyfus, 2007).

Reflection prompt

Consider the different texts children write, and identify the purposes and intended audiences for these texts?

How does the purpose of the text impact on the organisational structure of that text?

Children's early texts are often intended to recall events and to share their experiences with others, as seen in Figure 5.1.

As children's understanding of texts increases, they begin to write for a wider range of purposes and audiences. Figure 5.2 is an example of a child's recount text that provides some detail of the orientation and a clear sequence of events.

Figure 5.1   Simple recount

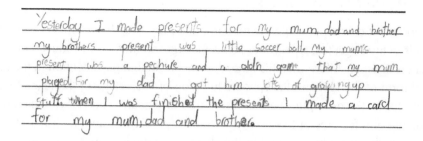

Yesterday I made presents for my mum, dad and brother my brothers present was little soccer ball. My mum's present was a pechure and n oldn game that my mum played. For my dad I got him kts of growing up stuff. When I was finished the presents I made a card for my mum, dad and brother.

Figure 5.2   Detailed recount

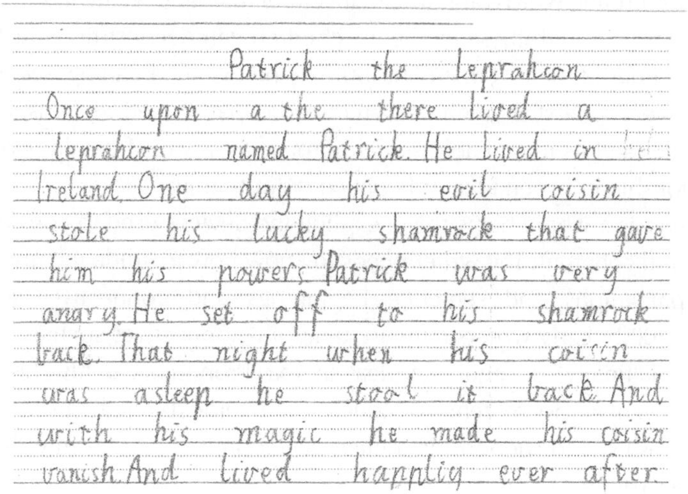

Patrick the Leprahcon
Once upon a the there lived a
leprahcon named Patrick. He lived in
Ireland One day his evil coisin
stole his lucky shamrock that gave
him his powers Patrick was very
anary. He set off to his shamrock
back. That night when his coisin
was asleep he stool it back And
with his magic he made his coisin
vanish. And lived happliy ever after

Figure 5.3   Narrative

Many children, after one or two years of formal instruction, begin to demonstrate sophisticated control over the linguistic structure of texts. The narrative text, Patrick the Leprechaun, (see Figure 5.3) shows the young writer's growing awareness of this text type, with the setting, complication, and resolution carefully described.

Teaching text structure

Kress (1994) argued that writing development necessarily includes knowledge of text types because the specific purposes for writing take on specific language structures. The explicit teaching of text types has been articulated more recently by writers such as Derewianka and Jones (2023) and Wing Jan and Taylor (2020). These writers advocate for processes of analysis, deconstruction, and construction, as children learn the social purpose, organisational structure, and language features of particular text types.

Providing models for analysis

It is important, if children are to write for particular purposes, that teachers expose them to models of the target text type. Model texts may be commercially produced or written by teachers or other children. At this time, the teacher should pay attention to the organisational form of the text and the specific function of each stage of the text (Wing Jan & Taylor, 2020). For example, see the description of recount texts above which details the structure and features of this text type. Similarly, when examining a narrative, the key stages of the text, (the setting, the details of the complication or problem, and the resolution) should be clearly identified. The particular linguistic elements of narratives can also be considered, including paying attention to the use of past tense, action verbs, adjectives as describing words, and the inclusion of dialogue (Wing Jan & Taylor, 2020). By becoming familiar with these elements, children can deconstruct a text, identifying the discrete sections of the text that contribute to the overall meaning (see also Chapters 9 and 10). However, a text should not be reduced to partitioned sections, but should be seen as a whole, and its identifiable social purpose as a way of gaining critical insights into the relationship between text and context (Wyatt-Smith, 1997).

Viewing texts as a whole helps make explicit the devices used to construct texts that are cohesive and coherent. The writer needs to know how to guide the reader through a text, using paragraphs and sentence beginnings and connectives to link ideas (Derewianka, 2022). Early writers may use temporal connectives such as "first," "then," "after that," and "finally" to sequence ideas in text. Pronouns can also be used to track a character or event across sentences. Model or mentor texts can be used to identify the cohesive devices used to support the logical development of ideas in written texts (see Chapters 9 and 10).

Developing meta-language

As children develop increased control over language structures and patterns, they often need a language to talk about language. Meta-language provides a shared language for teaching and learning about the features of language. Explicitly teaching the meta-language and related definitions of grammar enables young learners to describe language appropriately and accurately, to systematise language choices, and to explore how language is used in different contexts to achieve certain effects (Derewianka, 2022). This also suggests that teachers can assist children by increasing their own knowledge of grammar and how language is spoken about (Harper & Rennie, 2009). Terms to describe the linguistic structure of texts alongside grammatical terms such as nouns, pronouns, adjectives, verbs, and adverbs, together with terms such as clauses, sentences, and paragraphs, can be powerful tools for talking with children about their texts and how language can be manipulated to change or enhance the intended meaning.

Reflection prompt

Consider the language used to discuss text with young children: does this include the use of meta-language?

Graphic organisers

Graphic organisers help children to "identify key information and the interrelationships between the ideas they are presenting in their texts" (Department of Education Western Australia, 2013, p. 214). Types of graphic organisers that can be used to support children's writing include:

- Data charts – using headings, children can identify the category of information needed and organise information retrieved from a range of sources before writing, for example when writing an information report on an animal or insect, children might record what it looks like, where it lives, and what it eats.

- Story maps – similar to flow-charts, allow children to map the sequence of events when planning narrative texts (or recounts).

- Tree diagrams – can be used to record main ideas and the information that can be linked (for example, the main argument and supporting points in a persuasive text).

Sentence structure

Children's developing control over the patterns and forms of language is evident in their early speech, with the complexity of children's learning reflecting their experience of everyday language use. Their growth in language use is rapid, and quite early in their development most "children develop a deep, abstract and highly complex system of linguistic structure and use" (Lindfors, 1987, p. 90).

Children's earliest utterances show an awareness of word order, as they combine words that enable them to communicate their needs and ideas. For example, we often hear children connect agent and action (daddy push), action and object (read book) and possessor and possession (mummy nose) (Munro & McGregor, 2015). Beyond these two- and three-word utterances, young children begin using language to describe events in the here and now with language accompanied by action and events. Conversational partners familiar to the child provide a "knowing audience" that allows these messages to be understood.

Over time, children build a level of competence that enables them to express ideas beyond the immediate environment or communicate information to audiences at a distance (Raban, 2014). The development of language use is seen as "a gradual freeing of the child from dependence upon the immediate context" (Bridges et al., 1981, p. 120) as their use of more extended language forms increases the variety of messages communicated to a wider range of audiences. In turn, this signals to educators and teachers the need for them to model more complex syntactical variations typical of extended discourse (Vasilyeva & Waterfall, 2012). As students develop increasing control over a range of sentence types, they begin to use this for effect in their writing, making conscious choices about how to best express ideas and convey understandings (Scull & Nicolazzo, 2022).

Sentence structure and children's writing

From the perspective of teaching writing, it becomes imperative that teachers support the shift from conversational language to written language discourse structures, scaffolding children's lexical and grammatical competence. When children start to learn to write, they need to manipulate language in new ways, using their knowledge of word combinations to express more precise and nuanced meanings (Munro & McGregor, 2015). This moves beyond a focus on individual words and word meanings to "how words mean together" (Richgels, 2004, p. 473), including the use of sentences to organise their ideas.

The concept of a sentence poses particular challenges for many writers as the sentence relates to a pattern of language that occurs primarily in written text (Scull & Nicolazzo, 2022). Spoken language is not divided into sentences, with the term "clause complex," defined as a group of clauses that work together through some kind of a logical relationship, as a more appropriate term for spoken language use (Butt, Fahey, Feez, Spinks & Yallop, 2001, p. 30). As such, sentence boundaries need to be made explicit, through the texts that teachers model, and co-construct with young writers (see Chapter 10). Here we see a clear connection to punctuation, as capital letters and full stops/periods are used to signal the start and end of a sentence.

An increased control over sentence complexity is aligned with the need to share information with audiences, particularly those outside the immediate time and place, who may not have shared or common experiences with the writer. Early and later literacy learning requires writers to supply additional information to elaborate a topic. Figure 5.4 shows the use of simple, single-clause sentences that are combined, with details included to make the author's intended meaning clear.

To move beyond the use of single-clause sentences requires the combining of clauses to form compound sentences, with additive and temporal conjunctions used to link independent clauses. Most typical in the texts of young writers is use of the conjunction "and" and "and then" as children try to create a consolidated text (Teberosky et al., 2020). It is important that teachers support children to make a conscious choice to link and connect ideas, rather than reverting to the "clause complex" discourse patterns of oral language. Figure 5.5 below shows the use of simple and compound sentences, with a range of conjunctions used to connect clauses and develop ideas.

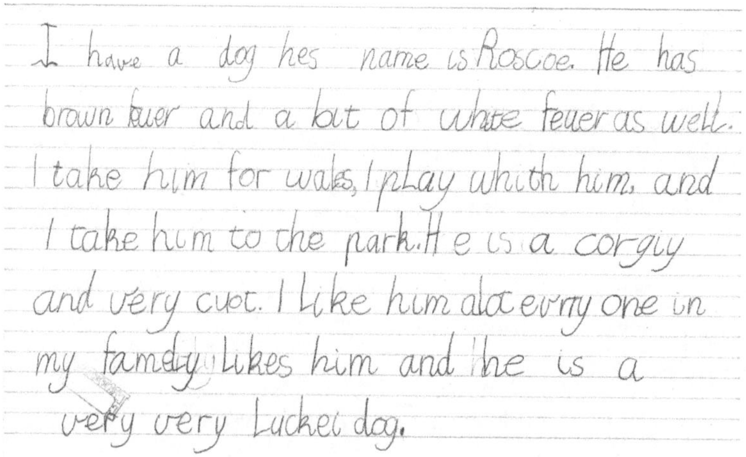

I have a dog hes name is Roscoe. He has
brown fuer and a bit of white feuer as well.
I take him for waks, I play whith him, and
I take him to the park. He is a corgy
and very cuot. I like him dla evvry one in
my famdy likes him and he is a
very very Lucke dog.

Figure 5.4   Use of simple, single-clause sentences

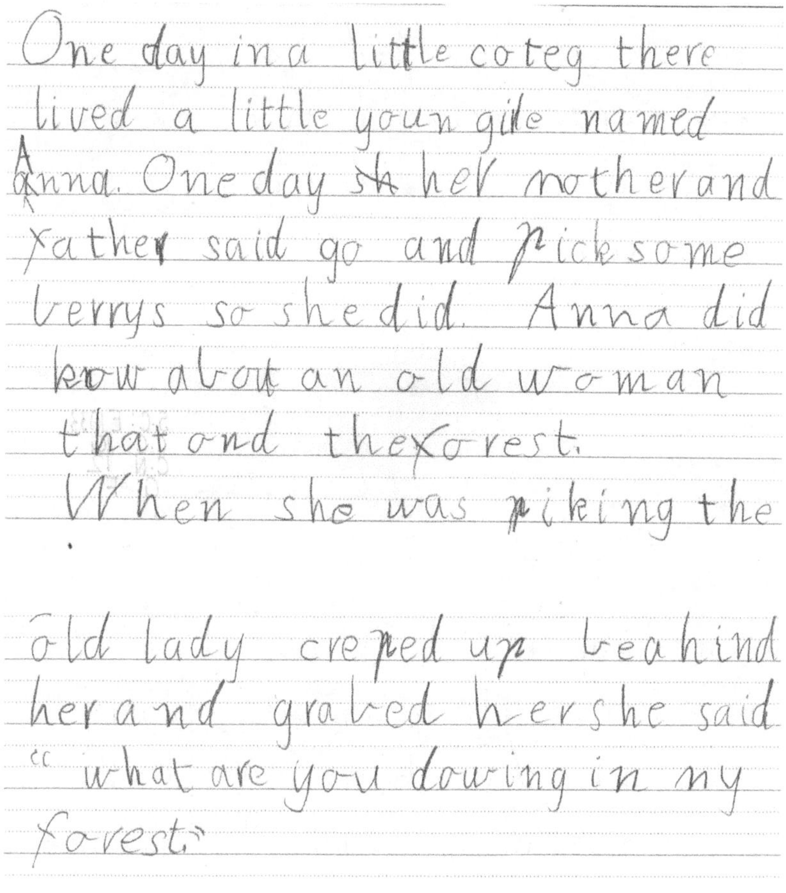

One day in a little coteg there
lived a little youn gile named
Anna. One day st her mother and
father said go and pick some
berrys so she did. Anna did
kow abot an old woman
that ond the forest.
When she was piking the

old lady creped up beahind
her and grabed her she said
" what are you dowing in my
forest."

Figure 5.5   Use of simple and compound sentences

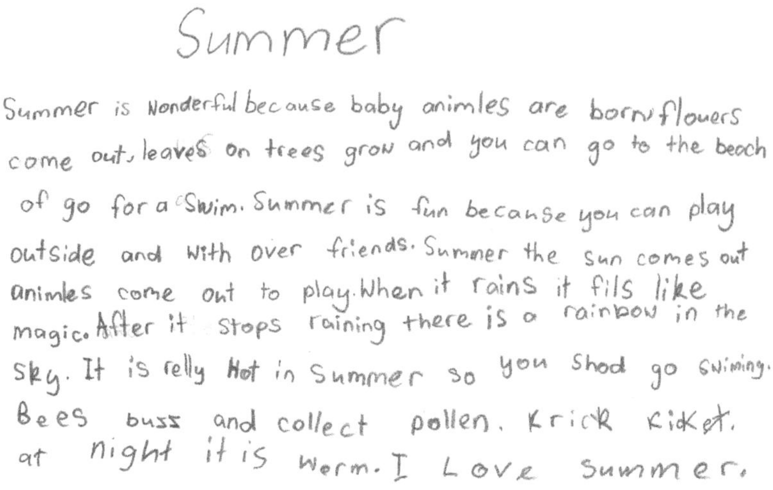

Summer

Summer is Wonderful because baby animles are born, flowers come out, leaves on trees grow and you can go to the beach of go for a Swim. Summer is fun because you can play outside and with over friends. Summer the sun comes out animles come out to play. When it rains it fils like magic. After it stops raining there is a rainbow in the sky. It is relly Hot in Summer so you shod go swiming. Bees buss and collect pollen. Krick kicket. at night it is worm. I Love Summer.

Figure 5.6   Use of causal conjunctions

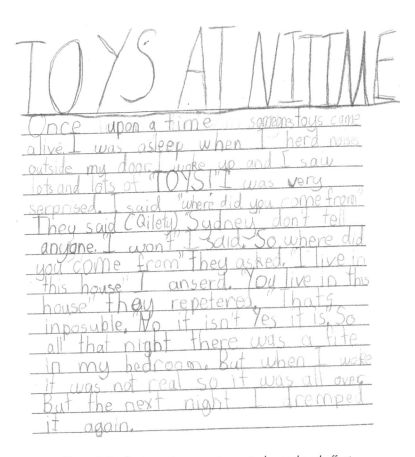

Figure 5.7   Sentence type use to control mood and effect

Syntactic control develops as young writers combine clauses to form complex groupings. Children's use of causal conjunctions results in dependent clauses that elaborate
on the message of the main clause, as illustrated in Figure 5.6.

As children develop an increased awareness of the patterns and forms of written discourse, they begin to use a variety of sentence types. They show evidence in their texts
of their conscious decisions to use a range of sentence types for effect. Figure 5.7 demonstrates the child's control over different sentence types to create mood and effect.

> **Reflection prompt**
>
> *Select a child's text to analyse. Can you identify the use of clauses, simple, com-
> pound, and complex sentences in the child's writing?*

Teaching sentence structure

Exposure to "complex language" forms (Dickinson et al., 2012) and opportunities
to engage in extended, connected verbal discourse are predictive of early literacy
(Mackenzie & Hemmings, 2014). The role of the teacher remains critical in supporting
children to use an increasing variety of sentence structures with confidence, which are
then available to the child as a resource for writing. Through explicit teaching interactions, teachers can demonstrate a range of sentence structures as well as variability of
sentence length and sentence beginnings to show how this can impact on the meaning
communicated in texts they create.

Extended conversations

As children engage in rich conversations, they experience and use flexible variations of
language, building a syntactic base to support literacy. In turn, this requires teachers to
move beyond conversational exchanges and to model syntactic complexity to support
familiarity with written discourse patterns. It may, for example, include asking children
to elaborate who was involved, when and where the event took place, and how they felt
about this. See Chapters 9 and 10 for examples of conversations with young children to
build language complexity.

Reading to children and dialogic reading

A primary source of engagement with more complex language occurs through book
reading; children who are read to will be more familiar with the structure of the language we write as distinct from the language we speak (Hill & Launder 2010). Book
reading introduces new syntactic structures to build and expand children's knowledge

of grammar (Breit-Smith et al., 2017) and impacts future academic achievement (Brown et al., 2022). There is now an extensive body of research that indicates text reading, and talk about text, fosters children's oral language development (Blewitt & Langan, 2016; Dickinson et al., 2012). When integrated, these activities create opportunities for children to hear and produce language, with conversations about texts shifting the focus of the talk from the present to beyond the "here and now" as they explore new ideas and concepts embedded in the pages of books. For example, the award-winning Australian book *Fox* by Wild and Brooks (2001) includes the following:

> With Magpie clinging to his back, he races through the scrub, past the stringybarks, past the clump of yellow box trees and into blueness. He runs so swiftly it is almost as if he is flying. Magpie feels the wind streaming through her feathers, and she rejoices. "Fly, dog, fly!"

Another example is from *Silver Buttons*, written by Graham (2013):

> Outside a pigeon nested under the roof. As Jonathan took his first step, a feather floated gently past the window like an autumn leaf.

As a stimulus for talk, texts invite dialogue and provide particular occasions for children to articulate understandings with attention to the grammar of written discourse. Their syntactic repertoire is enhanced as text structures are incorporated into talk interactions, extending children's command of language structures. For example, *Olivia* (Falconer, 2000) includes the line of text "Sometimes Olivia likes to bask in the sun". Alice, age 4, after having this book read to her, announced, "I think I'll go and bask in the sun now."

The impact of shared reading and the extra-textual conversations that occur about, around, and beyond the text, exposing children to new linguistic variations, is well recognised (Gonzalez et al., 2014). However, children's interactivity during shared reading is important, and high levels of engagement with adults are considered necessary. This prompts the child to produce language at the appropriate linguistic level while also promoting conceptual challenge as meanings are reinforced or new ideas are explored (Rowe & Snow, 2020).

Reflection prompt

Consider the books you read to children. What structural variations do these texts introduce? How might your interactions with young children encourage use of more complex language structures?

Mentor texts

The use of model texts or mentor texts (English, 2021) in classrooms provides an opportunity for children to learn firsthand from other writers and to become aware of decisions writers make in crafting their texts (Pytash & Morgan, 2014). The strategy "borrow a line" (Dorfman & Cappelli, 2007) is particularly useful for developing children's understanding of the grammatical features of a sentence. The teacher selects a sentence from a text and explains to the children that they will be writing something similar to the model provided. Guided by the teacher, the children examine the structure of the text to shape their own writing (Pytash & Morgan, 2014). For example, using a line of text from *Flood* (French & Whatley, 2011), "The rain fell gently onto the dry land" children will work with their teacher to explore the grammatical structure of the sentence: *The rain* (noun group), *fell* (verb), *gently* (adverb), *onto the dry land* (adverbial phrase). After a close examination of the mentor text, the children develop an in-depth understanding of how the text was crafted. Selecting new context or topic, such as a fire, earthquake, or hurricane, the children can then make substitutions to create a new text using the pattern discussed. For a further explanation of mentor texts in primary classrooms, see Chapter 9.

Sentence building activities

With a similar focus on the linguistic features of texts, young writers can also be encouraged to build and manipulate sentences. For example:

- Building and expanding noun groups – the *big, black, scary* spider;

- Adding adverbs – Simon sang *sweetly*; Kate ran *quickly*; and

- Including a range of adverbial phrases, to elaborate simple sentences to show where, when, why, how – We went to the shops *in High Street, on Saturday, to buy some bread, for our lunch, with my dad.*

- Extending single clause sentences to create a compound sentence – I like dogs *and my dog barks a lot* (adding an independent clause) and craft complex sentences – My dog barks *when he sees my neighbour's cat* (adding a dependent clause).

Punctuation – as markers of meaning

When we speak, we often use part sentences or clauses, and we use pauses or emphasis to break up our message; we do not often speak in sentences of the kind that we write. As such, punctuation conventions are associated only with written text forms and are used to group words into meaningful, grammatical units. Children begin to write without punctuation and need to be taught how to use punctuation to remove ambiguity from

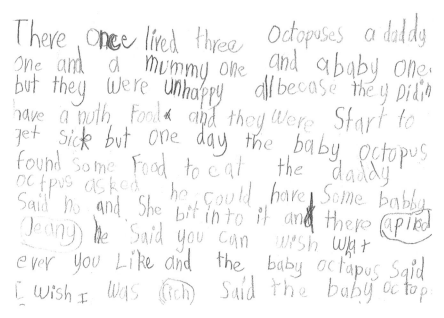

Figure 5.8   Random use of capital letters and full stops

their texts. In Figure 5.8 above, a Year 1 writing sample, the child has made some use of capital letters and full stops but has not used these correctly or consistently, although the reader can infer where the punctuation should have been inserted.

Reflection prompt

How would you approach the teaching of punctuation with the child who produced the text above?

In Figure 5.9 the child demonstrates some control over a variety of punctuation to enhance text meaning.

Some might suggest that it isn't until children begin to write like a reader that they truly see the purpose of punctuation.

Vocabulary and children's writing

In the previous sections we have discussed sentence structure or how words are put together to create both written and verbal utterances and how multiple sentences or utterances are combined to create texts for different purposes. We now move to a discussion which focuses on vocabulary as providing the building blocks of speech and written texts (Hiebert, 2020). Learning is dependent upon vocabulary knowledge and, as discussed

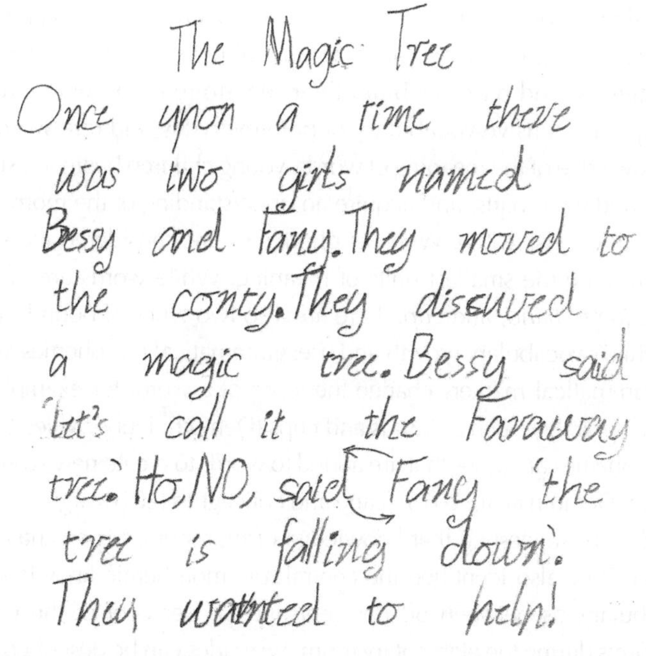

The Magic Tree

Once upon a time there
was two girls named
Bessy and Fany. They moved to
the conty. They discuved
a magic tree. Bessy said
'lit's call it the Faraway
tree.' Ho, NO, said Fany 'the
tree is falling down'.
They wanted to help!

Figure 5.9   Use of a variety of punctuation to support meaning

earlier in the chapter, oral language development is rapid in the early years. However, there is wide variability in children's vocabulary development (Munro & McGregor, 2015), and the gap between the vocabulary development of children from low and high socio-economic backgrounds is well documented (Schneider et al., 2023). While some of the language variation can be attributed to genetic factors, the environment plays a major role in explaining individual differences with language development dependent on the nature of the communicative experiences and the language models provided (Schneider et al., 2023). Hence, we appreciate that the universal acquisition of language reflects the unique opportunities for learning children experience, with this particularly evident in measures of vocabulary growth. It is also important to note that children's ability to understand words that they hear may be in advance of the words that they speak themselves, and their listening and speaking competency is usually well ahead of their reading and writing competence. Adults are the same – they may hear and understand a word, but not use the word when they speak or write. Sometimes it is simply a case of familiarity; the more they hear and see the word the more likely they will use the word. This suggests that the intentional teaching of vocabulary to young children is an equity issue with teachers able to close this learning gap for learners.

Vocabulary learning is largely the result of interaction with others and the opportuni-ties provided for children to engage in joint attention. Joint attentional skills begin in early childhood and occur when an adult and a child focus on the same object or point of reference (Tomasello et al., 2005). As adults gaze, point or touch, and label objects, these are noted by the child and in this way, they begin to build and extend their word knowledge (Munro & McGregor, 2015). Young children continually expand their command over single words with lexical acquisition extending across an individual's life span. From words to express close and familiar objects and relationships, children's experiences, interests, and passions build their repertoire of known words. Over time, children develop an extensive vocabulary of both everyday and rare words.

Alongside knowledge of the meaning of words, young children begin to explore the architecture of words and word parts, and acquire an understanding of the morphological structure of language (Richgels, 2004). Whereas phonemes are considered the smallest unit of sound, morphemes are the smallest units of meaning. While words are often single morphemes, such as *jump, hand,* and *cup,* there are also two types of bound morphemes that contribute to a child's vocabulary growth and use: grammatical morphemes and derivational morphemes. Grammatical markers change the tense of a word: for example, jumped and jumping, or signal plurality, such as hands and cups (Demuth, Dube, Miles & Tomas, 2015). Derivational morphemes are those that are added to words to create new words, for example teach/er, elect/ion (Demuth et al., 2015). Lane and colleagues (2010) argue for explicit teaching about morphemes suggesting that knowledge of morphemes is essential in learning to read and to spell. They also identified the central role morphemic knowledge plays in the growth of vocabulary, as between 60 per cent and 80 per cent of the new vocabulary acquired by students during the elementary (primary) grades can be described as morphologically complex (2010, p. 185). Refer also to Chapter 6 for further discussion of morphology.

Vocabulary for writing

"Learners need access to the meanings of words that are used by adults (particularly teachers) and other children, as well as those used in books and multimedia, if they are to participate in their community contexts and learn effectively" (Daffern & Mackenzie, 2015, p. 25). The importance of vocabulary development to literacy learning has been widely documented, with early vocabulary recognised as a predictor of later literacy growth (Biemiller, 2011). When we hear (or read) words, understand their meaning, and can pick up on the subtleties in text (oral or written), we can truly consider ourselves to have engaged with the meanings in the text. It is, therefore, important for children to build a mental lexicon, or vocabulary storehouse (Silliman et al., 2017), for learning generally but specifically for literacy learning. This starts early, with children from 3 years of age able to learn new words after hearing them only once or twice and schoolchildren able to learn five to ten new words per day during primary and high school (Hoffnung, et al., 2013). To learn a word, a learner needs to encounter the new word in context and understand its meaning, how it relates to other words around it, and how it may change in different contexts. To really know a word is to have the knowledge of the "multiple related meanings and shades of meaning for the word, knowledge of its semantic associations, knowledge of its meanings in different contexts, and knowledge of its different morphological forms" (Kieffer & Lesaux, 2012, p. 348).

> **Reflection prompt**
>
> *Consider the following: "If dynamite blows things up, then why did you just say, 'This is dynamite!' when you saw Uncle Mike's new house?" (Graves & Watts-Taffe, 2008, p. 185).*
>
> *Try to come up with another example that you could share with children.*

While the link between vocabulary and reading is often discussed, the importance of vocabulary to writing is not as well understood. Interestingly, Biemiller (2011) suggests that the impact of vocabulary on reading can be masked in the first three years of school by the use of texts (sometimes called *readers*) for reading instruction that have restricted vocabulary. It is often not until children reach Year 3 (Gee, 2004), when more topic-specific language is introduced, that their limited vocabulary can impact their comprehension. It is at this time that the children with rich vocabularies are greatly advantaged because vocabulary is critical to text reading and meaning-making processes. In fact, decoding skills, fluency skills and comprehension all draw upon a reader's known vocabulary.

> **Reflection prompt**
>
> *Have you ever read a word somewhere and thought you knew how to say it, only to hear the word and realise that you were saying it incorrectly? It happens to all of us – in the English language, the word needs to be in our mental lexicon for us to be sure we are "sounding it out" correctly.*

When children write, they select and combine words to create texts, with their written texts demonstrating their increasing awareness of appropriate vocabulary use – from use of everyday words to communicate messages and express meaning; to using a range of topic-specific words with an increasing awareness of context and audience; to selecting technically specific words to communicate unique field knowledge; alongside the use of figurative language to express meaning with precision and sophistication.

A writer may be described as lexically sophisticated if they are able to successfully use "difficult" or "mature" words when they write, while lexical density is used to describe the balance between content words (e.g., rainbow) and grammatical function words (e.g., the, it) (Hudson, 2009). As long as writing is not dependent upon accurate spelling, it is possible that children who are given genuine reasons to write will experiment with words in ways that they may not be seeing when they read. The following texts show children's vocabulary use from very simple through to a sophisticated use of words (see Figures 5.10, 5.11, 5.12, and 5.13).

I went to my hehs

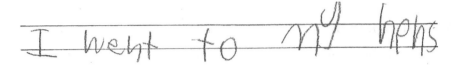

Figure 5.10 *Use of familiar, common words (went) and one, two, and three letter high frequency words (I, my, to)*

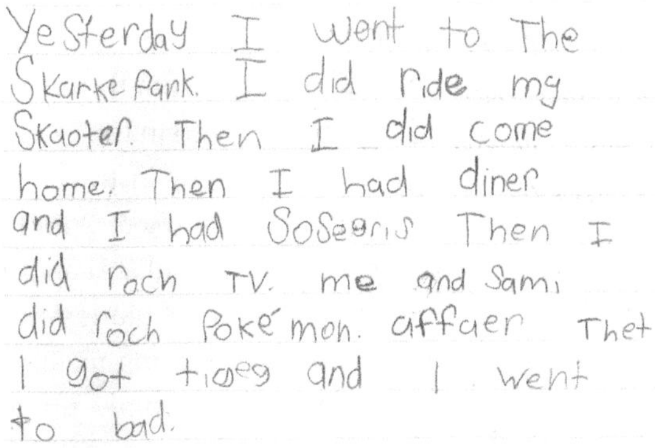

Yesterday I went to The Skarke Pank. I did ride my Skaoter. Then I did come home. Then I had diner and I had Soseoris Then I did roch TV. me and Sami did roch Poké mon. affaer Thet I got tioeg and I went to bad.

Figure 5.11 *Use of everyday, commonly used vocabulary plus proper nouns particular to the child's experience*

There once Lived a girl. She Lived in a Casle and there Lived a wicked wich and she Lived in a ugly old casle. the wicked wich went to the butuful. PINK girls Casle She went throw the door way fond the girl in her bedroom. the wicked wich opend the girls bedroom door and made her into a unicorn.

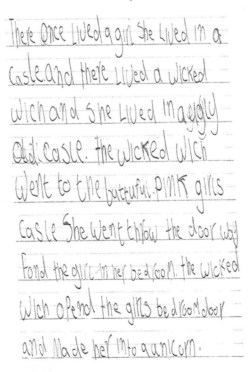

Figure 5.12 *Use of a variety of vocabulary choices and includes descriptive and emotive language*

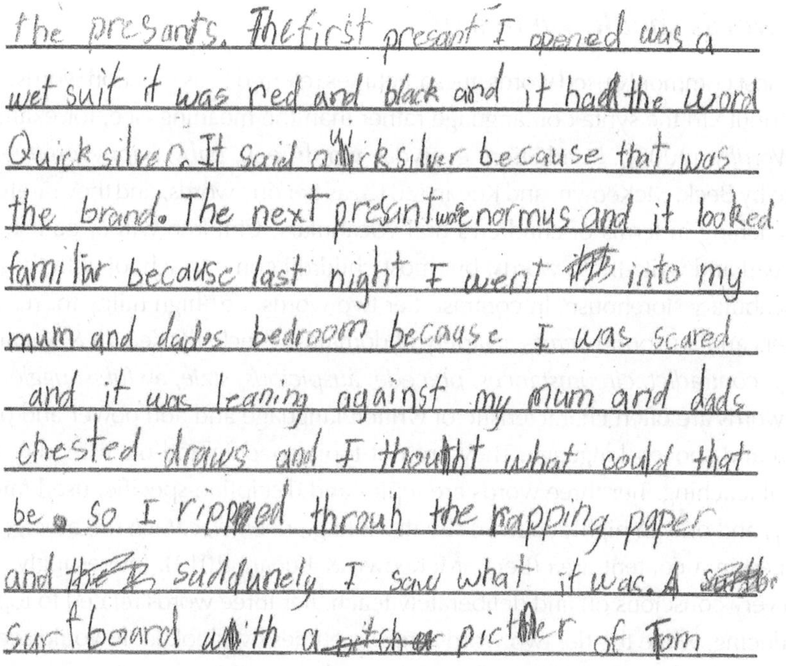

the presants. The first present I opened was a
wet suit it was red and black and it had the word
Quicksilver. It said Quicksilver because that was
the brand. The next present was enormus and it looked
familiar because last night I went into my
mum and dades bedroom because I was scared
and it was leaning against my mum and dads
chested draws and I thought what could that
be. so I ripped throuh the rapping paper
and the saddunely I saw what it was. A
surfboard with a picther of Tom

Figure 5.13   Use of example to the correct use of unique field or technically specific vocabulary

Teaching vocabulary

What "teachers know, do, and care about" is powerful (Hattie, 2003, p. 2) and this is very evident when it comes to teaching vocabulary. Opportunities for children to experience powerful vocabulary instruction are reliant upon: the teacher's own vocabulary and modelling of word usage; their interest in words and awareness of the need to teach vocabulary; their responsiveness to opportunities for incidental teaching but also their preparedness to teach explicitly (Lane & Allen, 2010). While it has been argued that incidental learning is the way we learn most new words, whether we are children or adults, incidental learning is not sufficient for the vocabulary learning necessary for school children, particularly those who may come from language impoverished backgrounds. Deliberate, explicit instruction will ensure that children will learn new words and their meanings, as well as how to use new words to enhance their text interpretation and text creation. The teaching of more sophisticated use of vocabulary, such as figurative language, metaphor, and analogy, are particularly dependent on a teacher's own use of language.

Reflection prompt

Do you consider yourself to be a wordsmith? Are the children in your care excited about words? How can you actively increase the vocabularies of the children in your care?

Which words should we teach?

The 100 most commonly used words are sometimes referred to as function words, because they contribute to the syntax of language rather than the meaning (see, for example, the *Oxford Wordlist* [2008]). In addition, everyday words (e.g., *baby, happy, pretty*) are also referred to by Beck, McKeown, and Kucan (2013) as tier one words, and they rarely require explicit teaching in terms of children's oral vocabulary. Children will of course need to learn to read and write these words, but most children come to school with these words in the vocabulary storehouse. In contrast, tier two words are "high utility for mature language users and are found across a variety of domains" (Beck, McKeown & Kucan, 2013, p. 9) (e.g., *contradict, circumstances, precede, auspicious, stale, awful, snuggle, twitch*). Tier two words are often characteristic of written language and add power and precision to written and spoken language. They are not topic-specific and often require explicit, intentional teaching. Tier three words are topic- and discipline-specific, used rarely (low frequency) and only in highly specific situations (e.g., *decibel, cataclysm, atom*) probably best learned in a content area (Beck, McKeown & Kucan, 2013). Interestingly, teachers are often very conscious of, and deliberately teach, tier three words related to topics they are introducing, while the tier two words are sometimes overlooked. It would seem however, that it is the tier two words that need the explicit teaching.

Explicit instruction

Explicit instruction in vocabulary is not just about teaching children how to locate dictionary definitions; rather it should provide children with opportunities to learn new words and how to use them as well as teaching them how to use already known words in new and different ways. Teachers who are "wordsmiths" will be quick to include jokes and puns into their daily talk but will also look for opportunities to include word games, crosswords, and anagrams into their lessons.

Reading aloud from good-quality, well-chosen texts is one of the best ways to build children's oral vocabulary. Some authors use rich language that provides numerous opportunities for discussions about words and their meanings. For example, *Miss Lily's Fabulous Pink Feather Boa* (Wild & Argent, 1999) provides numerous opportunities to explore tier two and three words:

> During dinner, the last Potoroo kept glancing nervously at Miss Lily's enormous snout, at her strong, sharp teeth.
>
> Suddenly her joy evaporated. "I can't take this," she whispered. "I did something dreadful. I wanted the boa so much that I stole a bit of it."

Prioritising read-aloud books that offer engaging stories and that also offer rich vocabulary opportunities will reap rewards. A conversation with your school or local librarian is sure to identify books for this purpose.

Table 5.1 Homophones, homonyms, and homographs

Word type	Definition	Examples
homophones	Words that are pronounced the same way, but have different spellings and meanings	"sow, sew, and so"; "flaw and floor"; "to, two and too"; "saw, sore and soar"; "there, their, they're"
homonyms	Words that have multiple meanings	"suit (clothes) or suit yourself" "fair – go to the fair or agree on a fair price"
homographs	Words that have the same spelling, but different meaning and pronunciation	"desert – to abandon" "desert – area of land" "bass – fish" "bass – instrument" "close – nearby" "close – to shut"

Homophones, homonyms, and homographs are confusing for children and therefore need to be part of any instruction that aims to expand children's word use (see Table 5.1).

Consider the following example of a homophone that would be considered a high frequency tier one word for most young English-speaking children:

James *read* his "home reader" to his Mum and then his dad came over to *read* to him from a new chapter book.

A quick search of the internet will help you find games and even instructional videos for children that use homophones, homonyms, and homographs. There are also books available that are based on homophones although the story lines are rather limited so choose carefully if you decide to use these resources. Further vocabulary activities can be found in the recommended reading at the end of the chapter.

Conclusion

Throughout this chapter we have highlighted the essential nature of language as a meaning-making process, used to communicate with others and explore ideas. We have demonstrated how children's oral language is foundational to written discourse, in particular how the authorial skills of writing – text structure, sentence structure, and vocabulary – build from children's spoken language repertoires. Further, as we examine the three authorial dimensions of writing closely, we see the reciprocity between children's receptive and expressive language skills. The language children hear spoken in conversations and via print, digital, and media sources and the language they use as active interlocutors and as authors of written texts to express meanings and communicate ideas are integrated and intertwined as a resource for language and literacy learning (Clay, 2004). We encourage all educators to explore the development of children's oral and written language, finding authentic contexts for children to use and expand their knowledge of language, and as authors of texts to handle new and complex variations with increasing facility and confidence.

Working with families

The authorial roles of the writer can be supported by:

1 Conversations about the language used in books that have been read aloud to children. Discussion of how sometimes a short simple sentence is the most powerful, but other times a sentence may need more complexity and include a number of phrases/clauses. This can bring in conversations about punctuation.

2 Discussion of how authors use punctuation – going beyond capital letters and full stops. Show children how punctuation allows for the construction of sentences – adding further meaning to the words. There are a number of excellent and entertaining books on punctuation (see for example, *The Perfect Punctuation Book*, by Kate Petty and Jennie Maizels (2006)– published by Dutton Children's Books – is a fun pop-up book that teaches punctuation in a playful way).

3 Playing with words – particularly exploring homonyms and synonyms. This can be done verbally or by exploring how words are used in books. Word games of all types can be powerful at expanding children's oral language, which then becomes a resource for their written language.

Glossary

Terminology: Meaning

Derivational morpheme: Formation of new words by adding prefixes or suffixes to base words, e.g., re + act = react; en + act = enact

Dialogic book reading: Adult and child/ren talking about a book as it is being read

Extra-textual conversations: Spontaneous conversation that occurs between reader and listener/s alongside a text read aloud

Semantic Associations: Direct or indirect relationship between two words in respect to meaning, e.g., *dog* and *poodle*

Written language registers: The way grammar, words, and expressions are selected for a piece of writing to make it appropriate for its intended context.

Recommended reading

Beck, I. L., McKeown, M. G., & Kucan, L. (2013). *Bringing words to life: Robust vocabulary instruction* (2nd ed.). Guilford Press.

Derewianka, B. (2022). *A new grammar companion for teachers* (3rd ed.). Primary English Teaching Association Australia.

Hiebert, E. H. (2020). The core vocabulary: The foundation of proficient comprehension. *The Reading Teacher, 73*(6), 757–768.

Wing Jan, L., & Taylor, S. (2020). *Write ways* (5th ed.). Oxford University Press.

References

Beck, I. L., McKeown, M. G., & Kucan, L. (2013). *Bringing Words to Life: Robust Vocabulary Instruction* (2nd ed.). New York: Guilford Press.

Biemiller, A. (2011, Winter). *Vocabulary: What Words Should We Teach? Better: Evidence-Based Education* (pp. 10–11). Johns Hopkins University School of Education Center for Research and Reform in Education. Retrieved from: www.oise.utoronto.ca/ics/UserFiles

Blewitt, P., & Langan, R. (2016). Learning words during shared book reading: The role of extratextual talk designed to increase child engagement. *Journal of Experimental Child Psychology, 150,* 404–410. https://doi.org/10.1016/j.jecp.2016.06.009

Breit-Smith, A., Kleeck, A., Prendeville, J. A., & Pan, W. (2017). Preschool children's exposure to story grammar elements during parent–child book reading. *Journal of Research in Reading, 40*(4), 345–364. https://doi.org/10.1111/1467-9817.12071

Bridges, A., Sinha, C., & Walkerdine, V. (1981). The development of comprehension. In G. Wells (Ed.), *Learning through Interaction: The Study of Language Development.* Cambridge, UK: Cambridge University Press.

Brown, M. I., Wang, C., & McLeod, S. (2022). Reading with 1–2 year olds impacts academic achievement at 8–11 years. *Early Childhood Research Quarterly, 58*(1st quarter), 198–207. https://doi.org/10.1016/j.ecresq.2021.09.008

Butt, D., Fahey, R., Feez, S., Spinks, S. & Yallop, C. (2001). *Using Functional Grammar: An Explorer's Guide.* Sydney, NSW: Macquarie University.

Christie, F. (2005). *Language Education in the Primary Years.* Sydney, NSW: University of New South Wales Press.

Christie, F., & Dreyfus, S. (2007). Letting the secret out: Mentoring successful writing in secondary English studies. *Australian Journal of Language and Literacy, 33*(3), 235–247.

Clay, M. M. (2004). Talking, reading and writing. *Journal of Reading Recovery,* Spring, 1–15.

Daffern, T., & Mackenzie, N. M. (2015). Building strong writers: Creating a balance between the authorial and secretarial elements of writing. *Literacy Learning: The Middle Years, 23*(1), 23–32.

Demuth, K., Dube, S., Miles, K. & Tomas, E. (2015). Morphology. In S McLeod & L. McCormack (Eds.) *Introduction to Speech, Language and Literacy* (pp. 231–265). South Melbourne, VIC: Oxford University Press

Department of Education, Western Australia (2013). *First Steps: Writing Resource Book. Department of Education WA.* Retrieved from: http://det.wa.edu.au/stepsresources/detcms/navigation/first-steps-literacy/

Derewianka, B. (2022). *A New Grammar Companion for Teachers* (3rd ed.). Newtown, NSW: Primary English Teaching Association Australia.

Derewianka, B., & Jones, P. (2023). *Teaching Language in Context* (3rd ed.). Newtown, NSW: Oxford University Press.

Dickinson, D. K., Griffith, J. A., Golinkoff, R. M., & Hirsh-Pasek, K. (2012). How reading books fosters language development around the world. *Child Development Research, 2012*. Article ID 602807, 15 pages. https://doi.org/10.1155/2012/602807

Dorfman, L. R. & Cappelli, R. (2007). *Mentor Texts: Teaching Writing through Children's Literature, K–6*. Portland, ME: Stenhouse.

Dyson, A. H. (2016). *Child Cultures, Schooling, and Literacy: Global Perspectives on Composing Unique Lives*. Routledge. https://doi.org/10.4324/9781315736518

Emmitt, M., Zbaracki, M., Komesaroff, L., & Pollock, J. (2014). *Language and Learning: An Introduction for Teaching* (6th ed.). South Melbourne, VIC: Oxford University Press.

English, R. (2021). Teaching through mentor texts. *Practical Literacy, 26*(1).

Falconer, I. (2000). *Olivia*. New York: Atheneum Books for Young Readers.

French, J., & Whatley, B. (2011). *Flood*. Lindfield, NSW: Scholastic Press.

Frow, J. (2015). *Genre* (2nd ed.). Abingdon: Routledge.

Gee, J. P. (2002). A sociocultural perspective on early literacy development. In S. B. Neuman & D. K. Dickinson (Eds.), *Handbook of Early Literacy Research* (pp. 30–42). New York: Guilford Press.

Gee, J. P. (2004). *Situated Language and Learning: A Critique of Traditional Schooling*. New York NY: Routledge.

Gibbons, P. (2002). *Scaffolding Language Scaffolding Learning*. Portsmouth, NH: Heinemann.

Gonzalez, J. E., Pollard-Durodola, S., Simmons, D. C., Taylor, A. B., Davis, M. J., Fogarty, M., & Simmons, L. (2014). Enhancing preschool children's vocabulary: Effects of teacher talk before, during and after shared reading. *Early Childhood Research Quarterly, 29*(2), 214–226. https://doi.org/10.1016/j.ecresq.2013.11.001

Graham, B. (2013). *Silver Buttons*. London: Walker Books.

Graham, S. (2018) A revised writer(s)-within-community model of writing, *Educational Psychologist, 53*(4), 258–279. https://doi.org/10.1080/00461520.2018.1481406

Graves, M. F., & Watts-Taffe, S. (2008). For the love of words: Fostering word consciousness in young readers. *The Reading Teacher, 62*(3), 185–193.

Halliday, M. A. (1975). *Learning How to Mean*. London: Edward Arnold.

Harper, H., & Rennie, J. (2009). 'I had to go out and get myself a book on grammar': A study of pre-service teachers' knowledge about language. *Australian Journal of Language and Literacy, 32*(1), 22–37.

Hattie, J. (2003). *Teachers Make a Difference: What Is the Research Evidence?* Paper presented at the *Australian Council for Educational Research Annual Conference on Building Teacher Quality*, Melbourne.

Hiebert, E. H. (2020). The core vocabulary: The foundation of proficient comprehension. *The Reading Teacher, 73*(6), 757–768.

Hill, S. & Launder, N. (2010). Oral language and beginning to read. *Australian Journal of Language and Literacy, 33*(3), 240–254.

Hoff, E. (2006). How social contexts support and shape language development. *Developmental Review, 26*(1), 55–88. https://doi.org/10.1016/j.dr.2005.11.002

Hoff, E., Core, C., & Shanks, K. F. (2020). The quality of child-directed speech depends on the speaker's language proficiency. *Journal of Child Language, 47*(1), 132–145. https://doi.org/10.1017/S030500091900028X

Hoffnung, M., Hoffnung, R. J., Seiffert, K. L., Burton Smith, R., Hine, A., Ward, L., & Swabey, K. (2013). *Lifespan Development: A Topical Approach*. Milton, UK: Wiley.

Hudson, R. (2009). Measuring maturity. In R. Beard, D. Myhill, J. Riley & M. Nystrand (Eds.), *The SAGE Handbook of Writing Development* (pp. 349–362). London: SAGE.

Kieffer, M. J. & Lesaux, N. K. (2012). Knowledge of words, knowledge about words: Dimensions of vocabulary in first and second language learners in sixth grade. *Reading and Writing: An Interdisciplinary Journal, 25*(2), 347–373. https://doi.org/10.1007/s11145-010-9272-9

Kress, G. (1994). *Learning to Write*. New York: Routledge.

Lane, H. B. & Allen, S. A. (2010). The vocabulary-rich classroom: Modelling sophisticated word use to promote word consciousness and vocabulary growth. *The Reading Teacher, 63*(5), 362–370.

Lindfors, J. W. (1987). *Children's Language and Learning*. Englewood Cliffs, NJ: Prentice-Hall.

Love, K. (2010). Literacy pedagogical content knowledge in the secondary curriculum. *Pedagogies, 5*(4), 338–355.

Mackenzie, N. M., & Hemmings, B. (2014). Predictors of success with writing in the first year of schooling. *Issues in Educational Research, 24*(1), 41–54.

Munroe, N. & McGregor, K. (2015). Semantics. In S. McLeod & J. McCormack (Eds.), *An Introduction to Speech, Language and Literacy* (pp. 181–230). Melbourne, VIC: Oxford University Press.

Myhill, D. (2021). Grammar re-imagined: foregrounding understanding of language choice in writing. *English in Education, 55*(3), 265–278. https://doi.org/10.1080/04250494.2021.1885975

New London Group. (2000). A pedagogy of multiliteracies: designing social futures. In B. Cope & M. Kalantzis (Eds.), *Multiliteracies: Literacy Learning and the Design of Social Futures* (pp. 9–37). Routledge.

Noble, C., Sala, G., Peter, M., Lingwood, J., Rowland, C. F., Gobet, F., & Pine, J. (2019). The impact of shared book reading on children's language skills: A meta-analysis. *Educational Research Review, 28*, 100290. https://doi.org/10.1016/j.edurev.2019.100290

Pytash, K. E. & Morgan, D. N. (2014). Using mentor texts to teach writing in science and social studies. *The Reading Teacher, 68*(2), 93–102. https://doi.org/10.1002/trtr.1276

Raban, B. (2014). TALK to think, learn, and teach. *Journal of Reading Recovery*, Spring, 1–11.

Raban, B., & Scull, J. (2023). Literacy. In D. Pendergast & S. Garvis (Eds.), *Teaching Early Years: Curriculum, Pedagogy and Assessment* (2nd ed., pp. 35–48). London: Routledge.

Richgels, D. J. (2004). Paying attention to language. *Reading Research Quarterly, 39*(4), 470–477.

Riordan, J., Reese, E., Das, S., Carroll, J., & Schaughency, E. (2022). Tender Shoots: A randomized controlled trial of two shared-reading approaches for enhancing parent-child interactions and children's oral language and literacy skills. *Scientific Studies of Reading, 26*(3), 183–203.

Rowe, M. L., & Snow, C. E. (2020). Analyzing input quality along three dimensions: Interactive, linguistic, and conceptual. *Journal of Child Language, 47*, 5–21. https://doi.org/10.1017/s0305000919000655

Schneider, J. M., Abel, A. D., & Maguire, M. J. (2023). Vocabulary knowledge and reading comprehension account for SES-differences in how school-aged children infer word meanings from sentences. *Language learning and development, 19*(4), 369–385. https://doi.org/10.1080/15475441.2022.2081573

Scull, J., Mackenzie, N. M., & Bowles, T. (2020). Assessing early writing: A six-factor model to inform assessment and teaching. *Educational Research for Policy and Practice*. https://doi.org/10.1007/s10671-020-09257-7

Scull, J., & Nicolazzo, M. (2022). Punctuation, Sentence Structure and Paragraphing. In D. Thomas & A. Thomas (Eds.) *Teaching and Learning Primary English* (pp 207–225). ISBN 9780190325725 Docklands, Vic: Oxford University Press.

Silliman, E., Bahr, R., Nagy, W., & Berninger, V. (2017). Language bases of spelling in writing during early and middle childhood: Grounding applications to struggling writers in typical writing development. In B. Miller, P. McCardle & V. Connelly (Eds.), *Development of Writing Skills in Individuals with Learning Difficulties*. Leiden, Netherlands: Brill.

Teberosky, A., Sepúlveda, A., Costa e Sousa, O. (2020). Orality, reading and writing in early literacy. In R. A. Alves, T. Limpo, R. M. Joshi, (Eds.). *Reading-Writing Connections*. Literacy Studies, vol 19. Cham: Springer. https://doi.org/10.1007/978-3-030-38811-9_6

Tomasello, M., Carpenter, M., Call, J., Behne, T., & Moll, H. (2005). Understanding and sharing intentions: The origins of cultural cognition. *Behavioral and Brain Sciences, 28*(5), 675–691.

Vasilyeva, M. & Waterfall, H. (2012). Beyond syntactic priming: Evidence for activation of alternative syntactic structures. *Journal of Child Language, 39*(2), 258–283. http://dx.doi.org/10.1017/S0305000911000055

Wild, M., & Argent, K. (1999). *Miss Lily's Fabulous Pink Feather Boa*. Melbourne, VIC: Picture Puffin.

Wild, M., & Brooks, R. (2001). *Fox*. St. Leonards, NSW: Allen & Unwin.

Wing Jan, L., & Taylor, S. (2020). *Write Ways* (5th ed.). Docklands, Vic: Oxford University Press.

Wyatt-Smith, C. (1997). Teaching and assessing writing: An Australian perspective. *English in Education, 31*(3), 8–21.

Developing spelling skills

Tessa Daffern

Introduction

Developing proficiency in Standard (conventional) English spelling is a critical part of becoming a literate writer. Yet conflicting perspectives on the typical course of spelling acquisition have emerged, and this has created uncertainty about the most effective way to teach spelling. Standard English spelling requires integration of "written symbols in conventional sequences (orthography) that represent speech sounds (phonology) and word parts that signal meaning and grammar (morphology)" (Garcia, Abbott & Berninger, 2010, p. 63). In this chapter, I explore some of the complexities of learning to spell and illustrate how spelling acquisition is a gradual process of becoming efficient in the coordination of multiple linguistic skills. The chapter begins by explaining why spelling is an important editorial skill and word-formation problem-solving process, and then shifts to an overview of the theoretical perspectives on spelling acquisition. Throughout the chapter, we will follow one child (Joshua) as he learns to spell. Examples of Joshua's phonological, orthographic, and morphological representations are presented in the context of his writing. This chapter also highlights the importance of explicitly teaching these three linguistic skills from the early years of learning to write.

Importance of learning to spell

Being able to automatically and accurately spell words is a crucial part of written communication (Hutcheon, Campbell & Stewart, 2012; Graham & Santangelo, 2014; Puranik & Al Otaiba, 2012). As Abbott, Berninger, and Fayol (2010, p. 296) assert, "spelling bridges idea generation and text generation," and it is considered one of the essential editorial processes and products of the written language (Bahr, Silliman, Danzak & Wilkinson, 2015; Hayes & Berninger, 2014; Puranik & Al Otaiba, 2012). Success with

DOI: 10.4324/9781003439264-6

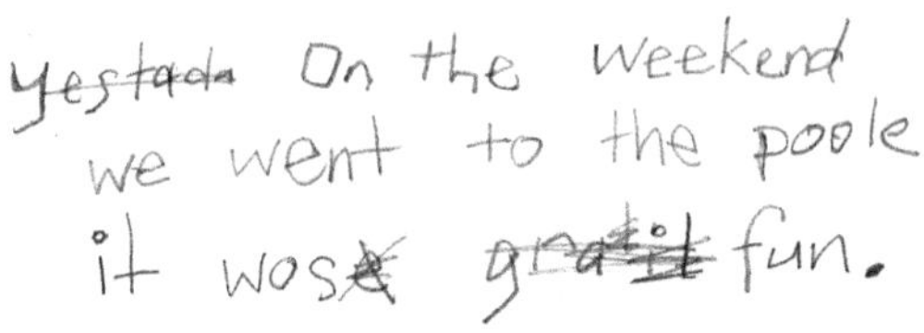

Figure 6.1   A child (age 5 years, 8 months) substitutes "tricky" words when writing

spelling in the first year of formal schooling is one of the key predicting factors of success with writing throughout school (Connelly, Dockrell, Walter & Critten, 2012; Kim,
Al Otaiba & Wanzek, 2015; Puranik & Al Otaiba, 2012). While proficiency in spelling
can positively influence writing competence (Graham, Gillespie & McKeown, 2013),
it is also associated with overall enjoyment, fluency, and comprehension in reading
(Graham et al., 2013; Martin-Chang, Ouellette & Madden, 2014; Treiman, 1998).

When spelling is problematic for a writer, the overall quality and precision of a written
text can be compromised. In particular, when young children begin to experiment with
alphabetic letter forms to represent written messages, substantial attention is often devoted
to the task of spelling individual words, and this may limit their capacity to use other cognitive resources required to craft a written text (Graham, Harris & Chorzempa, 2002;
Singer & Bashir, 2004). Some writers may also rely on words that they can confidently
spell, irrespective of whether or not more precise words could be used to convey their
intended message (Mackenzie, Scull & Bowles, 2015). To illustrate, Figure 6.1 shows what
a child (5 years, 8 months) does when attempting to write particular words in a recount of
an event that took place the previous weekend. In the example, the child encounters difficulty with the words "yesterday" and "great," and this is indicated by the crossing out as
well as by the substitution of those words. The child has attempted to write the word "yesterday" but then replaced it with "on the weekend." Similarly, the writer's unsuccessful
attempt to spell the word "great" has been substituted with the word "fun." In this instance,
the lexical substitutions have compromised the precision of the intended message.

Children who experience ongoing difficulties with spelling at school are less inclined
to take informed risks with written vocabulary (Daffern & Mackenzie, 2020; Kohnen,
Nickels & Castles, 2009). Some of these children may begin to avoid writing and
"develop a mindset that they cannot write," which could then lead to "arrested writing
development" (Graham & Santangelo, 2014, p. 1704). They may also develop greater
levels of anxiety and become less motivated to learn (Sideridis, 2005).

Reflection prompt

*Consider how you perceived yourself as a speller when you were learning to write
at school. Has this self-perception changed throughout your life? In what ways
have these self-perceptions influenced you as a writer?*

Theoretical perspectives on learning to spell

Assumptions underpinning spelling development have implications for the teaching of spelling. Stage and phase theories of learning to spell have offered descriptive accounts of qualitative changes in spelling development, and they have been particularly influential for the last four decades. These theories stem from "Piagetian theory and the notion that aspects of cognitive development proceed by way of qualitative stage-like change" (Gentry, 2000, p. 319). While the different theories are characterised by unique classifications for each stage or phase of development, they all broadly suggest that learning to spell follows a linear path whereby phonological knowledge is relied upon and established before orthographic knowledge, and that the development of morphological knowledge is dependent upon first establishing phonological and orthographic knowledge (Bahr, Silliman & Berninger, 2009). Table 6.1 presents a brief overview of the terms used to classify each stage or phase of development as identified by various stage and phase theorists.

Most instructional spelling programs and assessment frameworks draw on linear theories of spelling development (Kohnen et al., 2009), providing educators with a sequential framework from which to plan for instruction and assessment in a given classroom.

Table 6.1 Developmental theories of spelling

Theorists	Stages/Phases of Spelling Development
Gentry (2000)	Five distinct stages: Precommunicative (use of random letters or letter-like shapes). Semiphonetic (some evidence of sound to letter correspondence). Phonetic (correct representation of speech sounds in words). Transitional (increased knowledge of letter sequences in words). Correct/conventional (accurate phonological, orthographic and morphological representations).
Bear, Invernizzi, Templeton and Johnston (2012)	Five distinct stages: Emergent (use of random letters or letter-like shapes). Letter-name (some evidence of sound to letter correspondence). Within word patterns (some evidence of correct orthographic patterns). Syllables and affixes (some evidence of correctly spelled affixes). Derivational (evidence of how words derive from base words and word roots).
Ehri (2005)	Four successive phases: Pre-alphabetic (child may or may not know letters, but some words are spelled using memory of visual patterns in words). Partial alphabetic (some evidence of phonetic spelling). Full alphabetic (phonetically accurate spelling). Consolidated alphabetic (correct spelling).

Following a linear framework, instruction typically begins with a phonics and rote learning approach and much later may incorporate morphological skills. However, the view that spelling knowledge is acquired in a stage-like or phase-like manner has been refuted in recent times. For example, Devonshire, Morris, and Fluck (2013) posit that models of spelling development "must account for the impact of the child's environment" rather than a "predetermined path of intellectual development" (p. 87). Others argue that stage and phase theories offer an overly simplistic account of learning to spell as they cannot capture the range of difficulties or experiential advantages students encounter throughout their journey towards proficient spelling (Berninger, Abbott, Nagy & Carlisle, 2010; Daffern, Mackenzie & Hemmings, 2015). Research has shown that children are capable of using all strategies that are available to them to spell and that these may develop continuously and in parallel (Daffern, 2017; Lennox & Siegler, 1994; Sharp, Sinatra & Reynolds, 2008). In particular, with explicit instruction, it is possible for children to develop morphological awareness early in schooling (Apel, Brimo, Diehm & Apel, 2013; Daffern & Sassu, 2020; Nunes, Bryant & Olsson, 2003). According to Bowers, Kirby, and Deacon (2010, p. 171), morphological instruction is "at least as effective for students in the early stages of formal literacy instruction" as it is for older students.

Reflection prompt

How might your theoretical perspective on learning to spell influence how you teach spelling?

Triple Word Form Theory offers a non-linear perspective of learning to spell and has been validated in several neurocognitive and behavioural studies (Garcia et al., 2010; Richards et al., 2006; Daffern & Ramful, 2020). Underpinning this theory is the assumption that learning to spell in the English language involves learning to store and analyse in memory three interrelated linguistic word forms: phonological, orthographic, and morphological (Bahr, 2015; Garcia et al., 2010). Informed by this perspective, instruction in spelling should, from the beginning of formal schooling, be explicit and provide children with regular opportunities to coordinate (or "cross-map") phonological, orthographic, and morphological word forms until they become "unified representations" (Bahr et al., 2015, p. 74). Linguistic cross-mapping involves particular thinking processes when spelling. For example, phonological mapping may require "knowledge of how to segment spoken words into the smallest units of sound within words" and the capacity to encode word parts via direct speech sound-to-letter associations (Daffern, 2015, p. 34). Simultaneously, orthographic mapping requires visual sensitivity and awareness of the "legal" letter sequences within words, while morphological mapping requires the ability to "reflect, analyse and manipulate" the smallest meaningful units within words (Daffern, 2015, p. 34). Cross-mapping among the three word forms may be needed in order to spell a word that cannot be automatically encoded.

Developing spelling skills does not occur merely by memorising lists of words through rote learning methods. Instead, becoming proficient in spelling "involves learning how phonological, orthographic and morphological concepts can be combined to produce written words" (Daffern & Fleet, 2021, p. 68). This is a gradual process and one that demands quality explicit teaching and ample opportunities for children to consolidate their learning.

Reflection prompt

What thinking processes might you use when spelling difficult or less familiar words? Does it depend on what the word is? Why?

Meet Joshua

Joshua is the eldest of two boys with parents who are supportive and interested in their children's learning. While Joshua's dad is not an educator, his mother is. Joshua's parents have *read to him on a daily basis from birth*. Joshua has also been given many opportunities at home to paint, draw, sing, write, and tell stories (see Figure 6.2). Even before

Figure 6.2   Joshua (4 years, 6 months), drawing a playground

Joshua started formal schooling, he had developed a collection of his own illustrated stories, mostly scribed by his mother. He also became particularly curious and aware of the environmental print around him. At about 3 years of age, Joshua discovered that words could be represented using the alphabetic code, but he was not aware of the phonological regularities in the English spelling system at that point in time.

Beginning to spell

Children's first spelling attempts do not necessarily indicate that they have knowledge or control of the correspondences between phonemes (speech sounds) and graphemes (alphabetic letters that represent the phonemes) in words. Instead, their initial spelling attempts may reflect rudimentary sensitivity to the visual letter patterns in words that can be found in their physical environment, as well as words that are meaningful and important to them, such as their own name (Treiman, 2017). Indeed, many children begin to spell words by experimenting with the spelling patterns that they discover within their own name (Bissex, 1980; Levin, Both-De Vries, Aram & Bus, 2005). Cumulative experiences and exposure with words enable word-specific spelling patterns to become represented in the writer's vocabulary storehouse, or mental lexicon (Silliman, Bahr, Nagy & Berninger, 2017). Over time, specific orthographic patterns can then be retrieved from memory with little effort when writing, freeing attentional resources to other aspects of writing, such as idea generation or sentence structure.

Figure 6.3 illustrates how over a two-and-a-half-year span, Joshua's accumulated experiences with writing his own name have helped him to gain increasing control and automaticity in the spelling of his name. When Joshua started to learn to encode his own name, he did so through a visual-spatial process, rather than by systematically being able to map phonemes to graphemes. Between 3 and 4 years of age, Joshua often asked his parents to "show" him how to spell his name and they were always there to help. On many occasions, Joshua mimicked his mother as she slowly wrote his name, one letter at a time.

Building orthographic knowledge

According to Conrad, Harris, and Williams (2013), "orthographic knowledge … is acquired through repeated exposure to print" (p. 1226). By being immersed in reading and writing experiences, young children can gain increasing mastery of word-specific spelling patterns, a key aspect of orthographic knowledge, in familiar words such as family names (e.g., *Joshua, mum, dad*) and high-frequency words (such as *me, the, is*) (Reichle & Perfetti, 2003). At Joshua's request, favourite books were read to him by his parents, often multiple times in one reading session alone. The repetitive immersion with literary texts also enabled Joshua to recognise and attempt to write some words, despite

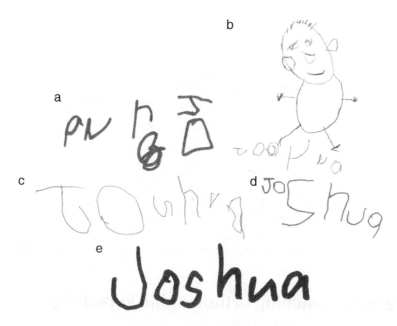

Figure 6.3   Joshua learns to spell his own name

Note. a. aged 3 years, 3 months; b. aged 3 years, 6 months; c. aged 3 years,
8 months; d. aged 4 years, 4 months; e. aged 5 years, 9 months.

Figure 6.4   Joshua writes a doctor's prescription (4 years, 7 months)

his lack of knowledge of the phonological constituents in those words. By the time
Joshua was 4½ years of age, he was able to write short messages during episodes of free
play, often with his friends or with his teddies (see, for example, Figures 6.4 and 6.5).
Sometimes, Joshua wrote messages by asking his mother or father how to spell particular
words or by copying words from books that he had found around the home. Other times,
he invented his own spelling.

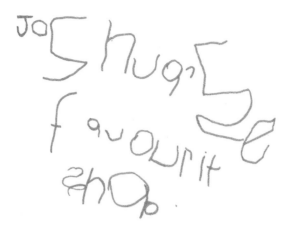

Figure 6.5   Joshua writes a sign for his imaginary shop (4 years, 11 months)

Strategies for teaching orthographic knowledge

In the preschool years, educators should actively encourage children to become aware of their environmental print. Facilitating children's growing awareness of environmental print is a critical strategy as it promotes emergent orthographic knowledge. This pedagogical practice may be visible in learning spaces where teachers display children's names on furniture, tables, birthday wall charts, art displays, and personal storage areas. Teachers may also display the names of other significant people, places, pets, and objects, both in the classroom and in outdoor areas. It is also important to actively help children recognise words that are present within their environment, and to encourage them to have a go at writing (by copying) those words when the occasions arise, especially during play-based activities. This also means that teachers should ensure children can readily access a range of tools (for example, paper, crayons, pencils, paint, paintbrushes, and chalk, to name a few) that enable them to express themselves through written words.

When reading to preschool children, teachers can use large picture books and e-books to enable them to attract children's attention to high-frequency words. Indeed, many preschool children are ready and eager to locate recurring words in familiar texts. Children can also be taught to identify, compare, and contrast letter patterns within those written words. For example, a preschool teacher may help some children count the number of letters contained in specific words. Teachers could also invite children to find words that contain a certain alphabetic letter (e.g., find words that start/end with the letter "a"/"A"). By constantly exposing young children to written words through varied means, they will begin to recognise that systematic sequencing of alphabetic letters will help them to communicate through writing.

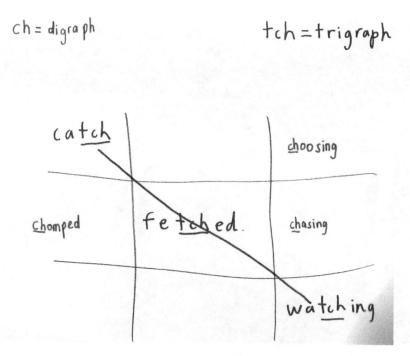

ch = digraph   tch = trigraph

catch   choosing

chomped   fetched.   chasing

watching

Figure 6.6   Partner word game (akin to "noughts and crosses")

In the early years of formal schooling, children should be given a variety of opportunities to build their awareness of plausible letter sequences within words, but also to develop fluency in the spelling of high-frequency words. Activities may involve sorting words according to specific orthographic categories (e.g., words containing the digraph *ch* and the trigraph *tch*); searching for common letter patterns in words from literary texts; partner word games (see, for example, Figure 6.6); and constructing high frequency words using a variety of mediums (e.g., Figure 6.7). Integrating handwriting instruction with the teaching of spelling is also recommended because the process of forming letters by hand can help commit new learning about the structure of written words into long-term memory (Graham, Harris & Adkins, 2018).

Building phonological knowledge

Integral to supporting children's early spelling attempts, and thus their writing vocabulary, is the development of phonemic awareness and oral language (Ehri, Nunes, Stahl & Willows, 2012; Mackenzie & Hemmings, 2014). Phonemic awareness is a "sub-skill of phonological awareness and refers to the ability to isolate and manipulate the sounds used in spoken language" (McLeod & McCormack, 2015, p. 600). Phonological awareness requires "conscious understanding of the sound structure of language" (McLeod &

Figure 6.7   Using magnetic letters to construct high frequency words

McCormack, 2015, p. 601). Phonological processing encompasses both phonological awareness and phonological working memory, and is one of the processes involved in spelling (McLeod & McCormack, 2015). Supporting children's development of phono-logical processing skills may involve phoneme and syllable manipulation tasks such as blending, segmenting, and elision (omission) (Yopp & Yopp, 2000).

It appears that children's growing sensitivity to hearing patterns in spoken language plays an important part in their early language and subsequent literacy learning (Richgels, 2004). From the earliest stages, children become attuned to speech sounds and develop receptive language skills to engage and respond to those around them. A baby's first cry marks the beginning of their journey in learning how to communicate. A baby rapidly learns to produce vowel-like sounds, and then learns to produce combinations of con-sonants and vowels to make intentional babbling sounds like *dadadada, bububu,* and *nanana* (Cox & McLeod, 2015). Between about 3 and 4 years of age, children should be able to masterfully produce most consonants and vowels in simple, monosyllabic words (Cox & McLeod, 2015). These young children can also respond to familiar voices and comforting tones, recognise the names of familiar objects, and can respond to simple requests. They use this implicit knowledge of the sounds of language to identify and create a wide range of spoken words and word sequences. Before starting formal school, children can also develop awareness that the speech stream is made up of a sequence of smaller components (Yopp & Yopp, 2000), noticing similarities between words and the constituent sounds within words, including sensitivity to rhymes (Raban, 2014). This aspect of phonological awareness is a crucial initial step in beginning to understand how written words work. Children can then learn to link individual speech sounds (phonemes) to alphabetic letters (graphemes), and this means they need to acquire a strong familiarity with the visual features of the alphabet. When young children are able to manipulate the phonemes in words, they can learn to map these to graphemes. Knowledge of how phonemes correspond to graphemes is important in learning to write as it enables young children "to construct the spellings of words in their spoken vocabularies" (Treiman, Tincoff, Rodriguez, Mouzaki & Francis, 1998, p. 1524). Research has shown that children who are able to demonstrate phonological awareness at 5 years of age are likely to succeed with compositional writing at age 11 (Savage, Carless & Ferraro, 2007). During the early childhood years, parents and educators can encourage children to develop phonological awareness by providing them ample "opportunities to talk and engage in conversation and also to attend to sounds in words, play word games such as 'I spy' and share rhyming songs and poems" (Cox & McLeod, 2015, p. 123).

Reflection prompt

What rhyming songs, poems and story books can be shared with young children to help build their phonological awareness?

We will now return to Joshua to consider how his phonological knowledge has been supported. Between 4 and 5 years of age, Joshua's interest with written words flourished. In response to Joshua's eagerness to write, his parents obtained a set of colourful magnetic letters (lower and upper case) and these were made available for Joshua to play with at home, on the fridge door in the kitchen. Joshua was encouraged to use the magnetic letters to "write" messages to his parents. Initially, he did so by randomly sequencing the magnetic letters, albeit in horizontal lines along the fridge door. In his first attempts, Joshua did not systematically include any spaces between the letter sequences; however, he often asked his parents to read the messages that he had created with those letters. In response, Joshua's parents attempted to phonetically decode Joshua's messages, pointing to each magnetic letter in a left to right direction. Obviously, the decoded messages were nonsensical, and Joshua found this hilarious. During these spontaneous and playful episodes at home, concepts of print such as phoneme to letter correspondences, left to right directionality, and word spacing, were casually introduced. Joshua was also encouraged to find the letters of his name and "make" his name on the fridge door (see Figure 6.8).

Joshua's curiosity with the alphabetic sign system was growing, so his parents started to introduce other words and they capitalised on the opportunity to talk about some similarities and differences in the spelling of those words. In doing so, it was not uncommon for Joshua's parents to incidentally show him how to create onset and rimes in one

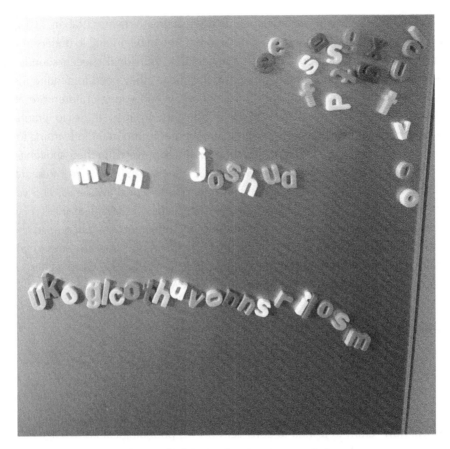

Figure 6.8   Playful encoding using magnetic letters

syllable words with the magnetic letters and also with coloured wooden blocks (e.g., *c-at, b-at, f-at, s-at, m-at, r-at, th-at*) (see Figure 6.9). An onset is featured at the start of a single syllable and refers to any consonants to the left of the vowel. The rime constitutes the coda in that syllable, which contains the vowel and any post-vocalic consonants (Cox & McLeod, 2015). Joshua was also exposed to many popular picture books which featured words with onset and rimes (such as *Hop on Pop* by Dr. Seuss).

By the time Joshua started his first year of formal schooling (at almost 5 years of age) he was able to read and write his own name, as well as a few simple high-frequency words (e.g., *the, a, I, and, is*) and some personally significant words (e.g., *mum, dah*). Joshua was also equipped with some knowledge of phoneme to grapheme correspondences and could name the letters of the alphabet. For example, he knew that the phoneme *sh* in *Jo* sh *ua* is written with two letters (*sh*), but that the letter *s* could also be used to represent a different speech sound, as in his brother's name, *Marcu* s. Joshua was making connections with words that were meaningful to him, and this helped him to implicitly combine rudimentary phonological and orthographic strategies to spell (and read) some words by the time he started school.

Figure 6.9   Using coloured blocks to explore onset and rime

Pedagogical strategies to support phonological knowledge

Before formal schooling begins, educators can support children's phonological knowledge in many ways. For example, preschool educators can explicitly show children how to identify and manipulate onset and rime patterns in spoken words. They can also regularly sing nursery rhymes with children and read literature that is abundant in rhyming and rhythmic patterns (authors may include, for example, Julia Donaldson, Mem Fox, and Pamela Allen). Preschool teachers should also ensure that children have many opportunities to develop their speaking skills. Importantly, educators also require the capability to identify whether or not children's phonological errors are typical for their age. While there are many educational resources available to educators that are designed to support the teaching and learning of phonological knowledge, one recommended resource that supports the development of spelling skills among young children is Daffern's manual, *Components of Spelling: Early Years*, available through her website (www.tessadaffern.com).

Educators also need to recognise that some children may begin formal schooling with no (or very limited) knowledge of sound-to-letter correspondences, while others may have grasped this linguistic skill reasonably well. This means that not all children in a given class require the same kind of phonological instruction when they start formal schooling. Indeed, each child is likely to present with a unique set of phonological skills, and teachers need to be able to identify what the instructional priority may be to help each child expand their phonological knowledge base. For example, some children may be able to recognise all the letters of the alphabet but find it particularly difficult to distinguish the difference between long vowel phonemes and short vowel phonemes in words (e.g., *hop* contains a short medial vowel; *hope* contains a long medial vowel). Therefore, this latter aspect of phonological knowledge may need to be an instructional priority for those children. For other children, a teacher may need to explicitly model how to segment and/or blend individual phonemes in words, while other children may benefit more by experimenting with syllable identification and manipulation using polysyllabic words. One way to manage the great diversity of student knowledge that may exist in any given class is to implement regular mini-lessons with small groups of children, rather than relying purely on the delivery of whole class instruction.

When children begin formal schooling, their existing phonological awareness should be refined and expanded by explicitly and systematically teaching phonic knowledge (the relationship between phonemes and graphemes). Instruction includes accurately modelling the process of segmenting words using taught phoneme-grapheme correspondences. For most children, instruction will begin with high-frequency, single-letter graphemes in words that follow a vowel-consonant structure (e.g., "at") and a consonant-vowel-consonant structure (e.g., "mat"). An effective instructional sequence should cover all phonemes and their corresponding graphemes in a cumulative manner, starting with high-frequency graphemes and progressing to less common graphemes for each phoneme. Teaching phoneme segmentation should begin with words comprising two and three phonemes and gradually increasing task complexity by using words comprising more phonemes and syllables.

Reflection prompt

Why are children's experiences prior to school so important in the development of spelling?

Building morphological knowledge

An important skill which impacts spelling is morphological awareness. Apel (2014) explains that morphological awareness encompasses four key components:

1   *Awareness of spoken and written forms of morphemes;*

2   *The meaning of affixes and the alterations in meaning and grammatical class they bring to base words/roots (e.g., -ed causes a verb to refer to the past as in walked; -er can change a verb to a noun, as in teach to teacher);*

3   *The manner in which written affixes connect to base words/roots, including changes to those base words/roots (e.g., some suffixes require a consonant to be doubled or dropped when attached to a base word/root in written form, such as in hop to hopping and hope to hoped);*

4   *The relation between base words/roots and their inflected or derived forms (e.g., knowing that a variety of words are related because they share the same base word/ root, such as act, action, react, and activity).*

(Apel, 2014, p. 200)

Instruction in spelling across the early years of school should not be limited to the teaching of phonological skills (Nunes & Bryant, 2006). Research has shown that with explicit instruction in "morphology, etymology, phonology and form rules" (Devonshire et al., 2013, p. 91), children as young as 5 years of age have the capacity to significantly improve in their spelling, more so than when a phonics instructional approach is used.

When Joshua was in Year 1, morphological aspects of his spelling required instructional attention. Persistent errors in his written compositions reflected limited understanding of how to correctly affix inflected suffixes (e.g., stop/stopped; activity/activities; make/making) and derivational suffixes (e.g., happy/happier) to base words (Figure 6.10).

As can be seen in Figure 6.11, Joshua's earlier writing also demonstrated difficulties with suffixes, as illustrated by errors in words such as *cuddlye* (cuddly), *lonley* (lonely), baby's (babies), *livd* (lived), and *happly* (happily).

In these two examples, Joshua's spelling errors revealed that he was relying on a phonological process to spell less-familiar words. At the time, Joshua's school implemented a commercial phonics program to teach spelling and he was encouraged by his teachers to "sound out words". This may explain why Joshua did not know how to apply morphological regularities when affixing suffixes to base words. As Devonshire et al. (2013) state, instruction in phonics only "may make it difficult for children to generate hypotheses about written language that go beyond sound-letter mappings; instead, they may treat words that do not conform to predictable phonic rules as exceptions that need to be learned in isolation" (p. 86).

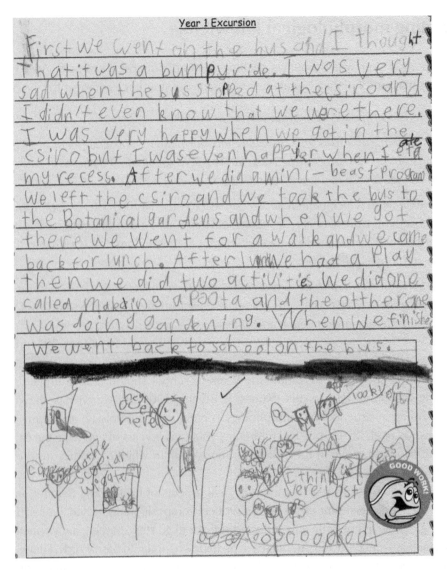

Figure 6.10   Joshua's (6 years, 9 months) writing contains incorrectly spelled affixed words

Strategies for teaching morphological knowledge

To nurture emerging morphological knowledge in the preschool years, educators need to ensure children have ample opportunities to speak, but also to listen to grammatically correct speech. The use of recasting and expansion is an important instructional technique that can be used when young children are speaking and listening. This technique involves rephrasing and/or elaborating a child's utterance in a grammatically correct or more sophisticated way, immediately after the child has spoken. For example, a child might say, "boy kick ball" and the teacher (or carer) may respond "Yes, the boy is kicking the ball".

Once upon a time
thor livd a Toy
Aog. She was kyook
and cudlye.

She was lonley

She had 3 dabys

and thai livd

haaly ever

after.

Figure 6.11   Errors with affixed words in Joshua's narrative (5 years, 7 months)

As children progress through the early years of primary school, children should be explicitly taught what a morpheme is. This includes explaining to children how morphemes can be distinguished as either *free* (a smallest meaningful unit that can stand alone, as in the base word, *dog*) or *bound* (a smallest meaningful unit that cannot stand alone, as in the inflected suffix, *s*, marking plurality in the word, *dogs*). Explicit teaching of high frequency homophones (e.g., too, two, too; eye, I; where, wear; there, their, they're) is also needed, and this should always occur through meaningful speaking, writing, and reading contexts.

At school, educators can facilitate children's inquiries into the functions of morphemes and the generalisations that may apply to those morphemes. For example, a teacher could capitalise on a familiar picture book and invite children to "hunt" for verbs that end in the bound morpheme *–ing* (see, for example, Figure 6.12). This morpheme is an example of an inflected progressive suffix that functions as a "process" or verb. Children could then sort those words according to how the affix is connected to the base words; for example, whether the base word remains the same (e.g., jump/jumping), or if the final consonant is doubled (e.g., spit/spitting), or if a final vowel letter is removed (e.g., ride/riding).

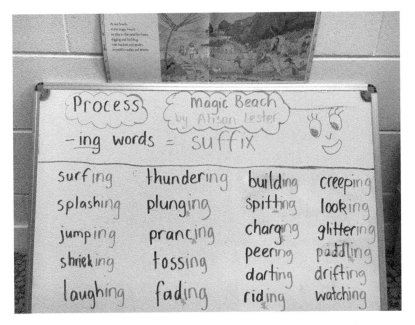

Figure 6.12   A teacher-guided inflected morpheme "hunt" using the picture book Magic Beach *by Alison Lester*

As an extension, children should be taught the various generalisations for using inflected suffixes. These include tense markers (*-ing, -ed, -s,* and *-es*), plural markers (*-s* and *-es*), comparative markers (*-er,* e.g., as in "bigger"), and superlative markers (*-est,* e.g., as in "biggest"). Common prefixes that do not require any change when they are attached to the start of base words should also be taught. Examples of common prefixes include *un-, re-, pre-,* and *dis-.*

Explicit morphological instruction should form part of any instructional approach in the early childhood years because it enables children to expand their vocabulary knowledge, including their knowledge of how to spell words correctly in the context of their writing (Nunes & Bryant, 2006).

Word study for young learners

Teaching spelling should also concurrently involve vocabulary instruction. It can occur as part of regular "word study," which entails a structured linguistic cross-mapping analysis of a carefully selected word (Daffern, 2023). For this activity, teachers allocate time each week for students to analyse the phonological, orthographic, and morphological properties of a new or challenging word that they have recently encountered when engaging with a text or when learning and writing about a topic. An example of a word study task is shown in Table 6.2. In this illustration, a series of questions are posed to

Table 6.2 An example of a word study task

Word: *sighed*

Phonological Component	*Orthographic Component*	*Morphological Component*
How many syllables can I hear? One syllable **How many phonemes can I hear?** Three phonemes **But how many letters can I see?** Six letters **What type of vowel can I hear?** long /i/ (in the middle) **What type of consonants can I hear?** /s/ (an unvoiced phoneme at the start) and /d/ (a voiced phoneme at the end)	**How many graphemes can I see?** Three: s – igh – ed (one for each phoneme) **Are there any tricky or new graphemes?** New grapheme: *igh* (trigraph) **Can I find smaller words?** I, sigh **Do any of the graphemes in this word remind me of other words?** sigh, high, light, fight, fright, bright, might **Are there any common patterns or generalisations?** Words never start with the grapheme, *igh*. The trigraph, *igh*, for the long /i/ is common when followed by the phoneme, /t/.	**What does the word mean?** The action of slowly and noisily breathing out to show a feeling of being tired or sad. **How can I use this word in a sentence?** I sighed when it was time to leave. **What is the base (free morpheme)?** sigh **Does this word have a suffix or a prefix? Is there a generalisation for this?** suffix: -*ed* (past tense). Just add -*ed* (because the base ends with a trigraph). **What other prefixes or suffixes can be used?** -*ing* (sighing) and -*s* (sighs) [tense markers]

Source: Table adapted with permission from Daffern, T. (2023, p. 362). *The Components of Spelling: Early Years. Instruction and assessment for the linguistic inquirer, 2nd Edition.* Literacy Education Solutions Pty Limited. ISBN: 978-0-6483430-5-9

target specific phonological, orthographic, and morphological properties of the word "*sighed*." With the teacher's guidance, students discuss their responses collaboratively.

Working with families

Educators can suggest engaging activities that parents or carers can do at home with their children to nurture an interest in words and support emerging spelling skills. For example, they can:

- encourage the child to sing nursery rhymes as this can help build phonological skills;

- read literature that is abundant in rhyming and rhythmic patterns;

- make writing tools (e.g., pencils and paper) readily available to the child;

- place magnetic lower-case and upper-case letters in a place that is accessible and regularly seen by the child (e.g., in the kitchen, on the fridge door);

- invite the child to use those magnetic letters to make personally significant words, with guidance as needed (e.g., the child's own name);

- model and encourage the child to sing the alphabet song while pointing to the letters;

- engage the child in daily conversations about words that they encounter when speaking and in texts they engage with. For example, talk about the speech sounds in a word, the letter names that correspond to those sounds, and the word's meaning.

In a school context, offering a parent/carer workshop on spelling can be powerful. The workshop should communicate the pedagogical approach that the school is adopting. For example, the information presented at the workshop can highlight the importance of teaching children about the phonological, orthographic, and morphological structures of words, rather than relying on methods that merely promote rote learning lists of words. With that insight, parents and carers should then be encouraged to regularly talk with their child about the spelling skills that they are learning at school. The series of questions shown in the suggested word study task (see Figure 6.13) can be used to guide conversations that may take place at home.

Families should also be regularly informed of the spelling skills that have been taught at school. For example, on a weekly basis, a teacher may communicate to parents/carers which phoneme-grapheme correspondences are introduced by the teacher. Those concepts can then be further consolidated at home by the child with the encouragement of a parent/carer. For example, a child can be encouraged to be a "word detective" as they read a text, identifying and writing words that feature the taught graphemes.

Teachers can also use spelling error analysis data to inform conversations that they have with a parent/carer about a child's progress in spelling. Spelling error analysis data provides valuable diagnostic information as it reveals how accurately students are applying their phonological, orthographic, and morphological skills to spell words. By

Figure 6.13   QR code to link to this YouTube video

referring to a child's error analysis data, a teacher can provide a parent/carer specific information about the types of spelling skills that a child is demonstrating and yet to learn. Error analysis is an important assessment as it informs instructional priorities. While it is recommended for all students, it is especially critical for children who find learning to spell challenging.

When supporting children who find learning to spell challenging, instruction should be tailored to the specific spelling needs of the individual child. This does *not* mean that a child with a diagnosed condition such as dyslexia or autism needs a "program" based on their condition. Similarly, an instructional approach should not be based on gender (Limbrick, Wheldall & Madelaine, 2012) or on a specific cultural background. For example, research has demonstrated that low-performing indigenous children can learn about written words just as effectively as similarly low-performing children who are not identified as indigenous, given they are afforded targeted, systematic, and explicit teaching that builds on specific skills in a cumulative manner (Wheldall, Beaman & Langstaff, 2010). Furthermore, where dialect differences in the pronunciation of a phoneme in a Standard English word (inevitably) arises, it is important to recognise and celebrate those differences while highlighting the corresponding grapheme, which remains consistent irrespective of the phoneme variation that is explained by dialect.

Essential to a targeted and systematic approach to teaching spelling is the use of valid and reliable error analysis data (Daffern, Thompson & Ryan, 2020). One example is the norm-referenced assessment, informed by Triple Word Form Theory, *The Components of Spelling: Early Years* (Daffern, 2023; Daffern, 2022). As summarised in Table 6.3, this assessment allows for a comprehensive analysis of the phonological, orthographic, and morphological skills in spelling.

Teachers should use error analysis data to determine the specific spelling skills that a child needs to be explicitly taught. Each child will have their own profile of spelling skills, and it is important for the teacher to be responsive to those identified needs when planning and teaching spelling.

Conclusion

Spelling is a complex problem-solving word formation process, and it is integral to becoming a literate writer. In this chapter, we have highlighted the importance of enabling children to access a range of opportunities, in and out of school, that can ignite their curiosity for words and how words work. We have also emphasised the importance of providing explicit instruction in the three overarching components that underpin Standard English spelling: (1) phonological, (2) orthographic, and (3) morphological.

While it is important to facilitate young children's knowledge of the spelling components, the primary goal is to help them develop efficient and accurate coordination of

Table 6.3 Overview of the structure of the *Components of Spelling Test: Early Years* (CoSTEY)

	Phonological Component		Orthographic Component		Morphological Component
	Part A	Part B	Part A	Part B	
Number of words the student writes	38	10	50	21	55
Number of error analysis items	114	10	50	26	55
Linguistic features	**Part A (monosyllabic words)** • Initial consonant graph • Medial short vowel graph • Final consonant graph • Consonant digraph • Initial and final consonant blend **Part B (disyllabic words)** • Disyllabic-word medial blending		**Part A (vowel graphemes)** • Long /a/ vowel • Long /e/ vowel • Long /i/ vowel • /oo/ vowel (as in "moon") • /oo/ vowel (as in "look") • /ow/ vowels (as in "cow" and "show") • /oy/ vowel (as in "boy") • /er/ and /ar/ vowels (as in "her" and "car") • /or/ vowel (as in "warm") **Part B (other positional constraints)** • Medial consonant doubling • /k/ graphemes • Unaccented final syllables • Final position /v/ • Final position consonant trigraphs		• Inflected suffixes (tense) • Inflected suffixes (plural) • Inflected suffixes (comparative & superlative) • Derivational suffixes • Prefixes • Homophones

Further information on the process of error analysis using this assessment tool can be viewed here: https://youtu.be/8dtXNYkfJVg

phonology, orthography, and morphology so that they can devote their attention to the craft of writing. For this to be realised, educators need to understand the linguistic complexities involved in spelling so that they can model correct spelling processes and apply appropriate metalanguage during instruction. With effective teaching of spelling, educators can help young children feel empowered to express themselves through the written language.

Reflection prompt

How might a teacher's linguistic knowledge impact upon the way in which spelling is taught in their classroom?

Glossary

Terminology: Meaning

Affix: A bound morpheme that is added to the beginning or end of a base or root (e.g., prefixes and suffixes).

Base word: A free morpheme, usually to which another morpheme can be added (e.g., *"swim"*)

Bound morpheme: The smallest meaningful unit that cannot stand alone as a single word (e.g., prefixes and suffixes).

Derivational suffix: A morpheme added to the end of a base/root that affects the meaning and/or part of speech (e.g., *-y* in *"sleepy"*).

Digraph: Two letters that represent one phoneme (e.g., *sh* in *"shop"*).

Free morpheme: The smallest meaningful unit that can stand alone to make a word (e.g., *"house"*).

Grapheme: A letter or group of letters that represent one phoneme (e.g., *ng* in *"ring"*).

Homophones: Words that sound the same but have different spelling and meaning (e.g., *see/sea*).

Inflected suffix: A morpheme added to the end of a base word that changes the tense (e.g., *-ed* in *"stopped"*) or number (e.g., *-s* in *"dogs"*), as well as a superlative (e.g., *-est* in *"biggest"*) and comparative (e.g., *-er* in *"bigger"*) marker.

Medial vowel: A vowel phoneme that is positioned somewhere in the middle of a spoken word (e.g., /a/ in *"sat"*)

Morpheme: The smallest meaningful unit in a word (e.g., a prefix, suffix, or base).

Phoneme: The smallest speech sound unit (e.g., the /s/ sound at the start of the word *"sun"*).

Prefix: A meaningful unit in a word that attaches to the beginning of a base word or word root to make a new word (e.g., *un-* in *"undo"*).

Suffix: A meaningful unit in a word that attaches to the end of a base word or root to make a new word (*-ing* in *"raining"*).

Syllable: A word part that feels like a beat and contains a vowel phoneme (e.g., "*rainbow*" has 2 syllables).

Trigraph: Three letters that represent one phoneme (e.g., *tch* in "*catch*").

Recommended reading

Daffern, T. (2022). *The Little Compendium of Standard English Spelling*. Shell Cove, Literacy Education Solutions Pty Limited. ISBN: 978-0-6483430-2-8

Daffern, T. (2017). What happens when a teacher uses metalanguage to teach spelling? *The Reading Teacher*, *70*(4), 423–434. doi: 10.1002/trtr.1528

Galuschka, K., Görgen, R., Kalmar, J., Haberstroh, S., Schmalz, X., & Schulte-Körne, G. (2020). Effectiveness of spelling interventions for learners with dyslexia: A meta-analysis and systematic review. *Educational Psychologist*, *55*(1), 1–20. doi: 10.1080/00461520.2019.1659794

Treiman, R. (2018). Teaching and learning spelling. *Child Development Perspectives*, *12*(4), 235–239. doi:10.1111/cdep.12292

References

Abbott, R., Berninger, V. & Fayol, M. (2010). Longitudinal relationships to levels of language in writing and between writing and reading in grades 1 to 7. *Journal of Educational Psychology*, *102*(2), 281–291. doi: 10.1037/a0019318

Apel, K. (2014). A comprehensive definition of morphological awareness: Implications for assessment. *Topics in Language Disorders*, *34*(3), 197–209. doi: 10.1097/TLD.00000 00000000019

Apel, K., Brimo, D., Diehm, E. & Apel, L. (2013). Morphological awareness intervention with kindergartners and first- and second-grade students from low socioeconomic status homes: A feasibility study. *Language, Speech & Hearing Services in Schools*, *44*(2), 161–173. doi: 10.1044/0161-1461(2012/12-0042)

Bahr, R. (2015). Spelling strategies and word formation processes. In R. Bahr & E. Silliman (Eds.), *Routledge Handbook of Communication Disorders* (pp. 193–203). Abingdon: Routledge.

Bahr, R., Silliman, E. & Berninger, V. (2009). What spelling errors have to tell about vocabulary learning. In C. Woods & V. Connelly (Eds.), *Contemporary Perspectives on Reading and Writing* (pp. 109–129). New York: Routledge.

Bahr, R., Silliman, E., Danzak, R. & Wilkinson, L. (2015). Bilingual spelling patterns in middle school: It is more than transfer. *International Journal of Bilingual Education and Bilingualism*, *18*(1), 73–91. doi: 10.1080/13670050.2013.878304

Bear, D. R., Invernizzi, M., Templeton, S. & Johnston, F. (2012). *Words their Way: Word Study for Phonics, Vocabulary, and Spelling Instruction* (5th ed.). Upper Saddle River, NJ: Pearson Education.

Berninger, V., Abbott, R., Nagy, W. & Carlisle, J. (2010). Growth in phonological, orthographic, and morphological awareness in grades 1 to 6. *Journal of Psycholinguistic Research*, *39*(2), 141–163. doi: 10.1007/s10936-009-9130-6

Bissex, G. (1980). *Gnys at Wrk: A Child Learns to Write and Read*. Cambridge, MA: Harvard University Press.

Bowers, P. N., Kirby, J. R. & Deacon, S. H. (2010). The effects of morphological instruction on literacy skills: A systematic review of the literature. *Review of Educational Research, 80*(2), 144–179. doi: 10.3102/0034654309359353

Connelly, V., Dockrell, J., Walter, K. & Critten, S. (2012). Predicting the quality of composition and written language bursts from oral language, spelling, and handwriting skills in children with and without specific language impairment. *Written Communication, 29*(3), 278–302. doi: 10.1177/0741088312451109

Conrad, N., Harris, N. & Williams, J. (2013). Individual differences in children's literacy development: The contribution of orthographic knowledge. *Reading and Writing, 26*(8), 1223–1239. doi: 10.1007/s11145-012-9415-2

Cox, F. & McLeod, S. (2015). Phonetics. In S. McLeod & J. McCormack (Eds.), *Introduction to Speech, Language and Literacy* (pp. 83–133). South Melbourne, VIC: Oxford University Press.

Daffern, T. (2015). Helping students become linguistic inquirers: A focus on spelling. *Literacy Learning: The Middle Years, 23*(1), 33–39.

Daffern, T. (2017). Linguistic skills involved in learning to spell: An Australian study. *Language and Education, 31*(1), 1747–7581 doi: 10.1080/095007822017.1296855

Daffern, T. (2022). Empowering teachers with an evidence-based spelling pedagogy. *Practical Literacy: The Early and Primary Years, 27*(2), 14–18.

Daffern, T. (2023). *The components of spelling: Early Years. Instruction and assessment for the linguistic inquirer* (2nd Ed.). Shell Cove, NSW: Literacy Education Solutions Pty Limited. ISBN: 978-0-6483430-5-9

Daffern, T. & Fleet, R. (2021). Investigating the efficacy of using error analysis data to inform explicit teaching of spelling. *Australian Journal of Learning Difficulties, 26*(1), 67–88. doi:10.10 80/19404158.2021.1881574

Daffern, T. & Mackenzie, N. M. (2020). A case study on the challenges of learning and teaching English spelling: Insights from eight Australian students and their teachers. *Literacy, 54*(3), 99–110. doi: 10.1111/lit.12215

Daffern, T., Mackenzie, N. M. & Hemmings, B. (2015). The development of a spelling assessment tool informed by triple word form theory. *Australian Journal of Language & Literacy, 38*(2), 72–82.

Daffern, T. & Ramful, A. (2020). Measurement of spelling ability: Construction and validation of a phonological, orthographic and morphological pseudo-word instrument. *Reading and Writing: An Interdisciplinary Journal, 33*, 571–603. DOI: 10.1007/s11145-019-09976-1 [share link: https://rdcu.be/bOCRB

Daffern, T. & Sassu, A. (2020). Building morphological foundations. *Practical Literacy: The Early and Primary Years, 25*(3), 35–37.

Daffern, T., Thompson, K. & Ryan, L. (2020). Teaching spelling in context can also be explicit and systematic. *Practical Literacy: The Early and Primary Years, 25*(1), 8–12.

Devonshire, V., Morris, P. & Fluck, M. (2013). Spelling and reading development: The effect of teaching children multiple levels of representation in their orthography. *Learning and Instruction, 25*, 85–94. doi: 10.1016/j.learninstruc.2012.11.007

Ehri, L. C. (2005). Learning to read words: Theory, findings, and issues. *Scientific Studies of Reading, 9*(2), 167–188. doi:10.1207/s1532799xssr0902_4

Ehri, L. C., Nunes, S. R., Stahl, S. A. & Willows, D. M. (2012). Systematic phonics instruction helps students learn to read: Evidence from the National Reading Panel's meta-analysis. In D. Wyse (Ed.), *Literacy Teaching and Education* (Vol. 4, pp. 184–236). London: SAGE Publications.

Garcia, N., Abbott, R. & Berninger, V. (2010). Predicting poor, average, and superior spellers in grades 1 to 6 from phonological, orthographic, and morphological, spelling, or reading composites. *Written Language & Literacy, 13*(1), 61–98.

Gentry, J. R. (2000). A retrospective on invented spelling and a look forward. *The Reading Teacher, 54*(3), 318–332.

Graham, S., Gillespie, A. & McKeown, D. (2013). Writing: Importance, development, and instruction. *Reading and Writing, 26*(1), 1–15. doi: 10.1007/s11145-012-9395-2

Graham, S., Harris, K. & Adkins, M. (2018). The impact of supplemental handwriting and spelling instruction with first grade students who do not acquire transcription skills as rapidly as peers: a randomized control trial. *Reading and Writing: An Interdisciplinary Journal, 31*(6), 1273–1294. doi:10.1007/s11145-018-9822-0

Graham, S., Harris, K. R. & Chorzempa, B. F. (2002). Contribution of spelling instruction to the spelling, writing, and reading of poor spellers. *Journal of Educational Psychology, 94*(4), 669–686.

Graham, S. & Santangelo, T. (2014). Does spelling instruction make students better spellers, readers, and writers? A meta-analytic review. *Reading and Writing, 27*(9), 1703–1743. doi: 10.1007/s11145-014-9517-0

Hayes, J. & Berninger, V. (2014). Cognitive processes in writing: A framework. In B. Arfe, J. Dockrell & V. Berninger (Eds.), *Writing Development in Children with Hearing Loss, Dyslexia, or Oral Language Problems: Implications for Assessment and Instruction* (pp. 3–15). London: Oxford University Press.

Hutcheon, G., Campbell, M. & Stewart, J. (2012). Spelling instruction through etymology: A method of developing spelling lists for older students. *Australian Journal of Educational & Developmental Psychology, 12*, 60–70.

Kim, Y., Al Otaiba, S. & Wanzek, J. (2015). Kindergarten predictors of third grade writing. *Learning and Individual Differences, 37*, 27–37. doi: 10.1016/j.lindif.2014.11.009

Kohnen, S., Nickels, L. & Castles, A. (2009). Assessing spelling skills and strategies: A critique of available resources. *Australian Journal of Learning Difficulties, 14*(1), 113–150.

Lennox, C. & Siegler, L. S. (1994). The role of phonological and orthographic processes in learning to spell. In G. Brown & N. Ellis (Eds.), *Handbook of Spelling: Theory, Process and Intervention* (pp. 93–109). Chichester, UK: John Wiley & Sons Ltd.

Levin, I., Both-De Vries, A., Aram, D. & Bus, A. G. (2005). Writing starts with own name writing: From scribbling to conventional spelling in Israeli and Dutch children. *Applied Psycholinguistics, 26*(3), 463–477.

Limbrick, L., Wheldall, K. & Madelaine, A. (2012). Do boys need different remedial reading instruction from girls? *Australian Journal of Learning Difficulties, 17*(1), 1–15. doi:10.1080/19404158.2011.648331

Mackenzie, N. M. & Hemmings, B. (2014). Predictors of success with writing in the first year of school. *Issues in Educational Research, 24*(1), 41–54.

Mackenzie, N. M., Scull, J. & Bowles, T. (2015). Writing over time: An analysis of texts created by Year One students. *The Australian Educational Researcher, 42*(5), 567–593. doi: 10.1007/s13384-015-0189-9

Martin-Chang, S., Ouellette, G. & Madden, M. (2014). Does poor spelling equate to slow reading? The relationship between reading, spelling, and orthographic quality. *Reading and Writing, 27*(8), 1485–1505. doi: 10.1007/s11145-014-9502-7

McLeod, J. & McCormack, J. (Eds.) (2015). *Introduction to Speech, Language and Literacy.* South Melbourne, VIC: Oxford University Press.

Nunes, T. & Bryant, P. (2006). *Improving Literacy by Teaching Morphemes.* Abingdon: Routledge.

Nunes, T., Bryant, P. & Olsson, J. (2003). Learning morphological and phonological spelling rules: An intervention study. *Scientific Studies of Reading, 7*(3), 289–307. doi: 10.1207/s1532799xssr0703_6

Puranik, C. S. & Al Otaiba, S. (2012). Examining the contribution of handwriting and spelling to written expression in kindergarten children. *Reading and Writing, 25*(7), 1523–1546.

Raban, B. (2014). Talk to think, learn, and teach. *Journal of Reading Recovery, Spring*, 5–15.

Reichle, E. & Perfetti, C. (2003). Morphology in word identification: A word-experience model that accounts for morpheme frequency effects. *Scientific Studies of Reading, 7*(3), 219–237. doi: 10.1207/S1532799XSSR0703_2

Richards, T., Aylward, E., Field, K., Grimme, A., Raskind, W., Richards, A., Nagy, W., Eckert, M., Leonard, C., Abbott, R. D. & Berninger, V. (2006). Converging evidence for triple word form theory in children with dyslexia. *Developmental Neuropsychology, 30*(1), 547–589. doi: 10.1207/s15326942dn3001_3

Richgels, D. J. (2004). Theory and research into practice: Paying attention to language. *Reading Research Quarterly, 39*(4), 470–477. doi: 10.1598/RRQ.39.4.6

Savage, R., Carless, S. & Ferraro, V. (2007). Predicting curriculum and test performance at age 11 years from pupil background, baseline skills and phonological awareness at age 5 years. *Journal of Child Psychology and Psychiatry, 48*(7), 732–739. doi: 10.1111/j.1469-7610.2007.01746.x

Sharp, A. C., Sinatra, G. M. & Reynolds, R. E. (2008). The development of children's orthographic knowledge: A microgenetic perspective. *Reading Research Quarterly, 43*(3), 206–226.

Sideridis, G. (2005). Attitudes and motivation of poor and good spellers: Broadening planned behavior theory. *Reading & Writing Quarterly, 21*(1), 87–103. doi: 10.1080/10573560590523685

Silliman, E., Bahr, R., Nagy, W. & Berninger, V. (2017). Language bases of spelling in writing during early and middle childhood: Grounding applications to struggling writers in typical writing development. In B. Miller, P. McCardle & V. Connelly (Eds.), *Development of Writing Skills in Individuals with Learning Difficulties* (pp. 99–119). Leiden, Netherlands: Brill.

Singer, B. & Bashir, A. (2004). Developmental variations in writing composition skills. In C. Stone, E. Silliman, B. Ehren & K. Apel (Eds.), *Handbook of Language and Literacy: Development and Disorders* (pp. 559–582). New York: Guilford Press.

Treiman, R. (1998). Why spelling? The benefits of incorporating spelling into beginning reading instruction. In J. Metsala & L. Ehri (Eds.), *Word Recognition in Beginning Literacy* (pp. 289–313). Hillsdale, NJ: Erlbaum.

Treiman, R. (2017). Learning to spell: Phonology and beyond. *Cognitive Neuropsychology, 34*(3–4), 83–93. doi:10.1080/02643294.2017.1337630

Treiman, R., Tincoff, R., Rodriguez, K., Mouzaki, A. & Francis, D. J. (1998). The foundations of literacy: Learning the sounds of letters. *Child Development, 69*(6), 1524–1540.

Wheldall, K., Beaman, R. & Langstaff, E. (2010). Mind the gap: Effective literacy instruction for Indigenous low progress readers. *Australasian Journal of Special Education, 34*(1), 1–16.

Yopp, H. K. & Yopp, R. H. (2000). Supporting phonemic awareness development in the classroom. *The Reading Teacher, 54*(2), 130–143.

Handwriting, keyboarding, or both?

Noella M. Mackenzie and Rebecca Spokes

Introduction

In this chapter, the authors bring together education and paediatric occupational therapy qualifications and experience to explore *how children record their writing on a page or a screen*. This has, in recent times, become a "hot topic" and source of confusion for many Early Childhood (EC) educators, Early Years (EY) schoolteachers and families. Twenty years ago, learning to write by hand was an important milestone associated with starting school. Handwriting instruction began with pencils and printing (manuscript), with children graduating to pen and cursive script as they moved into the fourth year of school. According to the Australian Curriculum (Australian Curriculum, Assessment and Reporting Authority, ACARA, 2023), this is still the expectation of Australian schools. However, in the last ten or so years things have changed rapidly, as tablets and smart phones have become commonplace in many homes, computers more visible in EC settings and EY classrooms, and the curriculum increasingly crowded. The accountability agenda that has resulted from high stakes testing has also impacted what teachers in schools prioritise. However, to be literate in 21st-century society requires the ability to flexibly create and interpret both print and digital texts. Most people use both keyboarding and handwriting at some stage throughout their day – as well as texting on their phone and/or using a touchscreen on a digital tablet. We provide a case for explicit instruction in both handwriting and keyboarding, as a means to support effective writing. Slow or awkward handwriting or keyboarding can hamper a writer's ability to record their messages efficiently. We acknowledge that handwriting and keyboarding are secretarial/editorial elements of writing and encourage the reader to consider this chapter alongside Chapters 5 (authorial skills) and 6 (spelling).

DOI: 10.4324/9781003439264-7

Current practices in Australia and beyond

In the Australian Curriculum (ACARA, 2023) handwriting is clearly identified as a requirement of literacy and English instruction. Children in the Foundation year are expected to learn how to "form most lower-case and upper-case letters using learned letter formations" (AC9EFLY09) although no particular script is mandated (ACARA, 2022, p. 14). Printing is the handwriting focus from Foundation to Year 2, with cursive script introduced in Year 3 and consolidated through to Year 6. In Year 3, students are expected to learn to *"write legibly and with growing fluency using un-joined upper-case and lower-case letters"* (AC9E2LY09). Handwriting features in the Australian Curriculum for all primary grades with the expectation that by the end of Year 7, children should have "a personal handwriting style that is legible, fluent and automatic and supports writing for extended periods" (ACARA, 2022, p. 22).

There seems to be an unwritten agreement across countries who use languages that are based on an alphabetic system that manuscript (printing, see Figure 7.1) is the first step in learning how to write. Starting scripts vary from *ball and stick* formations to those that have a more italicised appearance (see for example Figure 7.3). While cursive script is still a requirement in some parts of the world, the benefits of cursive (see Figure 7.2) are being questioned in other parts of the world. Proponents of cursive script demonstrate connections between cursive writing and academic success (Ose Askvik, van der Weel, & van der Meer, 2020). However, some children find cursive script difficult to read and it requires explicit intentional teaching and high repetition to develop fluency (Berninger & Wolf, 2009) at a time when the curriculum is more crowded than ever before. It has also been argued that limiting handwriting to one handwriting style (manuscript or cursive) promotes handwriting mastery by increasing speed, improving legibility, and promoting automatic letter formation (Blazer, 2010).

Reflection prompt

What can you remember about learning how to write by hand? How did you learn to use a keyboard?

The quick brown fox jumps over the lazy dog

Figure 7.1   Ball and stick manuscript

The quick brown fox jumps over the lazy dog

Figure 7.2   Cursive script

In Finland's current curriculum, cursive script is no longer a requirement of schools. Printing (manuscript) is instead combined with keyboarding skills. In the United States, the Common Core State Standards Initiative provides another case where cursive writing has been omitted from a national curriculum (Mo, Kopke, Hawkins, Troia & Olinghouse, 2014). There is, however, an expectation of schools implementing the Common Core State Standards that school children learn to print efficiently and be proficient in writing with a keyboard by the end of Year 4. In the United Kingdom, the British National Curriculum, introduced in 2014, has placed a greater emphasis on handwriting than in previous curricula (Medwell & Wray, 2014), with statutory requirements for the explicit instruction of handwriting to Year 6, but with a choice to join the letters or not (United Kingdom Government, 2014). In contrast, France re-introduced cursive writing in 2000. French children are taught "all gestures and moves required by handwriting" before they enter elementary school (Olive, Favart, Beauvais & Beauvais, 2009, p. 301). Explicit instruction and practise opportunities are a requirement of elementary school up to Year 4. After Year 4, the instruction is replaced with daily practise with the goals of speed, accuracy, and fluency by the end of Year 5. This suggests that handwriting is still emphasised in current school curricula around the world, although there are differences in regard to the teaching of cursive script. While the teaching of keyboarding skills is not a feature of all curricula documents, these skills are starting to feature as an expectation of school writing programs and high stakes testing.

Reflection prompt

Did you learn cursive script? Does your handwriting more resemble printing or cursive? Why do you think that is the case?

What is involved in handwriting?

Handwriting is the process of forming letters and words by hand using a tool, such as pen or pencil, in order to record a message. Teaching handwriting refers to the teaching of skills relating to letter formation, a process that has in the past been seen as a relatively easy to teach, and learn, mechanical skill. However, having the ability to produce writing by hand, quickly and legibly, using a pen or pencil, is both cognitively and physically demanding, until it becomes an automatic process (Lust & Donica, 2011). The hand and the kinaesthetic memory must be trained to "generate the correct mental codes for production of letters and translate these into motor patterns of letters – as a language act, rather than just a motor act used to record writing" (Medwell & Wray, 2014, p. 35). The complexity described by Medwell and Wray (2014) supports the work of Feder and Majnemer (2007), who argued that handwriting is a "complex perceptual-motor skill encompassing a blend of visual-motor coordination abilities, motor planning, cognitive, and perceptual skills, as well as tactile and kinaesthetic sensitivities" (p.

313). Lust and Donica (2011) also identify "sustained attention, sensory processing, and the presence of proper biomechanical components for posture and hand grip" (p. 560). To learn to write a letter, a child must learn how to scan that letter, and this assists with learning that letter. They must "focus on the detail of that particular letter: its size, shape, position, direction, detail etc." (Mackenzie, 2019, p. 159).

The case for continuing to teach handwriting to young children

The benefits of handwriting for young learners are strongly established in the literature (Gahshan-Haddad & Weintraub, 2023; Limpo & Graham, 2020; Roessingh & Nordstokke, 2019; Ihara et al., 2021;). Students who can handwrite efficiently are able to "express their knowledge, thoughts, and experiences while engaging in schoolwork such as note- or test-taking, writing essays, and stories" (Gahshan-Haddad & Weintraub, 2023, p.1). Research also suggests that the motor actions performed on the basis of letter shape seem to promote letter knowledge (and phonic knowledge), spelling, and reading acquisition (Labat, Vallet, Magnan & Ecalle, 2015). James (2017) claims that handwriting experience is necessary for children to develop the adult-like neuronal circuit of letter processing encompassing visual and motor areas of the brain. Proficient handwriting, in contexts where handwritten texts are the expectation, leads to success in composition (Medwell & Wray, 2014). Efficient (quick, automatic, and legible) handwriting has also been linked to academic achievement and literacy skills, especially composition length and quality in primary and secondary schooling (Doug, 2019; Limpo et al., 2020). Other recent research provides evidence that handwriting is a beneficial life skill (Alves, Limpo, Salas & Joshi, 2019; Limpo & Graham, 2020), with Mangen, Anda, Oxborough, and Brønnick (2015) arguing that there are "certain cognitive benefits to handwriting which may not be fully retained in keyboard writing" (p. 227). Frangou et al. (2019) also demonstrated that writing modality affected writer recall, with handwriting superior to keyboarding and touchscreen writing, confirming earlier research by Mangen and colleagues in 2015.

In a study conducted by Mackenzie, Scull, and Munsie (2013), where writing samples from 210 Year 1 children were examined in terms of authorial and secretarial skills (see Chapter 5), the range of control of handwriting was quite extraordinary for children who were all in the second half of Year 1 (See Chapter 8). Some children were already able to easily produce text that is "correct, consistent, legible and appearing to be fluent" while at the other end of the spectrum some young writers were still producing "letter like forms with some recognisable letters" (Mackenzie, Scull & Munsie, 2013). This variation in control over handwriting signals a gap in young writers' ability to record their messages efficiently in a handwritten form. It could also be argued that this is an equity issue that can be closed only with explicit, intentional teaching and the provision of time for children to practise the skills and movements needed to develop automaticity of handwriting.

Handedness and the challenges for left-handed writers

As English is written from left to right, some left-handed students are likely to find learning handwriting more difficult than right-handed students. While a right-handed student writes away from the body and pulls the pencil, a left-handed student writes toward the body and pushes the pencil (Dept of Education WA, 2017). Writing from left to right favours right-handed writers. As a right-hander writes a letter or word, their product is to the left of their hand, readily visible to them and clear of smudges. For left-handers, their left-hand tends to obscure their writing as it moves across the page (Ministry NZ, 2008). Further advice for teaching left-handers is provided throughout the chapter.

What needs to be taught?

It is still the expectation of a wide range of curriculum documents that printing, and for some, cursive script, will be taught in primary school although handwriting scripts and approaches to teaching and learning vary across countries and even across states and territories in Australia (see, for example, Figures 7.3, 7.4 and 7.5 below).

   The purpose of handwriting instruction is to help children develop a handwriting technique that is efficient, automatic, and legible so that they can focus on the content of writing tasks rather than the physical act of writing. The teaching of handwriting can be integrated into the writing process (for example, in Interactive Writing lessons, see Chapter 10) and during independent writing, when teachers can reinforce correct letter formations. While the Australian Curriculum (ACARA, 2022) provides guidance as to what should be taught and when it should be achieved, it does not provide support for how to teach handwriting. An appropriate pencil grasp (see Figures 7.6 and 7.7), sitting position, and posture (see Figure 7.8), correct letter formation (including where to start and which way to go – Figure 7.9) are all essential to efficient handwriting.

The quick brown fox jumps over the lazy dog

Figure 7.3   NSW Foundation script

The quick brown fox jumps over the lazy dog

Figure 7.4   Victorian script

The quick brown fox jumps over the lazy dog

Figure 7.5   Queensland script

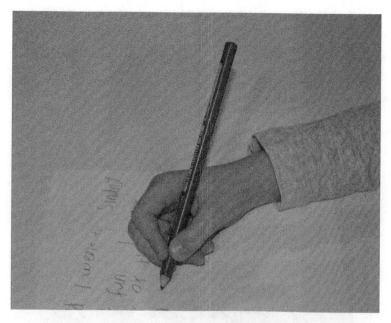

Figure 7.6   Tripod/mature pencil grasp

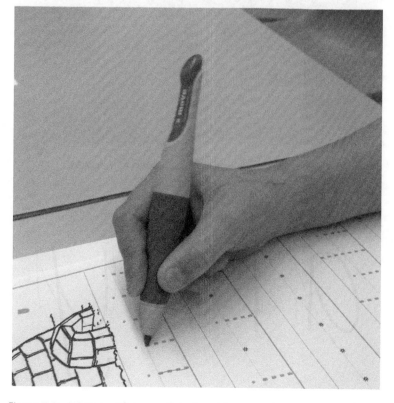

Figure 7.7   Writing with a pencil designed to support a mature pencil grasp

Figure 7.8   Appropriate sitting position and posture

Figure 7.9   Correct letter formation

These are far more important than which script is used. It is important to note here that pencil grasp can be learned and practised through experience with writing tools in non-writing contexts, with drawing providing a relaxed context for children to express themselves creatively while at the same time developing pencil grasp, sitting position, and posture that will support them when they begin to write.

In some countries (e.g., Finland) children are first taught to write in uppercase letters, although in others (e.g., Australia) it seems more common for children to be taught both upper- and lower-case letters simultaneously in the first year of school. This is a huge challenge for all school entrants, but particularly those who start school as young as 4 years and 6 months, or for those who may have little experience with pencils or crayons before starting school. While drawing is understood to be an important precursor to writing (Hoffnung et al., 2013), not all children come to school with experiences of drawing.

Posture

During handwriting instruction, a posture that encourages a stable base of support enables children to focus on letter formations rather than controlling their body (Benbow, 2006). Good posture enables free movement of the writing hand, allowing it to glide across the paper and allowing easy view of work in progress. Using the opposite hand to stabilise the paper also supports balance and posture (see Figure 7.8). It is important to encourage the use of furniture to support and promote the ultimate posture for writing.

Paper placement

Students should be encouraged to position their paper or book in a way which allows their arm to move freely across the paper as they write. Rather than positioning the paper in a vertical position, which limits the free movement of the arm across the paper, the paper should be positioned with a tilt parallel to the forearm. This allows the arm to follow the natural arch of the writing hand as it writes across the page. Left-handed students should position the page slightly to the left of them with the top left-hand corner tilted higher than the right (see Figure 7.10). Graham warns "left-handers who position their papers like right-handers are likely to develop an inverted grip, and this may decrease both the speed and legibility of their writing" (2009–2010, p. 53).

Pencil grasp

As children explore and learn to control and manipulate a pencil for the purpose of writing, their muscles and foundation motor skills will develop, and their pencil grasp will progress and alter (see Figures 7.6 and 7.7). Initially, young children will start with an

Paper position for handwriting

Left-handed

Position the top left corner
of the page slightly higher.

Right-handed

Position the top right corner
of the page slightly higher.

Figure 7.10   Paper position and hand support

immature grasp (see Figures 7.11–7.13), which engages the large muscles that originate from the forearm and shoulder. The child will adopt whole-arm movements for drawing and writing activities as he or she explores the process of meaning-making. In the long term, these movements are inefficient, often resulting in pain and fatigue, and cause writers to adopt compensatory postures or avoid writing (Berninger & Wolf, 2009).

As children experiment with different writing tools, they begin to refine the motor control required for drawing and writing. This engages the more efficient muscles of the hand, enabling them to adapt the way they hold their writing tool and adopt a mature pencil grasp. A mature pencil grasp balances stability and the ability to manipulate the pencil with finger-based movements. Some children will begin to develop a mature pencil grasp as young as 4 years of age, while other children will not be developmentally ready to begin using a mature grasp until somewhere between the ages of 5 and 7 years (Tseng, 1998).

The challenge in the classroom is to avoid inefficient pencil grasps and related postures becoming habitual. It is, therefore, important that through modelling, direct instruction, and close monitoring, teachers help children to develop and refine their pencil grasp to avoid long-term hand or arm injuries. When it comes to mature pencil grasps, the most common pencil grasp observed in the classroom is the dynamic tripod pencil grasp. This pencil grasp provides the best balance between finger stability and finger mobilisation by resting the pencil on the side of the first joint of the middle finger while holding the pencil with the thumb and index finger (see Figures 7.6 and 7.7).

However, other grasps have also been shown to facilitate the finger movements necessary to produce legible letters at functional speeds. Schwellnus and colleagues suggest that "occupational therapy practitioners and educators may reconsider the need for changing a child's pencil grasp when the child has adopted one of the four mature grasp

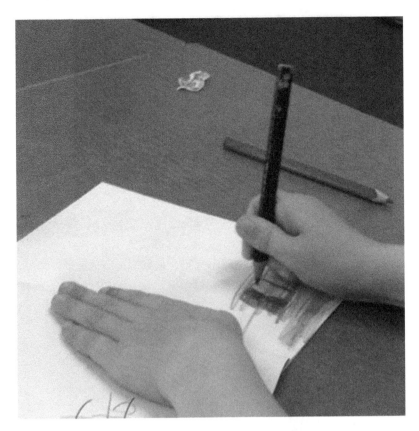

Figures 7.11–7.13   Examples of immature pencil grasps

patterns" (2012, p. 722). What is important is that the student develops a functional grasp that does not impact the legibility and speed of their writing (Schwellnus et al., 2012).

Left-handed writers can also employ any one of the mature pencil grasps but in order that their writing is not obscured, you might consider asking the left-handed learner to hold the implement at least 3 cm (a rubber band can mark the spot) from the tip or use a commercial triangular implement placed far enough up the barrel that the learner can see around his or her hand). They may also position their hand beneath the writing line with their wrist in greater extension, allowing them to see what they are writing and reducing the incidence of smudging their work as their hand glides across the page.

Start without too many restrictions

By providing authentic learning opportunities to explore drawing and writing in unrestricted ways, children learn how they can best control their pencil and which pencil grasp is most efficient for them. These authentic reasons for using drawing and writing tools in creative ways promote children's development of efficient tool use, which in turn supports meaning-making.

Reflection prompt

In your setting, what drawing and writing tools are children offered? What do they prefer?

Writing tools

Children need the opportunity to explore writing and drawing with a variety of good quality tools, pencils of different sizes and thicknesses (see Figure 7.14), and different hardness of leads as well as writing on different surfaces. Through exploration, children will gravitate towards the writing tools they find most comfortable and efficient to use, which leads to improved pencil control, legibility, and speed. Younger children may prefer shorter pencils with a large diameter as they are easier for them to hold, and triangle pencils can promote the development of a mature grasp. Soft lead pencils (e.g., 2B) are also recommended for early learners and left-handed learners, as they prevent the point digging into the page. In contrast, pencils with a thinner diameter encourage greater refinement of movements. Pencils with raised dots, indents, grooves, and built-in grips encourage the development of a mature pencil grasp.

Pencil grips are also designed with the specific purpose of assisting a child to hold a pencil with a mature and efficient grasp or to reduce hand fatigue and pain. The challenge with pencil grips is that every child will respond differently to each grip. Commercial pencil grips are something that should be introduced in consultation with an occupational therapist. The therapist will check to determine if there is an underlying cause for the poor pencil grasp and, if so, the best approach for remediation.

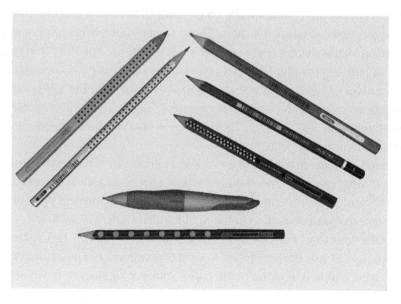

Figure 7.14   Examples of possible writing tools

Reflection prompt

What type of pen or pencil do you prefer? Does the type of pen influence the amount you write or the way you write?

Teaching correct letter formation

Achieving the correct movement is not easy, and lowercase letters are much more difficult than uppercase letters because they demand curved shapes and greater co-ordination of movements. Start with letter shape movements using large letters (paint, crayon, felt tip pens, sand trays, etc.). Concentrate on movement, direction, and shape, rather than size and orientation. Practise patterns and movements regularly in non-pressured situations, initially with fingers (e.g., in finger paint, sand trays, finger on the carpet and in the air) and then with brushes, crayons, and pencils (see Figure 7.14). Using the NSW Foundation script as an example, there are four basic movements for children to learn (see Figure 7.15):

1   clockwise ellipse
2   anti-clockwise ellipse
3   down strokes – vertical and diagonal
4   cross strokes – horizontal (usually left to right if written by a right-hander but left-handers often prefer right to left

These movements are ergonomically efficient for both wrist and arm movement and suit both right- and left-handed writers. These simple movements are combined and repeated to form letter shapes. These patterns assist children to "pick up" and "put down" the pencil as little as possible. This way, young writers can maintain consistency of size and slope. Curves or "wedges" are also used to assist with flow. The aim is that by practising these basic movements/patterns (see Figure 7.16), children will gradually develop their own fluent and legible style. These practise opportunities should sit alongside increased opportunities to write.

Left-handed students may choose a clockwise ellipse for some letters and numbers (e.g., O, Q, 0) where a right-handed student would choose an anticlockwise ellipse. Left-handers may also prefer to construct certain capital letters involving diagonal movements in a different order/direction to the right-handed student (e.g., X, Y, Z, L) and find it easier for the "crossbar" components of letters such as t, f, A, E, F, H, T to be drawn by pulling from right to left, rather than left to right (Department of Education, WA).

Initially, have children work on blank paper, introducing lines only when they have mastered most of the movement patterns. Provide lots of modelling and do not rely on

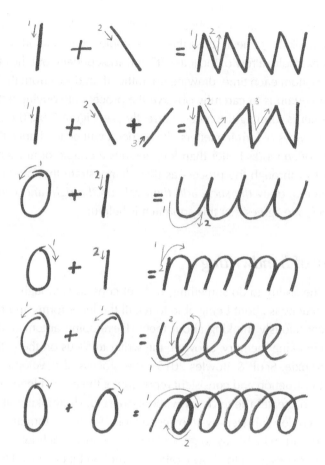

Figure 7.15   Basic handwriting movements

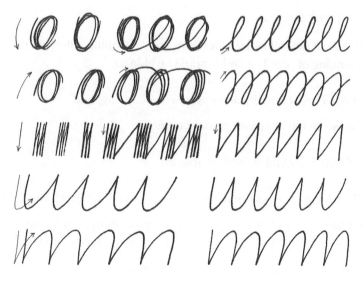

Figure 7.16   Basic handwriting movements/patterns

copying. It is important to be very observant at this early stage as children can often create letters that look the same as those they have copied, without following the correct movements. For example, a row of the letter "t" may look perfect, but the child may have started from the bottom each time, drawing up, rather than down from the top. The only way to know for certain is to carefully observe the process of copying letters, until you are sure the learner is forming the letters correctly (see Figure 7.9). The more children practise inefficient ways of forming letters, the harder it will be to change these practices later. *A little and often* works better than long lessons a couple of times a week. Some teachers like to talk through the process as they demonstrate the formation of a letter (e.g., *Start at the top, draw the stick, add the circle on the right and you have a "b"*), although not everyone agrees that this approach is helpful.

Automaticity of handwriting

Automaticity is the ability to do something without conscious thought. In handwriting, achieving automaticity is about being able to recall the letter forms and replicate these forms without consciously thinking about them. Developing automaticity with handwriting frees up working memory, allowing the writer to focus on the authorial aspects of writing (Mackenzie, Scull & Bowles 2015). The process of developing automaticity requires explicit instruction and consistent repetition of the correct letter formation until a young writer can create a letter form without consciously thinking about it. Scripts used in schools come with step-by-step instructions for letter formations. These will include where to start, which way to go and where to finish each letter. These instructions for teachers are designed to allow explicit instruction that will lead to automaticity.

Handwriting milestones

Children who meet the following milestones are developing automaticity:
   At the beginning of Year 1, a child should be able to:

- form all the letters correctly and easily when copying; and
- recite and write the alphabet in correct order.

At the end of Year 2, a child should be able to:

- form all the letters correctly and easily when copying and in response to letter names;
- write the whole alphabet from memory using correctly formed letters in alphabetical order in under one minute (this is a test of automaticity), and
- decide when it is appropriate to use neat handwriting.

This is based on the systems where children usually start school at 5 years of age (kindergarten) and therefore enter Year 1 after a year at school. In contrast, a child in Finland in Year 1 would be 7 years of age and have just started school.

What is involved in writing with a keyboard?

The past decade has seen a dramatic increase in the use of electronic devices by younger children. Most children are familiar with touchscreen devices such as tablets and smartphones and the process of using a tapping or swiping motion to create text and pictures. Whilst these are everyday forms of communication, they are typically utilised for short messages and not in the classroom for writing. In contrast, keyboarding, or typing on a computer keyboard, at this point in time, is often reserved for longer written texts as it allows for easy access to both text creation as well as the processes that support the writing process (e.g., formatting, fonts, cutting and pasting). Like handwriting, keyboarding is a secretarial skill and when efficient, allows a writer to focus on the process of composing a text.

Keyboarding involves the coordination of motor, perceptual, sensory, and cognitive skills in order to efficiently produce written text (Mangen & Velay, 2010). The sensory, motor, and perceptual skills for typing do, however, differ from handwriting. Unlike handwriting, which requires the refined finger and wrist motions necessary to control the pencil or pen to form letters, keyboarding requires the writer to use a search and tap motion to press keys (Alonso, 2015; Kiefer et al., 2015). This requires the use of different muscles and different motor and perceptual skills. Typing is also a bimanual task that requires the coordination of both hands (Alonso, 2015) as well as the coordination of sequential finger movements to type letters in correct order. It is a complex spatial learning process to identify where a letter is positioned on the keyboard and how to position and move the fingers to press the appropriate key (Mangen & Velay, 2010). Initially, someone learning to type will rely heavily on visual input, often adopting a search-and-peck motion (Weintraub, Gilmour-Grill & Weiss, 2010) to identify the location of a particular key. Through kinaesthetic input and the internalisation of the spatial coordinates of the keyboard, the typist then learns to accurately move the fingers from one key to another (Preminger, Weiss & Weintraub, 2004). Gradually, as they become more familiar with the location of the keys, they develop the motor coordination that matches the specific orthographic codes (Preminger et al., 2004). At this point, typing becomes increasingly automatic.

Reflection prompt

What do you write by hand and what do you write on a keyboard? What are you most efficient with?

As the Australian Curriculum (ACARA, 2023) highlights the importance of schoolchildren being able to confidently use technology and software programs to produce written work and from as early as the Foundation year children may be required to learn how to "construct texts using software including word processing" (ACARA, 2023), at the same time as they are learning to handwrite. There is no reference to typing or keyboarding in the curriculum although by the end of Year 6, children should demonstrate the ability to "use a range of software, including word processing programs, learning new functions as required to create texts" (ACARA, 2023).

The case for teaching young children how to type and use a computer keyboard

Although keyboarding is also intricately linked to the process of composing a text, it is discussed here as a discrete secretarial skill. Teaching keyboarding refers to the teaching of skills relating to typing on a keyboard and does not refer to "tapping" on a touchscreen device. Computers have been part of the landscape of Australian classrooms since the mid-1980s, with tablets introduced more recently. Many contemporary school children have grown up with access to at least one computer, if not multiple electronic devices and smart phones at home. While these devices can be used for writing, often in the home they have other purposes. Many children are commencing their education knowing how to swipe and single-finger point-tap on a touchscreen keypad, although they are often less familiar with typing on a keyboard. While any causal link between word processing and reading acquisition is yet to be established, Wollschied, Sjaastad, Tomte, and Lover (2016) found that children who used digital devices efficiently (they could touch type) wrote faster than those using pen and paper, enabling them to spend time thinking about what they were writing and to check, edit, and improve what they had written. In 2005, Freeman and colleagues suggested that keyboarding should be introduced prior to the grade level when computers would be used for academic work and yet computer-based high-stakes assessment has been introduced in Australia, without first ensuring that students have the skills needed for keyboarding. Students who do not have proficient mouse skills or efficient keyboarding skills are disadvantaged (Gong, Zhang & Li, 2022; Shute & Rahimi, 2017).

Regardless of the ease of access to digital devices and the integration of technology into people's everyday lives, children, when they start school, often find the use of computers for written work a new challenge, although it may be seen as novel, fun, and even a special reward (Poole & Preciado, 2016). Computers can also be used as a way to engage even those most reluctant writers to participate in writing tasks. Stevenson and Just (2014) argue that writers often have to choose between speed and legibility, and this can be overcome if they learn to use a keyboard. For school children who find that their handwriting is very slow or illegible, being able to use a keyboard can positively reinforce their skills as a writer (Tomchek & Schneck, 2006), and more competent writers may enjoy the added benefits of the editing tools provided on a computer. However, some young writers find computers challenging to navigate and the process of typing/keyboarding slow. Their hands and fingers are small, they are unsure of the locations of the keys, and they have difficulty coordinating their fingers to press keys in the correct order. This can make being asked to type frustrating, disengaging them from the writing process (Berninger & Wolf, 2009). Connelly, Gee, and Walsh (2007) found that without specific keyboard instruction, children were faster at handwriting. In their study, they found that the quality of typed essays by children in Years 5 and 6 was poorer than the quality of their handwritten ones but hypothesised that this would improve with more keyboard instruction (Connelly et al., 2007).

It is, therefore, important that schoolchildren are explicitly taught and given the time and practise opportunities needed to develop automatic typing skills if they are to be asked to compose texts on a keyboard. They need to be able to focus their attention on the content of the writing task, rather than the mechanical component of keyboarding (Medwell, 2012), and that can happen only if keyboarding is automatic. Poole and Preciado (2016) suggest that the easiest way to overcome the challenges of not knowing where the keys are is by learning to touch type through structured typing programs and lessons. These programs provide high repetition of the motor actions and spatial awareness of the location of the keys. It is through the repetitive nature of the programs that writers develop the motor programs associated for each letter, enabling them to develop the automaticity of typing. As with handwriting, keyboarding needs to be taught and practised if it is to be automatic. While the movements differ between handwriting and keyboarding, good fine-motor skills developed for handwriting facilitate keyboarding in acquiring both skills and speed (Freeman et al., 2005), connecting the motor learning of handwriting skills to that of keyboarding skills (Stevenson & Just, 2014).

Developing the skills necessary for handwriting and typing: the power of play

Developing the foundation skills that enable children to become proficient with handwriting and keyboarding (typing) begins long before children commence school. It is during the early years where children learn how to control their bodies and manipulate small objects in their hands, learn to visually track objects and how to differentiate between different yet similar objects and shapes. All these skills are essential building blocks for both handwriting and keyboarding and the best way to develop the skills is through play.

For young children, play is the way they explore and learn about their worlds. It is through play that they develop and refine their motor skills and develop a memory of how things look. It is through play that they understand that what they draw and make can convey meaning to others without using words. The following activities can be utilised in both the early childhood and school settings. They can also be easily shared with families as ways they can encourage children to explore and develop the skills necessary for drawing, handwriting and keyboarding in a fun play-based way. It is not about providing all these activities every day, but about being intentional about the play opportunities created for children by providing a wide variety of targeted activities that will build these skills.

Activities to build core strength

For children to be able to manipulate and use small objects efficiently in their hands they need a stable base of support which is provided by strong core muscles (see Figures 7.17 and 7.18) (Benbow, 2006). These muscles include those in the neck, back, abdominal region, and the pelvic area. By strengthening these muscles, the body can be held stable while the child uses their arms and hands to manipulate objects in refined movements.

Figures 7.17 and 7.18   Play to support core strength

There are many everyday activities that EC educators, EY teachers, and families can use to help children strengthen these muscles.

The focus is on children engaging the larger muscles in the body to help them learn to balance, coordinate their movements, and develop a greater sense of where their body is in space. Examples of activities for developing larger muscles include: climbing over frames, on playgrounds, and up ropes; swinging along monkey bars or swings; jumping on a trampoline; balancing on balance beams and walking on uneven surfaces; riding tricycles, bicycles, balance bikes, and scooters; ball games; running, jumping, skipping, and hopping activities; crawling through tunnels; parachute games; hopscotch and hula hoop play.

Activities to build shoulder control

For children to be able to use their hands to manipulate objects such as pencils, crayons, and felt tip pens or isolate their fingers to tap keys on a keyboard, they require good shoulder control to stabilise the top of their arm. Stabilising the top of the arm allows the muscles located in the forearm and hand to work freely as they manipulate small objects in their hands (Benbow, 2006). Activities that encourage the development of shoulder control include many of the core strength activities listed above, plus climbing up ladders; tug-of-war; making large movement actions with their arms such as parachute games, bubble wands, dancing ribbons; animal walking games (crab walking, crawling, bunny hops); wheel-barrow races; and painting and drawing on a vertical surface, for example, with art easels and window crayons or painting with water on the fence.

Bilateral coordination

Bilateral coordination is the ability to use both hands simultaneously to complete a task (Feder & Majnemer, 2007). During the infant and toddler years, children begin by doing the same thing with both hands (e.g., holding blocks and banging them together). As they refine these skills, they learn to use hands to do different components of tasks at the same time, (e.g., using scissors in one hand whilst holding and turning the paper in the other, banging a drum with alternating hands). For drawing and handwriting, children need to be able to hold and manipulate a pencil in one hand while stabilising and adjusting the paper in the other hand. For typing, each hand is required to tap different keys in a sequenced order. Activities that promote bilateral coordination development include popping bubbles with both hands; tearing up paper; crumpling and rolling up paper; playdough activities using tools, rolling snakes and balls, squeezing, modelling; construction activities using blocks and shapes; construction with cardboard, paper, straws, found objects; scissors activities; threading beads, pasta, straws onto a string; painting, drawing; making sandwiches and using cutlery; sewing, lacing cards; playing "Simon Says" and wheel-barrow races.

143

Figure 7.19   Painting on a vertical surface

Fine motor skills and hand strength

Being able to control a pencil or type on a keyboard requires highly refined fine motor skills. Fine motor skills incorporate a number of different components, such as grasping, finger dexterity, finger isolation, in-hand manipulation, and separation of the two sides of the hand (Benbow, 2006). Each skill contributes to the ability to control a pencil for handwriting and isolate the fingers for typing.

For children to be able to sustain fine motor activities, such as handwriting and typing, for extended periods of time, they also require sufficient hand strength. Improving hand strength also develops the muscles and the arches in the hand, altering how a

Figure 7.20   Developing bilateral coordination through sewing

learner can hold a pencil (Alaniz, Galit, Necesito & Rosario, 2015). There are many different activities that can target fine motor skills and hand strength, such as painting using different tools – fingers, paint brushes, rollers, stamps, cotton wool buds, straws, toothpicks; drawing using different tools – crayons of different shapes, pencils, markers, pens, chalk; drawing on different surfaces – paper, cardboard, windows, in sand, in shaving cream, in paint; beading, threading, sewing cards; cutting with scissors (using different textures and thickness of paper creates different degrees of resistance); playdough, clay, and putty (rolling, squeezing, stretching, pinching); board games such as Connect Four, Pop Up Pirate, and Snakes and Ladders; peeling and pressing stickers; mazes, tracing and dot-to-dots; peg boards; playing in the sandpit; playing with squeeze and stress balls and jigsaw puzzles.

Writing tool exploration

Even though it is not necessary to teach children how to handwrite or type before starting school (with perhaps the exception of their name), giving a child the ability to be able to use the writing tools with control will help prepare them to learn these skills (Ziviani & Wallen, 2006). Drawing and mark-making can be done in a variety of forms using a variety of tools. It can include traditional tools such as pencils, chalk, crayons, markers, paintbrushes, and pens or creative ways that require more refined skills such as cotton wool tips and tweezers holding cotton wool balls. It can be painting with water on the fence or wall, drawing on the path with chalk, using window crayons or etching

Figure 7.21   Cutting and pasting

in the sand with a stick. The goal is to explore and mimic drawing and writing. They will learn how they can adjust the way they grasp the objects to gain greater control and how the amount of pressure they apply to a tool will change how they make marks.

Developing visual skills

When children are learning to write and use a keyboard, they rely heavily on the integration of visual and motor skills to understand how to form letters or know where the keys are positioned (Benbow, 2006). The visual skills required include the ability to coordinate hand and visual skills (hand-eye coordination); recall how a shape looks (visual memory); copy forms; differentiate between similar shaped images (visual discrimination); visually scan along a line and a picture; locate specific information within a larger picture (figure ground); identify an image that is partially shown (visual closure); understand how an object is positioned in relation to others (visual spatial relations); and identify a shape regardless of size, colour, rotation (visual form constancy). Good visual skills help children understand what letters look like and how they differ from others, so they can copy, draw, or locate the correlating button on the keyboard

Figure 7.22   Children completing a jigsaw puzzle

(Benbow, 2006). Activities that promote visual skill development include: book reading, read-aloud opportunities where the child is able to see the text, writing opportunities, drawing opportunities, painting letters with water on a fence or paint on paper, making letters in sand or salt trays, mazes, dot-to-dots, spot-the-difference activities, copying shapes, construction tasks, jigsaw puzzles, and scavenger hunts.

These activities help to develop many of the different skills necessary for both writing and keyboarding. Opportunities for the development of these skills should be provided in early childhood settings (preschool and childcare), and the early years of school to increase young children's proficiency as young writers with the skills to be able to focus on making meaning.

Conclusion: The case for teaching both handwriting and keyboarding

Handwriting is a requirement of all curricula documents available when preparing this chapter, including those from the United Kingdom, the United States, France, Finland, and Australia. While many studies show how important handwriting is, we don't know what the long-term impact may be for children who are not taught how to handwrite. Anecdotal evidence based upon the referrals to occupational therapists suggests we already have a group of school children who are not automatic in handwriting or keyboarding, and this is making learning difficult for them. There is no research to show what happens if children are taught only to use keyboards and touchscreens. We do know that children who handwrite with automaticity are more successful with handwritten writing tasks and have a positive attitude towards handwriting, while children who have keyboarding automaticity are positive about keyboarding and experience positive outcomes with tasks written using a computer keyboard (Malpique, et al., 2023). However, we don't know if keyboarding will be replaced in the future with a currently unknown technology. Interestingly, digital ink is closer to handwriting than it is to keyboarding, and while voice recognition is improving, it is hard to imagine it replacing writing as a day-to-day process. Santangelo and Graham (2016) also argue that handwriting is still common at home and work; predominant at school; can influence teachers' judgements about the quality of a child's text; and can impact a writer's planning and text generation.

Many adults use both handwriting and keyboarding skills on a daily basis, selecting the best tool for the purpose. This should be the goal of our teaching: preparing students to be "hybrid writers" (Malpique et al., 2023) who can select and use both handwriting and keyboarding where appropriate, with equal efficiency. We need to teach both skills, with handwriting dominant in the first three years of school and keyboarding added in Year 3. Both skills need to be taught explicitly, with ample opportunities for practise aimed at automaticity. Integrating handwriting and keyboarding with text production will enable these two important secretarial skills to be included in the crowded curriculum.

Ideas for how families can support their young learners

During the early years, a broad range of play-based activities is the best way to promote the development of the skills required for handwriting and keyboarding. Educators can encourage parents to think about the type of play-based games they play with or set up for their children, looking for ways to promote handwriting and keyboarding development. It is important to focus on physical activities (both gross motor and fine motor) so young children not only develop the muscle strength and refined motor movements for writing and keyboarding, but also their spatial awareness.

Some simple play-based ideas that educators can provide parents include:

Gross motor tasks

- Spending time on swings and climbing equipment at home or at the playground
- Swimming
- Ball games
- Riding tricycles, bicycles, balance bikes, scooters
- Wheelbarrow races

- Ribbon dancing, bubble popping
- Sandpit play, water play, and gardening
- Simon Says

Fine motor tasks

- Drawing using a variety of tools on a variety for surfaces
- Colouring in
- Window chalk/crayons
- Nursery rhymes – Incy-Wincy Spider, Baa-baa Black sheep, Pat-a-Cake, Wind the Bobbin Up, etc.
- DUPLO, LEGO, Meccano, etc.
- Wooden trains and wooden blocks
- Painting – finger painting, painting on an art easel, on rocks
- Craft
- Cutting and pasting activities
- Playdough
- Beading, threading, and sewing
- Construction activities
- Nuts and bolts, hammer and nails (either plastic or under close supervision)
- Board games that require manipulation of small objects
- Games using tongs and tweezers.

Visual tasks

- Reading books together
- Spot the difference
- "I Spy" style books like "Seek and Find," "Where's Wally?" "Where's Waldo?"
- Jigsaw puzzles
- Paper and marble mazes
- Dot-to-Dots
- Hidden picture activities
- Matching and sorting games
- Patterning games.

Glossary of terms

Terminology: Meaning

Authorial skills: The component of writing tasks that includes text structure, sentence structure, and vocabulary.

Automaticity: The ability to do something without conscious thought.

Bilateral coordination: The ability to use both hands simultaneously to complete the task. The hands can either being doing the same action or different actions.

Bimanual tasks: Tasks that require the simultaneous use of both hands in order to complete.

Cognitive skills: Brain-based skills required for the acquisition of knowledge, the manipulation of knowledge, and reasoning. It includes skills such as attention, learning, memory, problem-solving, and abstract thinking.

Core strength: Strength of the muscles of the torso, shoulder, hip and neck region that aid in posture, balance, and stability of the body.

Cursive: The style of handwriting where individual letters or words are joined.

Digital ink: A form of technology that allows for handwriting and drawing to be added to documents electronically.

Explicit instruction: The overt teaching of a task by a teacher, through modelling and examples of each step.

Figure ground: The ability to distinguish objects of importance from their background.

Fine motor skills: Motor skills that involve the use of the smaller muscles of the hand.

Finger dexterity: How well a person can use their fingers to hold, grasp, and manipulate objects within their fingers to complete refined movements and tasks.

Finger isolation: The ability to move each finger in isolation of others.

Foundation year: The first year of formal education.

Hand-eye coordination: The way in which our hands and vision coordinate to complete tasks with speed and accuracy.

In-hand manipulation: The ability to manipulate objects within the hand without the use of the other hand to assist.

Kinaesthetic memory: The ability to recall a motor action based on the perception of body movements.

Manuscript script: The style of handwriting where individual letters or words are not joined.

Motor skills: Skills that require a physical/motor movement.

Orthographic codes: The detailed information about the order of letters and patterns in words

Pencil grasp: The grasp used to hold a pencil/pen for writing and drawing.

Pencil grip: A tool added to writing tools in assist in promoting an efficient pencil grasp.

Perceptual skills: The process of interpreting, understanding, and assigning meaning to sensory information.

Posture: The position in which a person holds their body to complete a task.

Secretarial skills: The component of writing tasks that includes handwriting, spelling, and punctuation.

Sensory skills: The skills required for receiving information from the external world. These include hearing, touch, smell, vestibular (balance and position in space), and proprioception (information from the muscles and joints)

Separation of two sides of the hand: The ability to disassociate the two sides of the hand when completing refined tasks. It includes the precision side (thumb, index finger and middle) which is responsible for the refined movements necessary for tasks; and the stability and power side of the hand (ring finger and little finger), which is responsible for stabilising the hand during refined tasks or providing additional power for tasks that require whole hand movements.

Spatial awareness: The awareness of the body's position in space in relation to visual input.

Visual closure: The ability to visual a complete object when provided with incomplete visual information.

Visual discrimination: The ability to identify differences in objects that are visually very similar.

Visual form constancy: The understanding that a form, shape, or object stays the same even if it changes in size, position or location in the environment.

Visual memory: The ability to recall visual information.

Visual motor integration: The coordination of visual skills, motor skills, and hand-eye coordination into an accurate motor action.

Visual spatial relations: The ability to perceive the position of two or more objects in relation to each other.

Working memory: The short-term storage and manipulation of information that is necessary in performing complex cognitive tasks such as learning, reasoning, writing, and comprehension.

Recommended reading

Finnish National Agency for Education. (2015). Writing by hand will still be taught in Finnish schools. Retrieved July 10, 2016, from www.oph.fi/chool/current_issues/101/0/writing_by_hand_will_still_be_taught_in_finnish_schools

Huffman, J. M. & Fortenberry, C. (2011). Helping preschoolers prepare for writing: Developing fine motor skills. *Young Children*, September, 100–103.

Mackenzie, N.M. (2019). Learning to 'look at' and 'write' the letters of the alphabet. In L. Beveridge, R. Cox, & S. Feez (Eds.), *The alphabetic principle and beyond: a survey of the landscape* (pp. 150–165). Newtown: Primary English Teaching Association (PETAA).

Santangelo, T. & Graham, S. (2016). A comprehensive meta-analysis of handwriting instruction. *Educational Psychology Review*, 28(2), 225–265. Doi:10.1007/s10648-015-9335-1

Shaturaev, J. (2019). The importance of handwriting in education. *International Journal of Advanced Research (IJAR)*, 7(12), 947–954.

Weintraub, N., Gilmour-Grill, N., & Weiss, P. (2010). Relationship between handwriting and keyboarding performance among fast and slow adult keyboarders. *The American Journal of Occupational Therapy*, 64(1), 123–132.

References

Alaniz, M. L., Galit, E., Necesito, C. I., & Rosario, E. R. (2015). Hand strength, handwriting, and functional skills in children with autism. *The American Journal of Occupational Therapy*, 69(4). https://doi.org/10.5014/ajot.2015.016022

Alonso, M. A. P. (2015). Metacognition and sensorimotor components underlying the process of handwriting and keyboarding and their impact on learning: An analysis from the perspective of embodied psychology. *Procedia – Social and Behavioral Sciences, 176*, 263–269.

Alves, R. A., Limpo, T., Salas, N., & Joshi, R. M. (2019). Handwriting and spelling. In S. Graham, C. A. MacArthur, & M. Hebert (Eds.), *Best practices in writing instruction* (3 ed., pp. 211–239). Guilford Press.

Australian Curriculum and Assessment and Reporting Authority (ACARA). (2022). *English: Version 9.0 Curriculum Content F-6.*

Australian Curriculum and Assessment and Reporting Authority (ACARA). (2023). *Australian Curriculum*. Retrieved June 23, 2023, from https://v9.australiancurriculum.edu.au/

Benbow, M. (2006). Principles and practices for teaching handwriting. In A. Henderson & C. Pehoski (Eds.), *Hand Function in the Child: Foundations and Remediation* (2nd ed., pp. 321–344): Missouri: Mosby Elsevier.

Berninger, V. & Wolf, B. (2009). *Teaching Students with Dyslexia and Dysgraphia: Lessons from Teaching and Science*. Baltimore, MD: Brookes Publishing Co.

Blazer, C. (2010). Should cursive handwriting still be taught in schools? *Information Capsule Research Services, 0916*, 1–8.

Connelly, V., Gee, D., & Walsh, E. (2007). A comparison of keyboarded and handwritten compositions and the relationship with transcription speed. *British Journal of Educational Psychology, 77*(2), 479–492.

Department of Education. (2017). *Handwriting guidelines (Revised)*. In: The Government of Western Australia.

Doug, R. (2019). Handwriting: Developing Pupils' Identity and Cognitive Skills. *International Journal of Education and Literacy Studies, 7*(2), 177–188.

Feder, K., & Majnemer, A. (2007). Handwriting development, competency and intervention. *Developmental Medicine & Child Neurology, 49*(4), 312–317.

Frangou, S.-M., Wikgren, J., Sintonen, S., Kairaluoma, L., & Vasari, P. (2019). The effect of writing modality on recollection in children and adolescents. *Research in learning technology, 27,* 1–13. https://doi.org/10.25304/rlt.v27.2239

Freeman, A. R., Mackinnon, J. R., & Miller, L. T. (2005). Keyboarding for students with handwriting problems. *Physical & Occupational Therapy in Pediatrics, 25*(1–2).

Gahshan-Haddad, N., & Weintraub, N. (2023). Underlying functions associated with keyboarding performance of elementary-school students. *Scandinavian journal of occupational therapy, ahead-of-print*(ahead-of-print), 1–9. DOI: 10.1080/11038128.2023.2188

Gong, T., Zhang, M., & Li, C. (2022). Association of keyboarding fluency and writing performance in online-delivered assessment. *Assessing Writing, 51,* 100575.

Hoffnung, M., Hoffnung, R. J., Seiffert, K. L., Burton Smith, R., Hine, A., Ward, L., & Swabey, K. (2013). *Lifespan Development: A Topical Approach*. Milton, Qld: Wiley.

Ihara, A. S., Nakajima, K., Kake, A., Ishimaru, K., Osugi, K., & Naruse, Y. (2021). Advantage of Handwriting Over Typing on Learning Words: Evidence from an N400 Event-Related Potential Index. *Frontiers in Human Neuroscience, 15,* 679191.

James, K. H. (2017). The Importance of Handwriting Experience on the Development of the Literate Brain. *Current Directions in Psychological Science, 26*(6), 502–508.

Kiefer, M., Schuler, S., Mayer, C., Trumpp, N. M., Hille, K., & Sachse, S. (2015). Handwriting or typewriting? The influence of pen- or keyboard-based writing training on reading and writing performance in preschool children. *Advances in Cognitive Psychology, 11*(4), 136–146.

Labat, H., Vallet, G., Magnan, A., & Ecalle, J. (2015). Facilitating effect of multisensory letter encoding on reading and spelling in 5-year-old children. *Applied Cognitive Psychology, 29*(3), 381–391.

Limpo, T., & Graham, S. (2020). The role of handwriting instruction in writers' education *British Journal of Educational Studies, 68*(3), 1–19.

Limpo, T., Vigario, V., Rocha, R., & Graham, S. (2020). Promoting transcription in third-grade classrooms: Effects on handwriting and spelling skills, composing, and motivation. *Contemporary Educational Psychology, 61,* 1–11.

Lust, C. A. & Donica, D. K. (2011). Effectiveness of a handwriting readiness program in Head Start: A two-group controlled trial. *AJOT: American Journal of Occupational Therapy, 65*(5), 560.

Mackenzie, N.M. (2019). Learning to 'look at' and 'write' the letters of the alphabet. In L. Beveridge, R. Cox, & S. Feez (Eds.), *The alphabetic principle and beyond: a survey of the landscape* (pp. 150–165). Newtown: Primary English Teaching Association (PETAA).

Mackenzie, N. M., Scull J., & Bowles, T. (2015). Writing over time: An analysis of texts created by Year One students. *Australian Educational Researcher, 42*(5) 568–593.

Mackenzie, N. M., Scull, J., & Munsie, L. (2013). Analysing writing: The development of a tool for use in the early years of schooling. *Issues in Educational Research, 23*(3), 375–391.

Malpique, A. A., Valcan, D., Pino-Pasternak, D., Ledger, S., & Kelso-Marsh, B. (2023). Shaping young children's handwriting and keyboarding performance: Individual and contextual-level factors. *Issues in Educational Research, 33*(4), 1441–1460

Mangen, A., Anda, L. G., Oxborough, G. H., & Brønnick, K. (2015). Handwriting versus keyboard writing: Effect on word recall. *Journal of Writing Research, 7*(2), 227–247.

Mangen, A., & Velay, J.-L. (2010). Digitzing literacy: Reflections on the haptics of writing. In M. Zadeh (Ed.), *Advances in Haptics* (pp. 385–402). INTECH Open Access Publisher.

Medwell, J. (2012). Handwriting and typing. In R. Cox (Ed.), *Primary English Teaching: An Introduction to Language, Literacy and Learning* (Revised Australian edition). Moorabbin, VIC: Hawker Brownlow Education.

Medwell, J., & Wray, D. (2014). Handwriting automaticity: The search for performance thresholds. *Language and Education, 28*(1), 34–51.

Ministry of Education. (2008). *Teaching Handwriting.* Wellington, New Zealand: Learning Media Limited.

Mo, Y., Kopke, R. A., Hawkins, L. K., Troia, G. A., & Olinghouse, N. G. (2014). The neglected 'R' in a time of Common Core. *The Reading Teacher, 67*(6), 445–453.

Olive, T., Favart, M., Beauvais, C., & Beauvais, L. (2009). Children's cognitive effort and fluency in writing: Effects of genre and of handwriting automatization. *Learning and Instruction, 19*(4), 299–308.

Ose Askvik, E., van der Weel, F. R., & van der Meer, A. L. H. (2020). The Importance of Cursive Handwriting Over Typewriting for Learning in the Classroom: A High-Density EEG Study of 12-Year-Old Children and Young Adults. *Frontiers in Psychology, 11,* 1–16.

Poole, D. M., & Preciado, M. K. (2016). Touch typing instruction: Elementary teachers' beliefs and practices. *Computers & Education, 102,* 1–14.

Preminger, F., Weiss, P., & Weintraub, M. (2004). Predicting occupational performance: Handwriting versus keyboarding. *The American Journal of Occupational Therapy, 58*(2), 193–201.

Roessingh, H., & Nordstokke, D. (2019). Handwriting at Grade 3: More Than a Matter of 'Neatness'. *Language & literacy (Kingston, Ont.), 21*(3), 38–63.

Santangelo, T., & Graham, S. (2016). A comprehensive meta-analysis of handwriting instruction. *Education Psychology Review, 28*(2), 225–265. 1

Schwellnus, H., Carnahan, H., Kushki, A., Polatajko, H., Missiuna, C., & Chau, T. (2012). Effect of pencil grasp on the speed and legibility of handwriting in children. *The American Journal of Occupational Therapy, 66*(6), 718–726. doi:10.5014/ajot.2012.004515

Shute, V. J., & Rahimi, S. (2017). Review of computer-based assessment for learning in elementary and secondary education: Computer-based assessment for learning. *Journal of Computer Assisted Learning, 33*(1), 1–19.

Stevenson, N. C., & Just, C. (2014). In early education, why teach handwriting before keyboarding? *Early Childhood Education, 42*(1), 49–56.

Tomchek, S., & Schneck, C. M. (2006). Evaluation of handwriting. In A. Henderson & C. Pehoski (Eds.), *Hand Function in the Child: Foundation for Remediation* (2nd ed., pp. 291–320). St. Louis: Mosby.

Tseng, M. H. (1998). Development of pencil grip position in preschool children. *OTJR: Occupation, Participation and Health, 18*(4), 207–224.

United Kingdon Government, Department of Education. (2014). Statutory guidance: National Curriculum in England: English programmes of study. Retrieved July 20, 2014, from www.gov.uk/government/publications/national-curriculum-in-england-english-programmes-of-study/national-curriculum-in-england-english-programmes-of-study

Wollscheid, S., Sjaastad, J., Tømte, C., & Løver, N. (2016). The effect of pen and paper or tablet computer on early writing – A pilot study. *Computers and Education, 98,* 70–80. doi:10.1016/j.compedu.2016.03.008

Ziviani, J., & Wallen, M. (2006). The development of graphomotor skills. In A. Henderson & C. Pehoski (Eds.), *Hand Function in the Child: Foundations for Remediation* (2nd ed., pp. 217–238). St. Louis: Mosby.

Assessing writing

Practices to support young writers

Janet Scull

Assessment practices are integral to teaching, informing the ways educators and teachers plan for learning, implement teaching tasks, and monitor children's performance over time (MacLachlan, Fleer & Edwards, 2018). Indeed, assessment is foundational to the effective teaching of writing and is deeply connected to the ways educators and teachers design and deliver daily teaching programs to support children's learning. While the many purposes and forms of assessing writing are acknowledged and appreciated, it is essentially "a social practice that involves noticing, representing, and responding to children's literate behaviours, rendering them meaningful for particular purposes and audiences" (Johnston & Costello, 2005 p. 258). This chapter will explore effective assessment practices for early writing, emphasising the need for the close scrutiny of multiple skills, situated within the context of purposeful, meaningful writing tasks, and also considers the way this information can be shared with young writers. To illustrate this process, an interactive writing analysis tool designed to analyse children's writing in terms of authorial and secretarial skill development will be discussed. Examples of children's written texts, teachers' analyses of these texts, and the teaching conversations that followed will be presented to demonstrate how the tool can be used to inform teaching decisions and support young writers.

Assessing children's writing

Summative and formative practices are often referenced when discussing assessment, with these terms used to signal the approach, timing, and purpose of the assessment. Summative assessment, sometimes referred to as "assessment of learning," generally takes place after instruction and "encapsulates all evidence up to a given point" (Taras, 2005, p. 468). It is generally designed to provide evidence of achievement in order to make judgements regarding the effectiveness of approaches to teaching and curriculum

DOI: 10.4324/9781003439264-8

choices (Black & Wiliam, 2003). It is an expectation that teachers summarise and report children's levels of writing achievement against curriculum standards to convey to parents, other educators, and key stakeholders how well children have performed against year-level expectations and to support classroom, school, and system-wide decision-making processes (Masters, 2017).

In contrast, formative assessment, sometimes referred to as "assessment for learning," is conducted with the specific goal of informing instruction and improving learning (Huot & Perry, 2009). In support of formative assessment practices, Tayler et al. (2023) suggest formative assessments assist early years teachers to respond to the strengths, interests, and abilities of individual children. Further, Wiliam (2013) explains the "term *formative* should apply not to the assessment but to the function that the evidence generated by the assessment actually serves" (p. 15). Formative assessment often occurs during the course of writing instruction to assist learning and is intended to ensure children understand exactly what they are to learn and what is expected of them, as they are given advice on how to improve.

Ideally, the strategies for assessing writing are integrated in teaching and learning sequences to promote children's understanding of the goals of learning, generating feedback that signals the relationship between current and desired performance, with children encouraged to take responsibility for their learning (Hawe & Parr, 2014, p. 212). Here we see the assessment and teaching of writing as integrated and iterative, with one informing the other (Leahy, Lyon, Thompson & Wiliam, 2005). However, for assessment to inform teaching and learning, the data must be made meaningful. This translates into practices where analysis is central to assessment. The analysis of children's written texts requires teachers to have a clear understanding of the ways in which children learn to write, knowledge of achievement patterns, and an awareness of the evidence that signals competence. What the educator knows about the writing process will determine what they are likely to notice; hence, it is important that teachers are supported to interpret assessment data in valid and reliable ways (Clay, 2019). As such, there is a need for assessment tools that capture the complex aspects of writing in ways that increase teachers' knowledge of children's developing skills (Troia, 2007) and that fit within classroom regular practice routines.

When working with young writers, teachers are expected to share their insights in ways that are relevant, providing useful information that builds on what the children can do to move the learning forward (Wiliam, 2016). Hattie (2003) points out that feedback needs to provide specific information relating to the activity or process of learning that fills a gap between what is understood and what is aimed to be understood. Further, feedback is more effective when it provides information about correct rather that incorrect responses, recognises and builds on previous attempts (Hattie & Timperley, 2007), and engages the learner in the process of learning, "transpiring during student-teacher interactions that are the fabric of learning activities" (Glasswell & Parr, 2009, p. 353).

Similarly, providing feedback and engaging parents in assessment conversations requires teachers to have a strong grasp of children's learning progressions as they provide information to families who are working in partnership with teachers to advance children's learning and development (Tayler et al., 2023). Parents and carers are genuinely interested in children's early and developing writing skills, and hence conversations should start with an appreciation of what the child has achieved. Parents can be encouraged to play a critical role in affirming children's efforts, contributing to their positive identity as writers and increasing the possibilities that they will enjoy writing and see value in the texts they produce (Wohlwend, 2008). This can be coupled with culturally sensitive and easy-to-access information to enhance writing experiences in the home (Nolan et al., 2016). Teachers can encourage parents and carers to share writing experiences with children as part of their everyday interactions, using the resources available and creating authentic opportunities for writing in the home.

Reflection prompt

Identify the various forms of assessment for writing used in your setting.
What is assessed, how is this assessed, and who is this information shared with?

Approaches to assessing and analysing early writing

The complexity of early writing requires that teachers assess the integrated aspects of early writing, drawing on authentic practices that reflect and measure what the child is learning (Clay, 2019). Approaches to writing assessment should be situated within meaningful writing tasks, where the purpose and audience of the writing is considered along with the social contexts that shape and surround the texts produced (Quinn & Bingham, 2019; Mackenzie & Scull, 2015). Similarly, engaging children in conversations as texts are constructed can be particularly useful as both children's own verbal commentary and their responses to an educator's prompts provide insights into the processes children use in text construction (Mackenzie, Scull & Thompson (Forthcoming).

Currently, early years educators have access to a number of writing measures in various forms; these examine particular aspects of learning to write, stages of development, processes of learning, and the range of texts children produce. Most often, multiple text samples are collected and analysed with these adequate to review performance and provide feedback that is instructionally relevant to children. The use of analytical scales or performance checklists can assist educators to make judgements about the quality of children's texts, based on the examination of skills across a range of criteria (Espin, Weissenburger & Benson, 2004).

A checklist for early writing developed by Clay (2019, p. 103) was based on her close observations of young children's explorations with writing. Clay's *Rating Technique for Early Writing* encourages educators and teachers to pay attention to young children's behaviours as they begin to master the complexity of the writing process. With reference to at least three texts, collected over consecutive days or a short period of time, the samples of writing are rated from 1 to 6 in each of three areas:

1   Language level – record the highest level of linguistic organisation used by the child, note the inclusion of letters, recognisable words and/or word groups, or sentences, a punctuated story (two or more sentences), or paragraphed story (two themes).

2   Message quality – describe the level of message complexity, record the child's use of signs and symbols, their concept of the message conveyed, indicate if the message was copied, the use of repetitive sentence patterns, the recording of their own ideas, or the production of a successful composition.

3   Directional principles – note control over directional patterns from no evidence of directional knowledge, part of the directional pattern is known, reversal of the pattern, correct directional pattern, directional pattern, and spacing between words, and extensive text with good arrangement and spacing.

Teachers of children in the primary school will find there is a vast range of checklists and rubrics available to analyse and assess children's writing; see, for example, Wing Jan and Taylor (2020) and Campbell (2017). In addition, teachers often create their own tools and rubrics matched to their children's needs and specific to learning tasks. In such cases, the criteria are tailored to the aims of the activity, with children often invited to engage in the process of establishing the measures of success and assessing the effectiveness of the texts created.

Similarly, mapping children's writing performance against milestone indicators, as described in Chapter 2, enables teachers to monitor children's performance over time and set appropriate targets for learning. Milestones are indicators or events that suggest advancement in children's knowledge, demonstrating their increasing flexibility and control over the written code. However, it is important not to read milestone achievements as a staged, sequenced approach to learning (Mackenzie & Scull, 2015). Avoiding a linear trajectory, we appreciate that children may take a range of different paths towards achieving similar outcomes (Clay, 2014), and we recognise that what children are able to do is closely related to their opportunities to learn (Askew, 2009).

Involving children in self- and peer assessment enhances their understanding of themselves as learners. "When children are actively involved in assessment they develop greater learning awareness, take increased responsibility and demonstrate independence" (Lowe, 2017, p. 32). Many teachers work closely with children to establish meaningful expectations for themselves and to monitor these learning goals. Goals may be related to a range of skills and strategies – from beginning writer competencies to more sophisticated skill sets. Teachers report that children's self-assessments are generally accurate, and children indicate that self-assessment benefits their understanding as they gain insight into their own learning (Leahy et al., 2005). The benefit of providing feedback to peers is also acknowledged. This requires children to think critically about the task, make careful comments based on their understanding of the skills required, with reference to another's work. When peers engage in feedback conversations, the learning opportunities are apparent for both the giver and receiver of the feedback.

Reflection prompt

Collect three texts from one child over several days. Take note of the contexts in which the texts were produced and the different supports available for the writer.

What insights about the child as a writer are evident?

What professional resources are available to support your judgements?

The discussion above highlights the need for well-informed, classroom-based assessment tools and analysis frames. Ideally, these will include processes for the systematic observation of children across a range of authentic tasks that capture a wide range of early writing skills, taking account of both the authorial and secretarial or editorial aspects of the writing process. The authorial aspect of writing takes into account the ways writers communicate meaning and express messages, translating thoughts into words and extended texts (Abbott, Berninger & Fayol, 2010). Learning to generate a message and convey this to oneself or to others involves developing competence about the ways texts are structured, sentences are formed, and vocabulary is selected to express precise meanings (Raban, 2014; Scull & Nicolazzo, 2022) (see also Chapter 5). Children must also learn to control the secretarial dimensions of writing as they work with the surface features or conventions of print. Control over the secretarial skills, including spelling, use of punctuation, and legibility of handwriting allows for thoughts and messages to be recorded and read by others (Daffern & Mackenzie, 2019; Mackenzie, 2018; Scull & Nicolazzo, 2022). For elaboration of these aspects of writing, see Chapters 6 and 7.

The Writing Analysis tool

The Writing Analysis Tool reported in this chapter addresses both the authorial and secretarial aspects of writing and was developed from the analysis of 210 texts randomly selected from a large dataset of Year 1 children's texts (Mackenzie, Scull & Munsie, 2013). The tool identifies six prominent dimensions of early writing evident in the texts analysed. Each dimension is described in Table 8.1. These dimensions were identified as markers of competency and challenge for young writers in the texts surveyed. The descriptions of each level of proficiency were based on the careful consideration of the writing samples, and this guided the development of the attainment sequence, rather than the use of any predetermined learning continuum or published curriculum level expectations. Examination of the texts revealed shifts in the levels of complexity evident in children's writing and resulted in the identification of six levels of competency (Mackenzie et al., 2013). The tool has subsequently been used to assess observable changes in children's writing (Mackenzie, Scull & Bowles, 2015) and to "identify various combinations of the dimensions of writing identified by the tool that may make teaching more focused and learning more efficient (Scull, Mackenzie & Bowles, 2020, p. 240).

To access an e-copy of the Writing Analysis Tool copy the following URL into your browser (either Mozilla Firefox or Google Chrome): https://doms.csu.edu.au/csu/file/832c364a-855c-4e39-aac5-1dc9a96fa8cf/1/Writing%20Analysis%20Tool.zip/Writing%20Analysis%20Tool/index.html

The Writing Analysis Tool encourages teachers to focus on discrete, yet related, areas to inform their teaching practice. Each of the dimensions identifies an aspect of early writing that contributes to children's writing development. As teachers look across children's texts and consider the dimensions of writing, children's profiles as writers may become apparent with teachers able to identify areas of strength and areas of need in the authorial and secretarial aspects of writing.

Table 8.1 Dimensions of the Writing Analysis Tool

Text structure	The sequence and complexity of information and ideas in the text. May include demonstration of features of text types.
Sentence structure	Sentence level grammar, control over sentence construction (e.g., simple, compound, and complex sentence usage).
Vocabulary	The range and precision of word choices (e.g., everyday language, topic-specific language, descriptive language).
Spelling	Accuracy of words recorded; includes use of phonetic knowledge, orthographic patterns, and spelling rules.
Punctuation	Use of conventional and appropriate punctuation to indicate the structure and organisation of the text to aid the reader.
Handwriting/legibility	Letter formation, size, spacing, position, and placement; ease of reading; apparent fluency.

The analysis tool also provides rich opportunities for the contextualised assessment of children's knowledge and use of phonics (Wyse & Bradbury 2022), as a key skill towards developing competency in spelling and writing more generally. When constructing their own messages, we see young writers attending closely to segmenting and synthesising sounds in words and to the features of letters as they compose and record messages (Mackenzie et al., 2015). Starting with children's texts, the tool directs teachers' attention to this complex range of skills, from noting children's early understanding of single letter sounds relationships, their control over semi-phonetic spellings, and the representations of consonant frameworks for words and dominant vowel sounds, to phonic spellings with students' spelling attempts showing most sounds in words represented. Further, the tool identifies the important shift to the use of orthographic patterns or common English letter sequences, necessary as children develop increasing command over irregular spelling patterns. When assessing the use of phonics and letter patterns through the texts children produce, teachers can monitor their intentional and effortful application of spelling strategies to encode a range of novel and varied words to communicate messages to self and others (Afflerbach, Pearson & Paris, 2008) (see also Chapter 6).

Reflection prompt

Use the Writing Analysis Tool to review a child's writing.
  First, describe what the child knows and can do as a young writer.
  Second, identify a specific teaching goal for this child.

Feedback conversations

The usefulness of the tool as a way of analysing writing and sharing information that might "feed forward" as children work on new texts was explored through a small study of practice. The study was intended to explore how teachers provide responsive advice to connect assessment to effective teaching interactions. Seven teachers from three schools were invited to collect two samples of writing from three children in the early years of schooling and analyse these texts using the Writing Analysis Tool. The teachers were asked to use their analysis to guide teaching conversations with individual children. These teaching conversations were audio-recorded and transcribed. Focus group interviews with teachers were also conducted to gain insight into their perceptions of the appropriateness of the tool to inform their feedback to children and their teaching decisions. Children's writing samples, teachers' analyses of texts, and the conversations teachers had with children are detailed below as illustrative examples of practice.

Writing sample 1

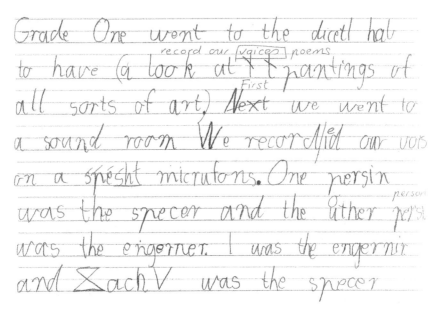

Figure 8.1   *A recount of a school excursion*

Teacher analysis – see also Appendix

Text structure	Four or more sequenced ideas. Clearly connected.
Sentence structure	Uses simple and compound sentence/s with appropriate conjunctions (e.g., and, but, then). Use of adverbial phrases to indicate when, where, how, or with whom.
Vocabulary	Uses a range of vocabulary, including topic-specific words (e.g., a story about going to the zoo might include animal names and behaviours).
Spelling	Phonetic spelling – plausible attempts with most sounds in words represented. Correct spelling of three- and four-letter high frequency words (e.g. the, like, come, have, went).
Punctuation	Some use of capital letters and/or full stops.
Handwriting/legibility	Regularity of letter size, shape, placement, orientation, and spacing.

Teacher–child conversation

Teacher: All right, [child's name], I've got a piece of writing that you did about our excursion to the digital hub and the arts centre.

Child: Yes.

Teacher: Brilliant. Okay. Really good use and you've got some great vocabulary there. We got some special vocabulary that we talked about and Dave talked about when we were at the digital hub. I want to ask you a question. Grade 1 went to the digital hub to have a look at paintings, of all sorts of art. Is that what we did at the digital art hub? Where did we look at the paintings?

Child: At the centre.

Teacher: At the art gallery, so we need to look at this. Grade 1 went to the digital hub. You haven't said when, okay, and remember, when we're recounting, we need to have – the who, the what, the where, and the when.

Child: And the when.

Teacher: And so that's one thing you've got to focus on when you go back and revisit this, so on Wednesday Grade 1 went to the digital hub to do what?

Child: Um, to –

Teacher: Not to have a look at art, to record –

Child: To record our voices.

Teacher: Record our voices. What particularly did we record? What have you written?

Child: A poem.

Teacher: Record the poems. First, not next, first because first we went to the sound room. We recorded the first bit you have put in order – your ideas are sequenced beautifully. What we do need though is recorded.

In this example, the teacher's feedback focused the child's attention on the authorial aspects of the text, building on the child's perceived strengths. The connections between vocabulary and the teacher's efforts to support the child's understanding of the structure and features of written recounts are interesting. By prompting the child to recall the location (digital hub), the teacher then supported the child to elaborate on the setting and provide precise details for inclusion in the orientation: "Remember when we're recounting, we need to have the who, the what, the where, and the when." The focus on text structure continued as the linguistic features of recounts were recalled, specifically, the use of temporal connectives (first) and past tense (recorded).

Writing sample 2

Teacher analysis – see also Appendix

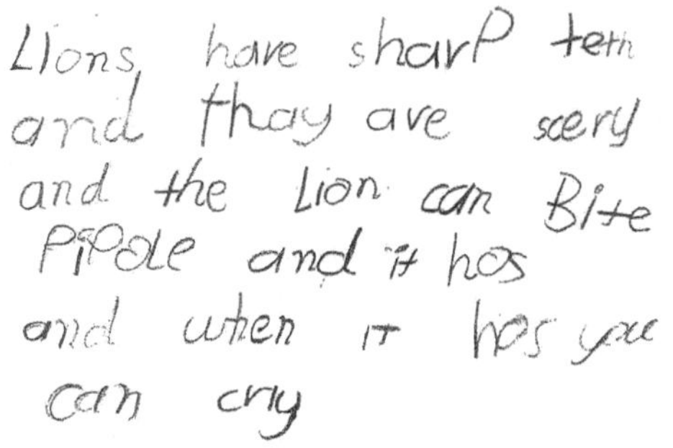

Figure 8.2   A report about lions

Text structure	Four or more sequenced ideas. Clearly connected.
Sentence structure	Uses simple clauses, with nouns, verbs, adverbs, which may be linked by "and". Meaning clear.
Vocabulary	Uses a range of vocabulary, including topic-specific words (e.g., a story about going to the zoo might include animal names and behaviours).
Spelling	Phonetic spelling – plausible attempts, with most sounds in words represented. Correct spelling of three- and four-letter high-frequency words (e.g., the, like, come, have, went).
Punctuation	Some use of capital letters and/or full stops.
Handwriting/legibility	Mostly correct letter formations yet may contain poor spacing, positioning, or messy corrections.

Teacher–child conversation

Teacher: Oh, wow. Fantastic. All right, let's look at what you've written about the lions. Have you got lots of ideas about lions?

Child: Yes.

Teacher: What's one of your ideas about lions?

Child: That you – like you don't go near because they could chase you.

Teacher: Yes. Have you got that in your writing though?

Child: No.

Teacher: You could add that if you wanted to add some more – they might chase you. I don't think you'd ever want to be near one, but you have one idea here that they have sharp teeth. Fantastic, and they are scary, so you've got lots of ideas written down about lions, haven't you? Okay. And I even saw that you were able to join some ideas together with the word "and."

Child: Yes.

Teacher: And you've got lots of words that tell us about lions. Which words are in this story that tell us about lions and not about too many other things? Which words did you use that are about lions? Have a look in your story.

Child: They have sharp teeth.

Teacher: Sharp teeth, yes, so they are words about lions, aren't they? And you wrote that they howl.

Child: Yes.

Teacher: Okay, fantastic, and they can bite. Okay. So, you've got quite a few words that are just about lions, and you said one before. What did the lion at the zoo use to scratch the rock?

Child: With his claws.

Teacher: Claws. That's another good word you use if you are writing about lions. So see if you can remember that when you continue writing next time.

In this example, the teacher also chose to focus on the child's strengths, building on the child's knowledge of topic-specific language. Together, the teacher and student recall the key words used in the text to describe the lion – "sharp teeth" and "howl." This leads to a discussion to expand on ideas for inclusion. Drawing on principles of formative assessment practices, the teacher makes clear what is expected and provides advice on how to improve their work – specifically around the use of adjectives.

Writing sample 3

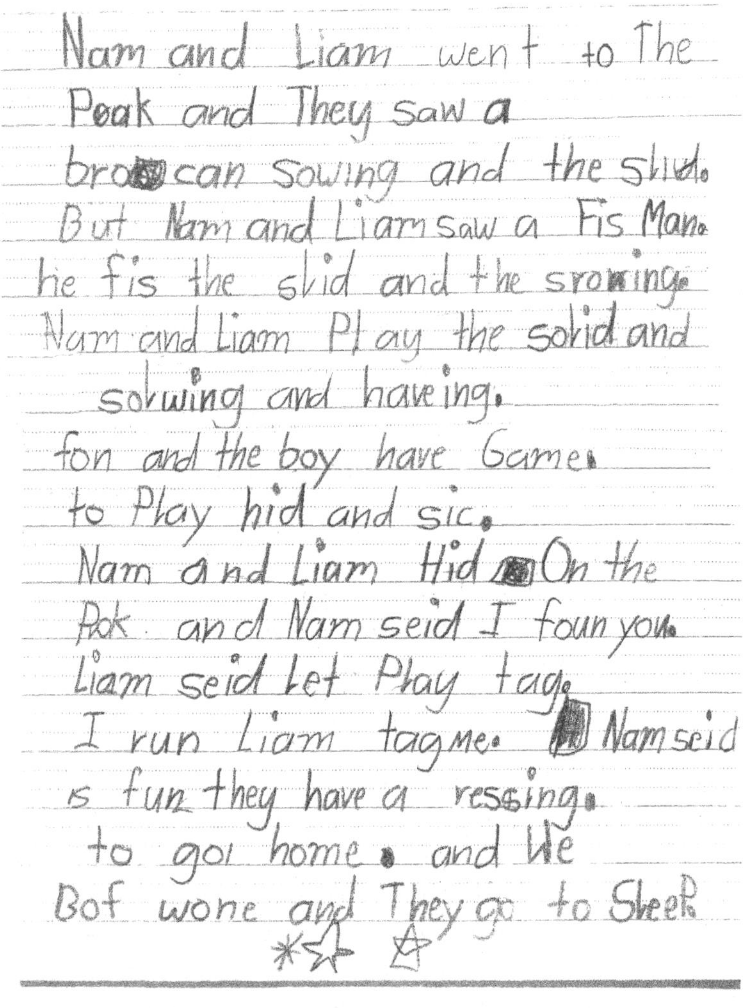

Nam and Liam went to The
Peak and They saw a
bro can sowing and the slid.
But Nam and Liam saw a Fis Man.
he fis the slid and the srowing.
Nam and Liam Play the solid and
   sowing and haveing.
fon and the boy have Game.
to Play hid and sic.
Nam and Liam Hid On the
Pok. and Nam seid I foun you.
Liam seid Let Play tag.
I run Liam tagme. Nam seid
is fun they have a ressing.
to goi home. and He
Bof wone and They go to Sleep

Figure 8.3   A recount about going to the park

Teacher analysis – see also Appendix

Text structure	Four or more sequenced ideas. Clearly connected.
Sentence structure	Uses simple and compound sentence/s with appropriate conjunctions (e.g., and, but, then). Use of adverbial phrases to indicate when, where, how, or with whom.
Vocabulary	Everyday vocabulary, for example using the Oxford Wordlist (the 307 most frequently used words) plus proper nouns particular to the child's cultural context (e.g., Fruit Fly Circus, Sydney Opera House).
Spelling	Phonetic spelling – plausible attempts with most sounds in words represented. Correct spelling of three- and four-letter high-frequency words (e.g., the, like, come, have, went).
Punctuation	Some use of capital letters and/or full stops.
Handwriting/legibility	Letters correctly formed, mostly well-spaced and positioned.

Teacher–child conversation

Teacher: All right, so read the first part for me.

Child: Nam and Liam went to the park, and they saw a broken swing and the slide.

Teacher: Right, stop. Good boy. So, let's have a look. What sounds can you hear in broken?

Child: B-r-o-k-e-n.

Teacher: All right, so you've got bro - -

Child: ca - -

Teacher: Now, what other letter makes "k"?

Child: K.

Teacher: Okay, so it's a K in that word. Good boy.

Teacher: Okay let's have a look at the word fix. What makes an "x" sound?

Child: E-r.

Teacher: There is an e-r on the end, you're right and we've got one more letter in here. What makes an "x"?

Child: s

Teacher: x

Child: k-s.

Teacher: No. It sounds like k-s, but there's a letter that makes that sound. Do you know what that letter is?

Child: No.

Teacher: It's an x.

Child: Oh.

Teacher: So it's f-i-x and you're right, it's e-r. Okay, so Nam and Liam saw a fixer man.

Child: Yes.

Teacher: Okay, so what should this be?

Child: He –

Teacher: Yes, but what should this letter be?

Child: A capital letter.

Teacher: A capital letter, good boy. He –

Child: Fix –

Teacher: Now, what letter should be at the end? Have a look at fixer.

Child: x

Teacher: Now, cross out the s. Okay, so we've got f-i-x. Do we say, "He fix the slide" or "He fixed the slide?"

Child: He fixed.

Teacher: Right, so what goes on the end?

Child: D.

Teacher: E-d.

Child: E-d.

Teacher: Good boy. He fixed the –

Child: Slide.

Using the Writing Analysis Tool, the teacher noted the student's control over the authorial aspects of writing. The performance indicators highlighted show evidence of the child's ability to recall and sequence ideas, providing a detailed description of his time at the park. Also clear is the child's control over a range of sentence structures, with the use of simple and compound sentences. Everyday vocabulary language choices are included. Hence, in contrast to the two examples above, this teacher has chosen to attend to secretarial aspects of writing – in particular, spelling. Importantly, partially correct responses have been identified for further teaching, with the child's use of phonetic spelling evident in his errors. The child has made a plausible attempt to spell both broken (bro can) and fix (fis), as all phonemes are represented. The teacher directs the child's attention to alternative letter choices for the phonemes "c" and "s." With support, the child is able to correct the first error, and for the second, the teacher provides the letter needed. Building on the child's knowledge of the word "fix," the teacher then directs the child's attention to the morphemes "er", to signal the person from the object of their occupation, and "ed" to show past tense.

> ### Reflection prompt
>
> *Record a conversation with a child about their writing. Consider the areas of writing you focus on, the errors attended to, and ways the child contributed to the discussion.*

Implications for practice

The teacher's use of the Writing Analysis Tool raises several key points that can be considered useful to guide and inform the assessment and teaching of writing.

A wide lens

The Writing Analysis Tool supports teachers to consider a broad range of skills to frame their teaching and assessment. This fits well with the intention to avoid narrowly focused, isolated skill development but rather promotes the teaching and learning of a range of writing components concurrently, while ensuring teachers have the "freedom to invent, adapt and modify instruction" (McNaughton, 2002, p. 43).

Writing requires attention to making connections and constructing meaning while using conventions that allow ideas to be communicated. Young children need to extend their range of vocabulary choices and build syntactic competence that permits self-expression while also developing control over grammar, spelling, and punctuation to record their ideas. The integration of skills related to the composition of messages and the recording of ideas draws on a range of conventions that allows messages to be encoded in texts. However, work with teachers suggests that when assessing early writing they often emphasise the conventions of writing (Mackenzie, 2014). Similarly, teachers' assessment practices prioritise quantity rather than quality and attend to the surface features of writing, with teaching focusing on the correction of errors (Hawe & Parr, 2014). That said, there is evidence to suggest teachers also consider learning to organise ideas and structure texts to be an important aspect of writing (McCarthey & Mkhize, 2013). Communicative purpose, attention to audience and to the ways ideas are expressed are central features of texts and are of equal importance; these aspects of writing need to be assessed and explicitly taught to support young writers.

The tool encourages teachers to examine children's writing using a broad framework and to take into account the integrated nature of aspects of writing processes. For example, vocabulary and text structure were connected in the examples of practice reported in the conversations above. The interview excerpts also show how the tool prompted the teachers to focus on a range of dimensions as they described their use of the tool, illustrated in the comments below:

I think we have to be really careful. Sometimes we just go straight and correct the spelling and put in the full stops and we don't have a really deep conversation about what the children are trying to say and what the purpose of the writing is and where they're going.

(Teacher, School 1)

It's a really good prompt ... because I think sometimes, we are looking at the secretarial [but] based on this rubric I would say okay, [child's name] needs to use a wider range of sentence structures in his writing and to use vocabulary to make his writing sound more interesting.

(Teacher, School 1)

It is proposed that when teachers address dimensions of the writing process in combination and move beyond isolated skill development, they strengthen teaching and maximise learning, working towards achievement at multiple levels rather than at singular levels of engagement.

Reflection prompt

Which areas of writing do you prioritise in your teaching and analysis of children's texts? Are you working with a narrow or more broadly conceptualised understanding of early writing?

Using data to inform teaching

While assessment is critical in monitoring children's writing progress across a wide range of skill areas, it is even more important as a means of establishing starting points for teaching and learning, with teachers clear about what they want children to learn. Essentially, assessment data should be used to describe "three key processes in learning – where the learner is right now; where the learner needs to be; and how to get there" (Wiliam, 2013, p. 16). The teaching conversations reported in this chapter are illustrative of the ways teachers used assessment data to make sensitive inferences to identify children's strengths alongside areas of need, and design teaching accordingly. Interview excerpts reference use of the tool when planning for teaching:

You could work out where they are at and where they need to go from there, and work with them, that sort of thing.

(Teacher, School 2)

So, you can pull out the right things at the right time for them and be more timely when you are planning.

(Teacher, School 1)

And moving her beyond what she is already doing, like, where to go next because she tends to … just do what she knows. It was good to see where I need to take her next.

(Teacher, School 3)

The careful observation and analysis of children's errors provides clear information to guide and refine our teaching decisions (Schwartz, 2005). There is evidence in a child's written errors or partially correct responses of what the child was attending to and the information that was neglected (Clay, 2001) as insights into the child's current level of understanding about writing. In the teaching conversations reported in this chapter, teachers attended to areas in the text a child had attempted to control, often identifying the errors just beyond the child's level of competency; that with further support might show improvement. Drawing on instructionally relevant data, the teachers were able to use what a child could do as a starting point for instruction and build from the known to the new to strengthen their writing, shifting the focus from *feedback* to efforts that *feed forward*. Similarly, when samples from a small group or the whole class are analysed, patterns across the group may become evident (Mackenzie & Scull 2015). With this information at hand, teachers are encouraged to employ flexible skill-focused groups, purposefully constructed based on children's learning needs, making targeted classroom instruction possible (Jones & Henriksen 2013) (see also Chapters 9 and 10).

Intentional teaching conversations

Teachers' deep appreciation of the breadth of the writing curriculum and their knowledge of children's specific learning needs facilitate intentional conversations to support learning. Such conversations are a key mediator for learning as teachers "design interactions, which purposefully challenge, scaffold, and extend children's skills" (Pianta, 2003, p. 5). Teachers' interview comments indicated how use of the analysis tool supported focused interactions:

[It] gives you something concrete to talk about … we knew what we were going to discuss with the child.

(Teacher, School 2)

I had pre-marked the rubric … The one-on-one time just made it incredible, to be able to sit down and have a discussion about what they need to do or what they are doing really well … I found it really helpful for feedback, not just great work … I could say I really like the way you did this and this and this … you used punctuation here or if you've improved on the goal that we set last time.

(Teacher, School 1)

I noticed their spelling needed work; basically, what I'm trying to say, having done this [analysed the writing] you knew what you could talk to them about and focus on and then get them to work on it further so that helped, that was good.

(Teacher, School 2)

Teachers also provided evidence of the ways children contributed to the interactions:

I went in with the focus of what I wanted to talk about with them. Sometimes things popped up in the conversation though, things that I wasn't going to discuss that the child brought it up.

(Teacher, School 1)

Teachers who engage in intentional teaching recognise that learning occurs in social contexts and that interactions and conversations are vitally important for learning (Department of Education, Employment and Workplace Relations, 2009). This highlights the importance of the carefully crafted ways teachers talk with children about their activities and the power of engaging children in conversations about learning (Hattie & Timperley, 2007).

However, many educators continue be challenged by ways to effectively involve children in rich conversation about their writing (Hawe & Parr, 2014). As Clay (2014) points out, teaching, like conversations, requires a two-way exchange, with the learner actively engaged and contributing to the problem being explored. When discussing children's writing, teachers may purposefully identify aspects of the text for discussion while also providing opportunities for children to contribute to the conversation. A simple way of doing this is to ask the children what they would like you to notice about their writing. "Thus the teaching and learning are reciprocal and responsive to the children's interests and engagement" (Margetts & Raban, 2011, p. 55).

Mapping transitions

Monitoring children's learning, mapping changes over time, is yet another dimension of effective assessment practices. The Writing Analysis Tool enables teachers to assess children's learning transitions and report their progress using meaningful descriptions of progress (Scull et al., 2020). This may show growth in individual areas of learning (e.g., sentence structure and punctuation) or more holistic development in the authorial or secretarial aspects of writing. However, writing progressions may not always follow a neat, linear sequence of development. The analysis of children's writing samples using the Writing Analysis Tool (Mackenzie et al., 2015) and that of Harmey and Rodgers (2017), who also looked at Year 1 children's writing, found performance may be variable before reaching stability, and as task demands in one area increase, other processes may be compromised.

Comparing children's writing profiles, taking into account the six dimensions of writing identified by the tool, may show classroom trends in areas of growth and learning, and also highlight children's shared learning needs. This process may prompt teachers to review their teaching priorities and revise their teaching goals. Importantly, the process provides the impetus for teachers to engage in collaborative professional learning conversations and collectively influence the design of classroom programs and school curriculum reform.

Conclusion

Educators and teachers make informed decisions as they assess the texts young writers create, taking into account the dimensions of writing to be assessed, the selection of assessment tools, and the way data is used to inform teaching and support children's learning. These choices have high stakes for young writers, as Wiliam, Lee, Harrison and Black (2004) remind us that teachers' effective use of assessment data can almost double the rate of children's learning. Given the clear connections between assessment and quality teaching, the challenge for all of us is to continue to examine ways we assess early writing competence to strengthen our teaching practice and advance children's learning.

Appendix Writing Analysis Tool (Mackenzie, Scull & Munsie, 2013)

Rating	Text Structure	Sentence Structure & Grammatical Features	Vocabulary	Spelling	Punctuation	Handwriting/Legibility
1	No clear message.	Random words.	Records words of personal significance, such as their own name or those of family members.	Random letters/letter like symbols.	No evidence of punctuation.	Letter-like forms with some recognisable letters.
2	One or more ideas (not related).	Shows an awareness of correct sentence parts including noun/verb agreement. Meaning may be unclear.	Uses familiar, common words (e.g. like, went) and one-, two-, and three-letter high-frequency words (e.g., I, my, to, the, a, see, me).	Semi-phonetic, consonant framework, alongside representation of dominant vowel sounds. Correct spelling of some two- and three-letter high-frequency words (e.g., the, my, to, can).	*Some use of capital letters and/or full stops*	Mix of upper- and lower-case letters and/or reversals or distortions. (e.g. hnr / a d / bp / v y / i l).

	Ideas	Sentence structure	Vocabulary	Spelling	Punctuation	Handwriting
3	Two or three related ideas. May also include other unrelated ideas.	Uses simple clauses, with nouns, verbs, adverbs, which may be linked by "and". Meaning clear.	Everyday vocabulary, for example Oxford first 307 word list plus proper nouns (particular to the child's cultural context, e.g., Fruit Fly Circus, Sydney Opera House).	*Phonetic spelling – plausible attempts with most sounds in words represented. Correct spelling of three- and four-letter high frequency words (e.g., the, like, come, have, went).*	Correct use of capital letters and full stops at the start and end of sentences.	Mostly correct letter formations yet may contain poor spacing, positioning, or messy corrections.
4	*Four or more sequenced ideas. Clearly connected.*	*Uses simple and compound sentence/s with appropriate conjunctions (e.g. and, but, then). Use of adverbial phrases to indicate when, where, how or with whom.*	*Uses a range of vocabulary, including topic specific words (e.g. A story about going to the zoo might include animal names and behaviours).*	Use of orthographic patterns or common English letter sequences. If incorrect they are plausible alternatives (e.g., er for ir or ur; cort for caught). Use of some digraphs (ck, ay). Correct use of inflections (ed, ing). Correct spelling of common words (e.g. was, here, they, this).	Some use, either correct or incorrect, of any of the following: • Proper noun capitalisation, • Speech marks, • Question mark, • Exclamation mark. • Commas for lists, • Apostrophe for possession.	Letters correctly formed, mostly well spaced and positioned.

(continued)

175

(continued)

Rating	Text Structure	Sentence Structure & Grammatical Features	Vocabulary	Spelling	Punctuation	Handwriting/Legibility
5	Evidence of structure and features of text type. e.g., recount, narrative, report, letter.	Uses a variety of sentence structures: simple, compound, and complex. Pronoun reference is correct to track a character or object over sentences. Verb agreement.	Demonstrate a variety of vocabulary choices. Includes descriptive or emotive language.	Use of some irregular spelling patterns (e.g., light, cough) Application of spelling rules (e.g., hope/hoping, skip/skipping). Correct spelling of more complex common words (e.g. there, their, where, were, why, who).	Uses a range of punctuation correctly.	*Regularity of letter size, shape, placement, orientation and spacing.*
6	Complex text which shows strong evidence of the features of text type, purpose, and audience.	Demonstrates variety in sentence structures, sentence length, and uses a range of sentence beginnings. Sentences flow with logical sequence throughout the text and show a consistent use of tense.	Correct use of unique field or technically specific vocabulary. Use of figurative language such as metaphor and/or simile.	Correct spelling of most words including multisyllabic and phonetically irregular words. Making plausible attempts at unusual words.	Demonstrates control over a variety of punctuation to enhance text meaning.	Correct, consistent, legible, appearing to be fluent.

Rating	Text Structure	Sentence Structure & Grammatical Features	Vocabulary	Spelling	Punctuation	Handwriting/Legibility
1	No clear message.	Random words.	Records words of personal significance, such as their own name or those of family members.	Random letters/letter like symbols.	No evidence of punctuation.	Letter-like forms with some recognisable letters.
2	One or more ideas (not related).	Shows an awareness of correct sentence parts including noun/verb agreement. Meaning may be unclear.	Uses familiar, common words (e.g. like, went) and one-, two-, and three- letter high-frequency words (e.g., I, my, to, the, a, see, me).	Semi-phonetic, consonant framework, alongside representation of dominant vowel sounds. Correct spelling of some two- and three- letter high-frequency words (e.g., the, my, to, can).	*Some use of capital letters and/or full stops*	Mix of upper- and lower-case letters and/or reversals or distortions. (e.g., hnr / a d / bp / v y / i l).
3	Two or three related ideas. May also include other unrelated ideas.	*Uses simple clauses, with nouns, verbs, adverbs, which may be linked by "and". Meaning clear.*	Everyday vocabulary, for example Oxford first 307 word list plus proper nouns (particular to the child's cultural context, e.g., Fruit Fly Circus, Sydney Opera House).	*Phonetic spelling – plausible attempts with most sounds in words represented. Correct spelling of three- and four-letter high-frequency words (e.g., the, like, come, have, went).*	Correct use of capital letters and full stops at the start and end of sentences.	*Mostly correct letter formations yet may contain poor spacing, positioning, or messy corrections.*

(continued)

(continued)

Rating	Text Structure	Sentence Structure & Grammatical Features	Vocabulary	Spelling	Punctuation	Handwriting/Legibility
4	**Four or more sequenced ideas. Clearly connected.**	Uses simple and compound sentence/s with appropriate conjunctions (e.g., and, but, then). Use of adverbial phrases to indicate when, where, how, or with whom.	**Uses a range of vocabulary, including topic specific words (e.g., A story about going to the zoo might include animal names and behaviours).**	Use of orthographic patterns or common English letter sequences. If incorrect they are plausible alternatives (e.g., er for ir or ur; cort for caught). Use of some digraphs (ck, ay). Correct use of inflections (ed, ing). Correct spelling of common words (e.g. was, here, they, this).	Some use, either correct or incorrect, of any of the following: • Proper noun capitalisation, • Speech marks, • Question mark, • Exclamation mark. • Commas for lists, • Apostrophe for possession.	Letters correctly formed, mostly well spaced and positioned.
5	Evidence of structure and features of text type. e.g. recount, narrative, report, letter.	Uses a variety of sentence structures: simple, compound, and complex. Pronoun reference is correct to track a character or object over sentences. Verb agreement	Demonstrate a variety of vocabulary choices. Includes descriptive or emotive language.	Use of some irregular spelling patterns (e.g., light, cough) Application of spelling rules (e.g., hope/hoping, skip/skipping). Correct spelling of more complex common words (e.g., there, their, where, were, why, who).	Uses a range of punctuation correctly.	Regularity of letter size, shape, placement, orientation, and spacing.

| 6 | Complex text which shows strong evidence of the features of text type, purpose, and audience. | Demonstrates variety in sentence structures, sentence length, and uses a range of sentence beginnings. Sentences flow with logical sequence throughout the text and show a consistent use of tense. | Correct use of unique field or technically specific vocabulary. Use of figurative language such as metaphor and/or simile. | Correct spelling of most words including multisyllabic and phonetically irregular words. Making plausible attempts at unusual words. | Demonstrates control over a variety of punctuation to enhance text meaning. | Correct, consistent, legible, appearing to be fluent. |

Rating	Text Structure	Sentence structure & grammatical features	Vocabulary	Spelling	Punctuation	Handwriting/Legibility
1	No clear message.	Random words.	Records words of personal significance, such as their own name or those of family members.	Random letters/letter-like symbols.	No evidence of punctuation.	Letter like forms with some recognisable letters.
2	One or more ideas (not related).	Shows an awareness of correct sentence parts including noun/verb agreement. Meaning may be unclear.	Uses familiar, common words (e.g., like, went) and one-, two-, and three- letter high-frequency words (e.g., I, my, to, the, a, see, me).	Semi-phonetic, consonant framework, alongside representation of dominant vowel sounds. Correct spelling of some two- and three-letter high-frequency words (e.g., the, my, to, can).	*Some use of capital letters and/or full stops*	Mix of upper- and lower-case letters and/or reversals or distortions. (e.g., hnr / a d / bp / v y / i l).
3	Two or three related ideas. May also include other unrelated ideas.	Uses simple clauses, with nouns, verbs, adverbs, which may be linked by "and". Meaning clear.	*Everyday vocabulary, for example Oxford first 307 word list plus proper nouns (particular to the child's cultural context, e.g., Fruit Fly Circus, Sydney Opera House).*	*Phonetic spelling – plausible attempts with most sounds in words represented. Correct spelling of three- and four-letter high-frequency words (e.g., the, like, come, have, went).*	Correct use of capital letters and full stops at the start and end of sentences.	Mostly correct letter formations yet may contain poor spacing, positioning, or messy corrections.

	Sentence structure	Vocabulary	Spelling	Punctuation	Handwriting
4	*Four or more sequenced ideas. Clearly connected.* *Uses simple and compound sentence/s with appropriate conjunctions (e.g., and, but, then). Use of adverbial phrases to indicate when, where, how or with whom.*	Uses a range of vocabulary, including topic-specific words (e.g., A story about going to the zoo might include animal names and behaviours).	Use of orthographic patterns or common English letter sequences. If incorrect they are plausible alternatives (e.g., er for ir or ur; cort for caught). Use of some digraphs (ck, ay). Correct use of inflections (ed, ing). Correct spelling of common words (e.g., was, here, they, this).	Some use, either correct or incorrect, of any of the following: • Proper noun capitalisation, • Speech marks, • Question mark, • Exclamation mark. • Commas for lists, • Apostrophe for possession.	*Letters correctly formed, mostly well spaced and positioned.*
5	Evidence of structure and features of text type. e.g. recount, narrative, report, letter. Uses a variety of sentence structures: simple, compound and complex. Pronoun reference is correct to track a character or object over sentences. Verb agreement	Demonstrate a variety of vocabulary choices. Includes descriptive or emotive language.	Use of some irregular spelling patterns (e.g. light, cough) Application of spelling rules (e.g., hope/hoping, skip/skipping). Correct spelling of more complex common words (e.g., there, their, where, were, why, who).	Uses a range of punctuation correctly.	Regularity of letter size, shape, placement, orientation and spacing.

(continued)

(continued)

Rating	Text Structure	Sentence structure & grammatical features	Vocabulary	Spelling	Punctuation	Handwriting/Legibility
6	Complex text which shows strong evidence of the features of text type, purpose and audience.	Demonstrates variety in sentence structures, sentence length, and uses a range of sentence beginnings. Sentences flow with logical sequence throughout the text and show a consistent use of tense.	Correct use of unique field or technically specific vocabulary. Use of figurative language such as metaphor and/or simile.	Correct spelling of most words including multisyllabic and phonetically irregular words. Making plausible attempts at unusual words.	Demonstrates control over a variety of punctuation to enhance text meaning.	Correct, consistent, legible, appearing to be fluent.

Recommended reading

Campbell, R. (2017). Assessing writing for effective teaching. In H. Fehring (Ed.), *Assessment into Practice: Understanding Assessment Practice to Improve Children's Literacy Learning* (pp. 89–99). Sydney, Australia: Primary English Teaching Association Australia.

Clay, M. M. (2019). *An Observation Survey of Early Literacy Achievement* (4th ed.). Auckland, New Zealand: Heinemann.

Mackenzie, N. M., & Scull, J. (2016). Using a Writing Analysis Tool to monitor student progress and focus teaching decisions. *Practical Primary: The Early and Primary Years*, *21*(2), 35–38.

References

Abbott, R. D., Berninger, V. W., & Fayol, M. (2010). Longitudinal relationships of levels of language in writing and between writing and reading in grades 1 to 7. *Journal of Educational Psychology*, *102*(2), 281–298.

Afflerbach, P., Pearson, P. D., & Paris, S. G. (2008). Clarifying Differences between Reading Skills and Reading Strategies. *The Reading Teacher*, 61(5), 364–373. https://doi.org/10.1598/rt.61.5.1

Askew, B. J. (2009). Using an unusual lens. In B. Watson & B. J. Askew (Eds.), *Marie Clay's Search for the Impossible in Children's Literacy* (pp. 101–127). North Shore, New Zealand: Pearson Education.

Black, P., & Wiliam, D. (2003). In praise of educational research: Formative assessment. *British Educational Research Journal*, *29*(5), 623–637.

Campbell, R. (2017). Assessing writing for effective teaching. In H. Fehring (Ed.), *Assessment into Practice: Understanding Assessment Practice to Improve Children's Literacy Learning* (pp. 89–99). Sydney, Australia: Primary English Teaching Association Australia.

Clay, M. M. (2001). *Change Over Time in Children's Literacy Development*. Auckland, New Zealand: Heinemann.

Clay, M. M. (2014). *By Different Paths to Common Outcomes*. York, ME: Stenhouse Publishers.

Clay, M. M. (2019). *An Observation Survey of Early Literacy Achievement* (4th ed.). Auckland, New Zealand: Heinemann.

Daffern, T., Mackenzie, N. M. (2019). The challenges of learning and teaching English spelling: Insights from eight Australian students and their teachers. *Literacy*. *54*(3), 99–110. https://doi.org/10.1111/lit.12215

Department of Education, Employment and Workplace Relations (DEEWR). (2009). *Belonging, Being and Becoming: The Early Years Learning Framework for Australia*. Canberra, Australia: Commonwealth of Australia. https://www.acecqa.gov.au/sites/default/files/2018-02/belonging_being_and_becoming_the_early_years_learning_framework_for_australia.pdf

Espin, C. A., Weissenburger, J. W., & Benson, B. J. (2004). Assessing the writing performance of children in special Education. *Exceptionality: A Special Education Journal*, *12*(1), 55–66. http://doi.org/10.1207/s15327035ex1201_5

Glasswell, K., & Parr, J. (2009). Teachable moments: Linking assessment and teaching in talk around writing. *Language Arts*, *86*(5), 352–361.

Harmey S. J., & Rodgers, E. M. (2017). Differences in the early writing development of struggling children who beat the odds and those who did not, *Journal of Education for Students Placed at Risk (JESPAR)*, *22*(3), 157–177, https://doi.org/10.1080/10824669.2017.1338140

Hattie, J. (2003, October). *Teachers Make a Difference*. Paper presented at the *Building Teacher Quality ACER Annual Conference*, Auckland, New Zealand.

Hattie, J., & Timperley, H. (2007). The power of feedback. *Review of Educational Research, 77(1)*, 81–112.

Hawe, E., & Parr, J. (2014). Assessment for learning in the writing classroom: An incomplete realisation. *The Curriculum Journal, 25(2)*, 210–237. http://doi.org/10.1080/09585176.2013.862172

Huot, B., & Perry, J. (2009). Toward a new understanding for classroom writing assessment. In R. Beard, D. Myhill, J. Riley & M. Nystrand (Eds.), *The SAGE Handbook of Writing Development* (pp. 423–435). Los Angeles, CA: SAGE. http://doi.org/10.4135/9780857021069.n30

Johnston, P., & Costello, P. (2005). Principles for literacy assessment. *Reading Research Quarterly, 40(2)*, 256–267. http://doi.org/10.1598/RRQ.40.2.6

Jones, C. D., & Henriksen, B. M. (2013). Skills-focused small group literacy instruction in the first grade: An inquiry and insights. *Journal of Reading Education, 38(2)*, 25–30.

Leahy, S., Lyon, C. J., Thompson, M., & Wiliam, D. (2005). Classroom assessment: Minute-by-minute and day-by-day. *Educational Leadership, 63(3)*, 18–24. http://connection.ebscohost.com/c/articles/18772694/classroom-assessment-minute-by-minute-day-by-day

Lowe, K. (2017). Literacy learning: Assessing what, for whom and why. In H. Fehring (Ed.), *Assessment into Practice: Understanding Assessment Practice to Improve Children's Literacy Learning* (pp. 30–36). Sydney, Australia: Primary English Teaching Association Australia.

Mackenzie, N. M. (2014). Teaching early writers: Teachers' responses to a young child's writing sample. *Australian Journal of Language and Literacy, 37(3)*, 182–191.

Mackenzie, N. M. (2018). *Handwriting and keyboarding: skills for writing*. South Australian Department for Education, http://tiny.cc/BestAdviceLit

Mackenzie, N. M., & Scull, J. (2015). Literacy: Writing. In S. McLeod & J. McCormack (Eds.), *An Introduction to Speech, Language and Literacy* (pp. 396–443). Melbourne, VIC: Oxford University Press.

Mackenzie, N. M., Scull, J., & Bowles, T. (2015). Writing over time: An analysis of texts created by year one children. *The Australian Educational Researcher, 42(5)*, 567–593. http://doi.org/10.1007/s13384-015-0189-9

Mackenzie, N. M., Scull, J., & Munsie, L. (2013). Analysing writing: The development of a tool for use in the early years of schooling. *Issues in Educational Research, 23(3)*, 375–391.

Mackenzie, M. N., Scull, J., & Thompson, N. (Forthcoming) Researching young children's writing transitions. In A.-W. Dunlop, S. Peters & S. L. Kagan (Eds.), *The Bloomsbury Handbook of Early Childhood Transitions Research)*. London: Bloomsbury.

MacLachlan, C., Fleer, M., & Edwards, S. (2018). *Early Childhood Curriculum: Planning, assessment and Implementation*. Sydney: Cambridge University Press.

Margetts, K., & Raban, B. (2011). *Principles and Practice for Driving the EYLF*. Melbourne, VIC: Teaching Solutions.

Masters, G. N. (2017). Is there another way to think about schooling? In H. Fehring (Ed.), *Assessment into Practice: Understanding Assessment Practice to Improve Children's Literacy Learning* (pp. 11–16). Sydney, Australia: Primary English Teaching Association Australia.

McCarthey, S. J., & Mkhize, D. (2013). Teachers' orientations towards writing. *Journal of Writing Research, 5(1)*, 1–33.

McNaughton, S. (2002). *Meeting of Minds*. Wellington, New Zealand: Learning Media.

Nolan, A., Raban, B., & Smith, R. (2016). Understanding home literacy practices of young children in vulnerable communities: What we can learn from the research. In J. Scull & B. Raban (Eds.), *Growing Up Literate: Australian Literacy Research for Practice* (pp. 37–50). South Yarra, Vic: Eleanor Curtain Publishing.

Pianta, R. C. (2003). *Standardized Classroom Observations from Pre-K to 3rd Grade: A Mechanism for Improving Access to Consistently High Quality Classroom Experiences and Practices during the P–3 Years*. New York: Foundation for Child Development.

Quinn, M. F., & Bingham, G. E. (2019). The nature and measurement of children's early composing. *Reading Research Quarterly, 54*(2), 213–235.

Raban, B. (2014). TALK to think, learn, and teach. *Journal of Reading Recovery, 14*(2), 1–11.

Schwartz, R. (2005). Decisions, decisions: Responding to primary children during guided reading. *The Reading Teacher, 58*(5), 436–443. http://doi.org/10.1598/RT.58.5.3

Scull, J., Mackenzie, N., & Bowles, T. (2020). Assessing early writing: a six-factor model to inform assessment and teaching. *Educational Research for Policy and Practice*, 19, 239–259. https://doi.org/10.1007/s10671-020-09257-7

Scull, J., & Nicolazzo, M. (2022). Punctuation, Sentence Structure and Paragraphing. In D. Thomas & A. Thomas (Eds.), *Teaching and Learning Primary English* (pp 207–225). ISBN 9780190325725. Sth Melbourne, Vic: Oxford University Press.

Taras, M. (2005). Assessment – summative and formative – some theoretical reflections. *British Journal of Educational Studies, 53*(4), 466–478. http://doi.org/10.1111/j.1467-8527.2005.00307.x

Tayler, C., Ishimine K., & Page, J. (2023). Assessment. In D. Pendergast & S. Garvis (Eds.), *Teaching Early Years Curriculum, Pedagogy, and Assessment* (2nd Ed.,. pp. 215–228). London: Routledge.

Troia, G. (2007). Research in writing instruction: What we know and what we need to know. In M. Pressley, A. Billman, K. Perry, K. Refitt & J. M. Reynolds (Eds.), *Shaping Literacy Achievement: Research We Have, Research We Need* (pp. 129–156). New York: Guilford Press.

Wiliam, D. (2013). Assessment: The bridge between teaching and learning. *Voices from the Middle, 21*(2),15–20. www.ncte.org.ezp.lib.unimelb.edu.au/journals/vm/issues/v21-2

Wiliam, D. (2016). The secret of effective feedback. *Educational Leadership, 73*(7), 10–15.

Wiliam, D., Lee, C., Harrison, C., & Black, P. (2004). *Teachers developing assessment for learning: Impact on student achievement. Assessment in Education: Principles, Policy and Practice, 11*(1), 49–65.

Wing Jan, L., & Taylor, S. (2020). *Write Ways: Modelling Writing Forms*. (5th Ed.) South Melbourne: Oxford University Press.

Wohlwend, K. E. (2008). From 'What did I write?' to 'Is this right?': Intention, convention, and accountability in early literacy. *The New Educator, 4*(1), 43–63.

Wyse, D., & Bradbury, A. (2022). Reading wars or reading reconciliation? A critical examination of robust research evidence, curriculum policy and teachers' practices for teaching phonics and reading. *Review of Education*, 10, e3314.

Teaching writing

Marian Nicolazzo and Noella M. Mackenzie

Introduction

In this chapter, the authors share a number of strategies that teachers can use to teach young writers what they need to learn. Importantly, we consider the teaching of the authorial and secretarial aspects of writing, both independently and as complementary processes as children learn to write. The strategies introduced offer differing levels of support from the teacher and broadly fall into four categories: modelled writing strategies, shared or co-construction writing strategies, guided writing strategies, and strategies to support individual writing. The chapter pays particular attention to the *Shifting Levels of Support Cycle*, *Interactive Writing*, and *Mentor Texts* as powerful strategies for teachers to use in the early years of school. Australian Aboriginal and Torres Strait Islander groups are not identified specifically because all strategies shared in the chapter are seen as supporting any and all children in early years classrooms. However, further discussion of how to support children who are learning English as a second language or dialect can be found in Chapter 12, while Chapter 13 explores supports for children who are finding learning to write more challenging than most. Draw, Talk, Write and Share is described in Chapter 10.

Writing is a complex process. As children learn to write, they need to master what Peters and Smith (1993) described as the authorial and the secretarial aspects of writing. The authorial role requires the writer to consider the selection and organisation of ideas and vocabulary to communicate effectively with the intended audience. Complementary to this is the secretarial (or editorial) role, where writers focus on the conventions of writing such as spelling, punctuation, and handwriting or keyboarding. These roles are considered in more detail in Chapters 6–8.

Classroom culture and authentic reasons and audiences for writing

To support children in the challenging task of learning to write, it is important for teachers to create a classroom culture in which children see writing as purposeful and worthwhile and themselves as writers. As such, children should be provided with a wide range of opportunities to write every day for authentic purposes and audiences. Time for children to share their writing with others is also important. Also essential is time for adult–child interactions focused on an individual child's writing. This one-on-one time allows for on-the-spot constructive feedback (comments that feed forward) focused on the intended message of the writing and the child's developing skills as a writer. A range of digital technologies – for example, computers, software programs, interactive whiteboards and digital cameras–allows for the production of multimodal texts combining print and visual images. While written language is central to most texts, in contemporary times, other modes are playing an increasingly important role (see Chapters 10 and 11 for discussion of multimodal text creation).

> ### Reflection prompt
>
> *Did you know that most writing children do at school is only ever read by the teacher and themselves? What might be some authentic contexts and purposes for writing in your context? How can you organise an audience for children's writing?*

Where do you start?

Prior to starting school, children develop a range of methods of sharing meaning. Usually, they are happy to share stories and make meaning orally, through drawings or paintings and through role play (e.g., in the dress-ups corner). As they become more aware of conventional texts (late preschool or early in the first year of school) a teacher might invite them to draw and talk about their drawing and then add some writing. If they do, they will observe a range of varied responses:

- Many will add their name to their drawing;
- Some will add a sentence or more to their drawing, using a mix of known words and invented texts, that can be read by the teacher;
- Some will add some known random words to their drawing;
- Some will add random letters to their drawing;
- Some will add some "letter-like" symbols or scribble to their drawing;

- Some will be happy with their drawing, but make no attempt to add text in any form; and

- Others will be unsure about even drawing, perhaps resorting to the scribbles associated with a much younger child.

Given this huge range, it is sometimes hard to know where to start. The "Draw, Talk, Write, Share" (Mackenzie, 2011, 2022) strategy works very well at this point (see Chapter 10).

Shifting levels of support

Explicit and intentional teaching of the skills and knowledge needed to craft a range of different texts is necessary for all schoolchildren. This teaching can occur within a range of different instructional strategies with varied levels of teacher support and shifting levels of responsibility for learning between teachers and children. All instructional strategies should take place within meaningful contexts which will facilitate a focus on selected aspects of writing – authorial and/or secretarial/editorial.

The level of support provided by the teacher will be dependent on the needs of the children and challenges inherent in the texts they are creating. In other words, as children become more proficient writers (or proficient at a particular type of writing), the level of teacher support provided should decrease. Teachers should make strategic use of a range of instructional strategies requiring varying degrees of responsibility from the child. This requires the teacher to balance explicit teaching and guidance, with provision of opportunities for both collaborative and individual text construction. In addition, the teacher will monitor the learning of individual children and respond to specific needs as they arise. A simple way of thinking about the shifting levels of support is provided by the cycle seen in Figure 9.1. The cycle can be used flexibly to meet the varied and changing needs of children.

The "shifting levels of support cycle" draws from a genre approach to teaching writing (Derewianka & Jones, 2023; Hakim, 2023; Tardy, Sommer-Farias & Gevers, 2020), starting with Phase 1 and moving through the identified phases of the cycle as necessary. The cycle can be used to assist children across all stages of schooling to learn about writing for a range of different purposes and audiences and across a range of discipline-specific text types. The teacher's role is as a knowledgeable writer who apprentices or inducts children into the types of writing particular to various curriculum areas. As indicated above, the phases are not intended to be followed in a rigid manner; rather, the teacher works with particular phases depending on children's needs.

At each phase, the instructional strategies involve varying degrees of responsibility for writing from both the teacher and the children. Over time, the intention is that there is a gradual release of responsibility that requires the teacher to shift the level of support provided from assuming all the responsibility for performing a writing task, to a situation in

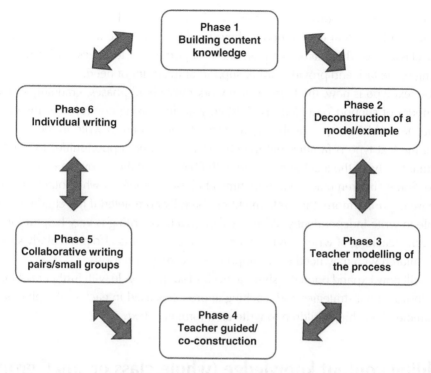

Figure 9.1   Shifting levels of support cycle

which the students assume most of the responsibility when engaging with a familiar text type and topic. The gradual release of responsibility model (Fisher, Frey & Akhavan 2019, p.12), first proposed by Pearson and Gallagher (1983), underpins the cycle as the responsibility or cognitive load needed for writing a particular text type gradually shifts from the teacher to the children as they become more competent and independent writers (Fisher, Frey & Akhavan 2019). As with the shifting levels of support cycle, the components of the gradual release of responsibility model are not designed in a linear or prescriptive manner. In any given learning sequence, the teacher can choose the appropriate supports dependent upon the demands of the writing tasks and the identified learning needs of the children.

The shifting levels of support cycle begins with Phase 1, building content knowledge. This phase is crucial to building children's content knowledge and developing the topic-specific vocabulary needed for engaging successfully with writing. In Phase 2, the teacher thinks aloud as she guides children in the deconstruction of an example of the target text type. She also thinks aloud as she constructs an example of the target text type in Phase 3. In guided co-construction (Phase 4) some of the responsibility is transferred to the children as the teacher, while still holding the pen, takes suggestions from the children and guides the construction of a new shared text. This can be a whole class or a small group. Interactive Writing could also be utilised at Phase 4 (see below). In Phase 5, a small group of two or three children will construct a text together. In this phase the group takes shared responsibility and enjoys shared success. In Phase 6, children work on their own individual text, although they should always have access to their teacher and/or classmates. The teacher can use these opportunities to check children's understanding of the task and provide further support at the point of need.

If the text type is new, the teacher may work through all phases, gradually reducing the amount of support provided, as children gain increasing control over the content knowledge and language (vocabulary and structure) needed to write in the target text type. If the text type is familiar but the children need more opportunities to practise a particular text type, the teacher may start with Phase 1 and then move to Phases 4, 5, or even 6. Some children may need more time at Phases 4 and/or 5 while others are ready for Phase 6. Furthermore, the cycle might not be fully completed if the children are not yet able to write independently. While this approach to writing is very helpful for scaffolding the teaching of writing in mainstream classrooms, it is also particularly supportive of children who may need extra support for a variety of reasons.

We will now expand upon the shifting levels of support cycle with further explanation of the instructional strategies and teaching approaches used in each of the phases with an example of teaching children to write an informative text.

Building content knowledge (whole class or small group)

In Phase 1, the teacher and the children build up shared content knowledge of the chosen topic. The aim is to ensure that the children have sufficient background knowledge to write about the topic successfully (Derewianka & Jones, 2023). Topics for writing do not need to be additional to those already being studied in other disciplines. Writing linked to other disciplines, for example, Science, Social Sciences, and Health, provide an opportunity to work with content that students are already learning about. Guest speakers, excursions, reading and viewing, information gathering, note-taking, class discussions, and debates all support students to build up the necessary language and content knowledge to create texts in the later phases.

Information report Phase 1: Building content knowledge

In this example from a Year 1/2 classroom, the children are involved in a study of the importance of bees, linked to their Science inquiry learning. In order to build the children's knowledge of the topic and to provide content and vocabulary for their writing later on, the teachers invite a beekeeper to visit the classroom. Here, the children ask prepared questions and later record some of the information gathered. The children are also involved in many reading and viewing opportunities where further facts about bees are collected and recorded in different ways (Figures 9.2 and 9.3).

Figure 9.2   Visit from beekeeper

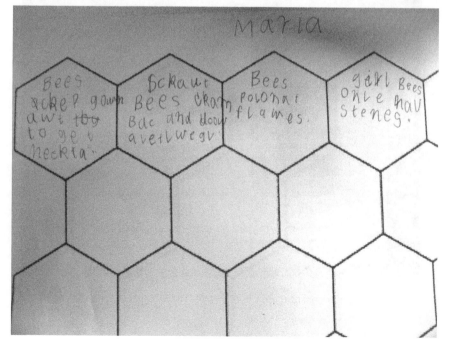

Figure 9.3   Bee facts

Deconstruction of a model/example (whole class or small group)

At Phase 2, the teacher shares an example of the type of writing being introduced to the children. It may be one the teacher has created or an example they have located from elsewhere. Together, the teacher and the children deconstruct the text. They identify the structure and features of the text and the types of language used. They discuss how language has been used to achieve the purpose of the target text type. Phase 2 ensures children are familiar with this text type and understand some of the building blocks to create this text type.

Information report Phase 2: Deconstruction of a model/example

The teacher and children are engaged in shared reading sessions where the teacher provides strong models of information reports about other animals. These texts, such as the one in Figure 9.4, are deconstructed with a focus on how over-all text structure and the use of language in particular ways serve to achieve the

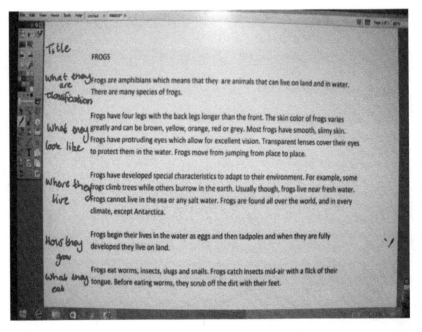

Figure 9.4   Text deconstruction on interactive whiteboard in Year 1/2 classroom

social purpose of information reports. In this example, a report about frogs is presented on the interactive whiteboard. As children will be expected to write a report about bees individually towards the end of the unit, a report about another animal is chosen here by way of example. After reading through the text together and discussing unfamiliar and technical vocabulary, the children's attention is drawn to how the author has organised the information into chunks or paragraphs. Here, a software program (ActivInspire) is used to annotate the sections of the text on the whiteboard. On subsequent days, this activity is repeated with other information reports and children are engaged in various activities, such as sequencing a "jumbled" report text and composing subtitles for each paragraph, in order to reinforce understanding of the structural organisation of this text type.

Teacher modelling of the process

When modelling writing (Phase 3), the teacher takes full responsibility for the writing. This strategy can be employed with the whole class group or with a small group of children with similar needs. It provides an opportunity for the teacher to demonstrate the thoughts and actions of a proficient writer while composing and recording a text. The writing may be recorded on large sheets of paper, a whiteboard, an interactive whiteboard, or on a screen to ensure it can easily be seen by all the children involved. The children's role is to observe what the teacher is writing and to listen as skills, strategies, procedures, and understandings are verbalised by the teacher. Here, children learn from seeing and hearing "enactments of those inner mental processes that are the essence of literate behaviour so they can appropriate them and deploy them for themselves" (Wells, 1991, p. 88). In other words, as a result of the demonstration, it is hoped that children will attempt an aspect of writing the teacher has modelled when they are writing. As this approach offers a high level of support, it is very useful when introducing a new concept about writing to children and particularly relevant to children for whom English is an additional language (see Chapter 12). It is important to move quickly through this, and the text should not be too long. The teacher may even start with a partially written text, explain what has already taken place, and then build on this while the children watch and listen. Alternatively, she may construct the text over a few lessons across the week.

Information report Phase 3: Teacher modelling of the process

The teacher creates an information report in front of the children, thinking out loud and demonstrating how the text is constructed. The text is then deconstructed in the same way the first text was. Text is displayed where it can be used as a reference point. The key elements of the information report are drawn from the process and provided with the example (What kinds of words are used? How is the text structured? What is its purpose? Who is the intended audience?)

Teacher guided co-construction

In teacher guided co-construction (Phase 4) the teacher and children collaborate to compose and co-construct a single text. Again, this strategy can be used with the whole class or small groups of children. The children's role is to offer ideas and suggestions, and listen to the teacher as she makes decisions using her knowledge as a proficient writer. While considering and responding to these ideas, the teacher takes responsibility for recording the writing on a large piece of paper, board, or screen and negotiating with the children which ideas will be incorporated into the text. Often, the focus is on authorial aspects of writing, with the teacher guiding the discussion in an attempt to craft a well-structured, meaningful, and effective piece of writing with the child (Interactive Writing could substitute here – see below).

Information report Phase 4: Teacher guided co-construction

The teacher and children co-construct a report about bees using both the content and language knowledge learned in previous sessions. Using the shared writing approach, the teacher takes responsibility for the recording of the new text, selecting suggestions offered by the children to guide the crafting of the text. In the first of these sessions the teacher focuses on composing the first paragraph of the text, namely, the Classification stage of the report. Discussion centres on the function of this stage of the text, which is to classify bees within a scientific taxonomy. Attention is also given to the use of the relating verbs *are* and *have* in the sentences to help achieve this purpose. Over a number of days, the teacher and children continue to compose and record further paragraphs of the text, describing different features and behaviours of bees (Figure 9.5).

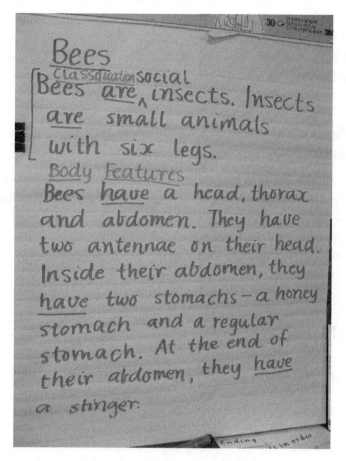

Figure 9.5   Joint construction bees

Collaborative writing in pairs or small groups

In collaborative writing (Phase 5), the responsibility for recording moves to the children. The teacher engages a small group of children (or individual children) with a particular focus, either authorial or secretarial aspects of writing, in mind. For example, the focus may be on writing an orientation for a narrative or, alternatively, on revising an already completed text for spelling and punctuation. After a short introduction by the teacher, which might include some modelling, the children create a shared text. The teacher is available to offer support and guidance, talking with the group to extend or clarify their ideas and thinking as they write. Co-construction is a step away from individual writing and can often provide just enough support to allow children to work without teacher support. This may be an alternative to guided writing and offers the teacher further flexibility; allowing for differentiation of instruction at this critical phase. Some children co-construct in pairs or threes, while the teacher guides the writing of other children who need more support before being asked to create the particular text type individually.

Information report Phase 5: Collaborative writing in pairs or small groups

In Phase 5, children work in pairs or small groups to create an information report, with reference to the previously created samples and the key elements of information reports identified in Phase 3. They check to see that they have met all the requirements of this text type (perhaps with help from the teacher). The pair or group creates a co-constructed text.

Individual writing

In individual writing (Phase 6), the children are given an opportunity to use all the strategies, skills, and understandings introduced by the teacher and practised through the collaborative processes outlined above, as they take more responsibility for their own writing. Children create their own text as independently as possible. The teacher will move amongst the children, holding individual writing conferences. In this way, the teacher is still able to provide varying levels of scaffolding at the point of need.

Information report Phase 6: Individual writing

Finally, the children are given an opportunity to apply their new learning as they independently compose a report about bees. The children feel confident with the content knowledge, drawing on all the learning from the building content knowledge phase. Specific linguistic knowledge introduced in earlier phases is also employed here as children think about how to use language to achieve the social purpose of this particular text type. The teacher is still available to assist children as she roves around the classroom, offering additional support to individual children at the point of need.

Children could be encouraged to use the "Draw, Talk, Write, Share" approach (see Chapter 10) for individual text construction (Figure 9.6).

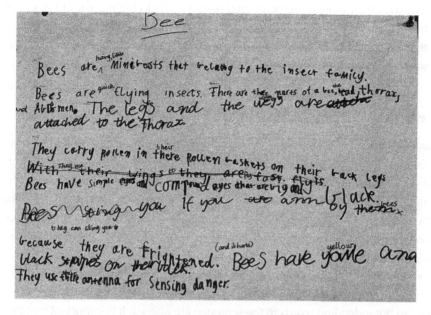

Figure 9.6   Individual report

Mentor texts

Description

In this strategy, rich examples of children's literature, both fiction and non-fiction, are used as mentor texts for the children's own writing. "A mentor text is a piece of literature that can be used as a model to demonstrate effective reading and writing skills" (English, 2021, p. 37). The examination of these texts should encourage children to read like writers, noticing new, rich vocabulary and interesting sentence structures that can be incorporated into their own independent writing. The language choices and patterns employed by the author are adopted and adapted by young writers. Here, the strong connection between reading and writing is emphasised. Children use the mentor texts to *"read like writers,* to notice what works in their mentor texts, to appropriate interesting structures that are new to them, and to take syntactic risks" (Newman, 2012, p. 28) in their own writing. It must be remembered however, that children should not think that they should be able to write like a professional, published author. They need to understand that even published authors have a great deal of help with their writing and texts can take years to go from initial idea to published text.

Process

This strategy relies on a classroom where children are regularly exposed to quality texts, read aloud to them, primarily for enjoyment. From this rich range of texts read, mentor texts are carefully selected as strong models of various aspects of the author's craft. Subsequently, these texts are revisited with opportunities to "zoom in" on particular aspects and uses of language employed by the author to craft the text. It is the teacher's responsibility to guide the children to actively notice what works well in the mentor text. The talk focuses on how the author makes effective language choices to create particular types of meaning. Attention can be drawn to language at the word level, with new words substituted for original words or at the sentence level, where the sentence structure is maintained but individual words in the sentence are altered. It is important that the mentor texts are used as resources, but are not destroyed through over-analysis.

The teacher and children work collaboratively to compose a new text which is then available for reading. Opportunities may also then be provided for children to work in pairs or small groups, independent of the teacher, to create their own texts, scaffolded by the structures explored in the mentor text.

Mentor texts in action in the classroom

In a Year 1/2 classroom, the children are involved in an author study exploring picture books by Aaron Blabey. All of his books have been read aloud to the class for enjoyment, over a period of up to week.

Step 1: The teacher leads discussions around aspects of the text, for example, new vocabulary, and the author's message after the books have been shared.

Step 2: The teacher helps the class to examine some of these texts to look more closely at how Blabey uses language to create his stories.

Step 3: The teacher re-reads *Pearl Barley and Charlie Parsley* (Blabey, 2007) and focusing on the sentence level, the teacher invites the children to look at how Blabey compares the different traits of the two main characters ["While Pearl Barley likes to … Charlie Parsley likes to …"]. Particular attention is given to the conjunction "while" and how this word functions to join the two ideas expressed in the sentence and to show comparison.

Step 4: The children experiment with word order and discuss how the conjunction could either start the sentence or be placed between the two clauses. The teacher then uses that structure to model new sentences in a shared writing session and encourages children to write their own sentences about the differences between the characters.

Step 5: The new sentences are published by the teacher and illustrated by the children. This co-authored class text is now used for independent reading both in the classroom and at home. It is also interesting to note that some of the children also appropriate some of the less common vocabulary, for example, "runs amok" from the text in their new sentences (Figure 9.7).

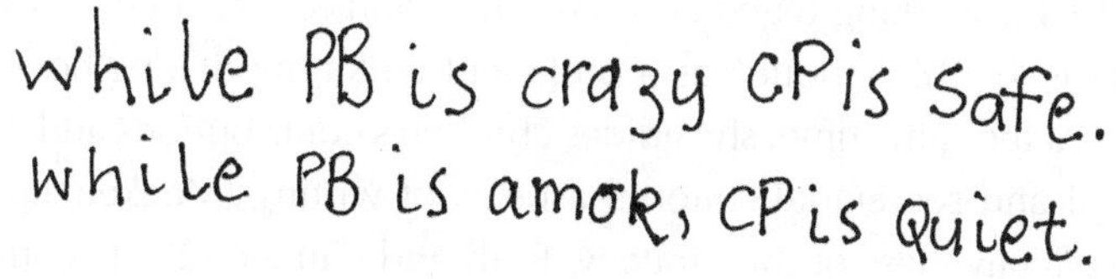

while PB is crazy CP is Safe.
while PB is amok, CP is Quiet.

Figure 9.7 Rough draft of page from Aaron Blabey book

While Pearl Barley runs amok,
Charlie Parsley is quiet.
Angus

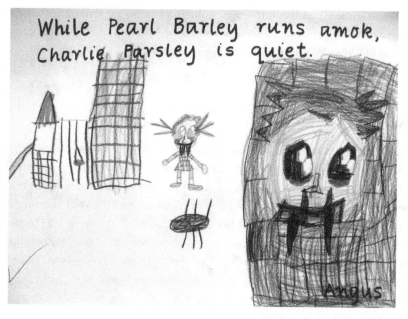

Figure 9.8 Picture from class created book

Reflection prompt

What are the advantages of this strategy? What age children could it be adapted for?

Interactive Writing

Description

"The purpose of interactive writing is to mediate students' understanding of what it means to write" (Williams, 2017, p. 523). The strategy utilises what students already *know and can do collectively* (Mackenzie, 2010) and provides a supportive forum for them to learn new skills. The teacher and children "share the pen" (McCarrier, Pinnell & Fountas, 2000), working together to compose and record a co-constructed text. The teacher's role is to "think aloud" as a proficient writer, modelling how to organise and record a text. At the same time, she guides children's contributions and explicitly teaches both authorial and secretarial/editorial aspects of writing (Mackenzie, 2015). In a US study of the effectiveness of this strategy, Roth and Guinee (2011) compared a control group of 52 children with an Interactive Writing group of 49 children and found that the children in the Interactive Writing group

> not only improved in their overall independent writing, but also made greater gains on nine out of 10 of the individual subcomponents of writing measured: Ideas, Organization, Word Choice, Sentence Fluency, Spelling of High-Frequency Words, Spelling of Other Words, Capitalization, Punctuation, and Handwriting.
>
> (p. 331)

Process

Interactive Writing ideally operates for about ten to fifteen minutes each day across a school week. With very young writers, the text should be limited to one sentence per day, increasing the length and complexity as children become more experienced writers. One sentence a day allows the creation of a five-sentence text (beginning sentence, 3 middle sentences and a concluding sentence). Classes that have used the strategy for some time and are writing more efficiently may perhaps write two sentences, but the aim is to have short, sharp mini-lessons every day, rather than longer lessons once or twice a week. The text grows from Monday to Friday; each day building on from the previous, so that by the end of the week the text is complete. The aim is to create a short, cohesive text across the week. It is possible to use Interactive Writing to create a wide range of text types.

Before the first lesson: The subject will have been determined by the teacher and will come from topics being studied in a curriculum area such as Science or Social Studies or a shared experience such as an excursion or visitor. The shared knowledge and vocabulary help all children to contribute to the task. This process will also help deepen their understanding of the topic and associated vocabulary. The children will also be reading the text each day and using the finished text as an exemplar for their own writing.

Organisation: The teacher has a pen and there is one for the children to share. The group sits on the floor in front of the interactive whiteboard, whiteboard or chart stand, and each child has their own small whiteboard, pen, and eraser on their laps (they can sit on these until needed). These small boards are ready for learning a high-frequency word or practising a letter or word, while one child is adding to the shared text – this keeps all children engaged and allows for quick teaching of words, word parts, and letters the teacher feels are important.

If you are using chart paper to record the text, a column can be drawn on the right-hand side of the page where a confident child may be encouraged to "have a go" at a new word the teacher thinks they may know. The teacher can also use this space to explicitly teach appropriate skills, for example, spelling patterns or starting points for letter formation. After this, the child can write the word correctly within the text on the left. This results in a polished piece of writing at the end of the session. If you are using an interactive whiteboard the process is easier and there is room for quick attempts and also for easy corrections.

Day 1

Composing: At the start of the week the teacher engages the children in discussion and together they decide how to start their text. This first sentence should be a beginning sentence. While children make suggestions, it is important that the teacher takes ownership of the sentence construction, ensuring that the text is grammatically correct and has consistent tense across the week. Teachers often write the sentence (as it is composed) on their own small whiteboard or on paper to help them remember it and to help them decide what to teach and what to leave.

Teacher Decision-making: The teacher decides which of the words they think they will write, which will be written by children (and perhaps who), which part-words may be written by children (and perhaps who,) and if there is a high-frequency word, spelling strategy, letter, or perhaps a print convention, they want to teach the group. It will depend on the group and the time of year. Teachers will ask the children to use their small whiteboards to write letters or a new high-frequency word or to try a spelling strategy (e.g., analogy – *you know the word "sing," we need "bring" – have a go at using "sing" to help you write "bring." The two words rhyme and end with the same* *suffix)*. It is important however, not to do too much on any one day. Instead, teaching points are strategically selected "to illustrate the principles that can take the student further in their learning" (McCarrier, Pinnell & Fountas, 2000, p.11). Children are shown how to use classroom resources like "the word wall" or "the alphabet chart" as a resource (e.g., *Let's all learn this new and important word (to) and I will also add it to our word wall).*

Sharing the Pen: A very young child with very limited control over words and letters may be asked to contribute the first letter of their name; a child who has learned a particular word may volunteer (or be encouraged) to write that word. You can even make certain children responsible for a new high-frequency word (e.g., *This week during Interactive Writing I want you (Jo) to be responsible for the word "the" – every time we need "the" you will write it for us.)* The teacher writes the challenging aspects of the text, while inviting specific children to record words or parts that they know how to write. This assumes teacher knowledge of the writing development of each child in the group.

Co-construction: The sentence is repeated orally a couple of times and then the first word written by a child or the teacher. The children are then asked: *What word comes next? How can we remember? We can re-read from the start of the sentence.* This is repeated until the sentence is complete.

Days 2–5

Each following day the lesson begins with the teacher guiding the children to re-read the text from the previous day/s and to decide what will come next. Remember, children give suggestions, but the teacher determines the sentence structure. The writing process continues as per Day 1. There should be a beginning sentence (Day 1), approximately three middle sentences (Days 2–4), and a concluding sentence (Day 5). The Interactive Writing strategy provides opportunity for *celebration of the known*, and *introduction to the new* through the shared construction of a simple text. This builds engagement as the children see an authentic purpose for writing and take shared ownership of a text.

Follow-up reading: In many classrooms, the teacher prints out a copy of the week's text (A4) for each child to illustrate and take home to share with families as "home reading." In some classes, a large copy (A3) of the shared text is printed, illustrated, and displayed or turned into a class book.

   The example in Figure 9.9 came from a Foundation classroom, where the children and teacher had been studying frogs and the teacher had been reading both fiction and non-fiction texts about frogs. They were studying the life cycle of frogs in science.

Title: Frogs

Monday	Our class is learning about frogs.
Tuesday	Frogs are cold-blooded and live near ponds, lakes and dams.
Wednesday	They lay eggs in water and the eggs hatch into tadpoles.
Thursday	Tadpoles grow legs and turn into frogs.
Friday	Frogs are amphibians.

Figure 9.9   Example of Interactive Writing in a foundation classroom

Interactive Writing in the classroom

In Figure 9.9, from a Foundation classroom early in the school year, the teacher brings in a plant for the children to examine, touch and talk about. All the children are seated in a circle on the floor. This fits with their inquiry learning related to the Science topic "The Living World".

After a short discussion, the teacher guides the children as together they compose and rehearse what they will write about the plant. Together they decide to write a list of the things a plant needs to survive.

As the group gathers around a sheet of poster paper, there is some initial discussion around the structure of a list. Punctuation such as a dash to start the list and a dot point on each new line to introduce each item is highlighted. They decide on the title –and the teacher writes "Things that" and then asks Hannah to write the initial sound for the word *help* as she knows that Hannah is familiar with this letter as it is the first letter in her name. Hannah writes the *"h"* in lower case showing flexibility with this letter and then indicates that she can hear the sound */p/* at the end of help and knows how to write *"p"*. The teacher writes the *"el"* and Hannah adds the *"p"*. Each day the teacher encourages individual children to add letters they know for sounds they can hear, and she writes the remaining letters. A few minutes are used to discuss the letters used to make the *"/sh/"* blend at the beginning of the word *shade* and some children offer other words such as *shop* which begin with the same consonant blend. A similar process is followed each day as the teacher guides different children to record the remaining words in the list. While the teacher uses a different colour pen to the contributing children, that is a choice and not necessary. In this example however, it makes it easy to see what the children wrote and what the teacher added. Each day the children read what has been written in previous days before the new words are added. At the end of the week the teacher gives a printed copy of the list to each child to illustrate and keep (see Figure 9.10). Note: Another example (Year 1) with detailed explanation can be found at https://noellamackenzie. com/2019/08/23/putting-the-power-into-interactive-writing/

Figure 9.10   Interactive Writing example

Reflection prompt

What knowledge about each child's writing development does the educator need to have in order to engage young children successfully in interactive writing?

Conclusion

Learning to write in English is a complex process that needs to be explicitly taught to children as a meaning-making process which follows set rules and conventions. Writing is also critical to literacy in the 21st century, with children required to create both print-based and multimodal texts for a variety of social purposes. When most children come to school, they already use drawing and other forms of meaning-making such as singing and painting, and will learn more about writing as a new system of meaning-making (Mackenzie, 2011). At school, they will need many opportunities to hear models of written language through a range of reading activities and to practise writing in shared, guided, collaborative, and individual contexts. It is the teacher's responsibility to understand the nature of the written language that children will be expected to master at school and to employ a range of instructional strategies, offering appropriate levels of support, to enable children to write effectively.

Working with families

Teachers should:

1 regularly share examples of co-constructed texts and children's individual texts (drawing and writing) including drafts, with families and encourage parents/carers to create texts with and in front of their children, for example, shopping lists and birthday cards.

2 show parents how learning to write involves learning both authorial and secretarial skills. They can help parents understand that writing is more than spelling and handwriting but they should help parents understand the importance of these skills.

3 encourage parents to provide a range of writing tools for children to use at home (crayons, pencils, felt-tip pens, etc.) and blank scrap books for children to write in at home.

4 encourage parents to play word games with children – both board games and oral games like "I spy …"

Recommended reading

Brittney, S.-S., & Kerri-Lynn, T. (2021). The many forms of a mentor: Using mentor texts and author engagement to improve students' writing. *Practical Literacy, 26*(3), 12–15.

Mackenzie, N.M. (2015). Interactive writing: A powerful teaching strategy. *Practical Literacy: The Early and Primary Years, 20*(3), 36–38.

Mackenzie, N.M. (2020). Writing in the early years. In A. Woods & B. Exley (Eds), *Literacies in Early Childhood: Foundations for Equity and Quality* (pp. 179–192). Melbourne, VIC: Oxford University Press.

References

Blabey, A. (2007). *Pearl Barley and Charlie Parsley*. Australia: Penguin.

Derewianka, B. & Jones, P. (2023). *Teaching Language in Context*. Docklands, VIC: Oxford University Press.

English, R. (2021). Teaching through mentor texts. *Practical Literacy, 26*(1), 37–38.

Fisher, D., Frey, N., & Akhavan, N. L. (2019). *This is balanced literacy, grades K–6*. Corwin: A SAGE Company.

Hakim, A. (2023). Genre-related episodes as a lens on students' emerging genre knowledge: Implications for genre-based writing pedagogy, collaborative tasks, and learning materials. *Journal of second language writing, 60*, 101001. https://doi.org/10.1016/j.jslw.2023.101001

Mackenzie, N. M. (2010). Motivating young writers. In N. J. Fletcher, F. Parkhill & G. Gillon (Eds.), *Motivating Literacy Learners in Today's World* (pp. 23–32). Auckland: New Zealand Council for Educational Research (NZCER).

Mackenzie, N. M. (2011). From drawing to writing: What happens when you shift teaching priorities in the first six months of school? *Australian Journal of Language and Literacy*, *37*(3), 182–191.

Mackenzie, N. M. (2015). Interactive writing: A powerful teaching strategy. *Practical Literacy: The Early & Primary Years*, *20*(3), 36.

Mackenzie, N.M. (2022). Multimodal text creation from day 1 with Draw, Talk, Write, Share. *The California Reader (TCR) 55*(1), 9–14.

McCarrier, A., Pinnell, G. S. & Fountas, I. C. (2000). *Interactive Writing: How Language and Literacy Come Together, K–2*. Portsmouth, NH: Heinemann.

Newman, B. M. (2012). Mentor texts and funds of knowledge: Situating writing within our students' worlds. *Voices from the Middle*, 20(1), 25–30. September 2012.

Pearson, P. D., & Gallagher, M. C. (1983). The instruction of reading comprehension. *Contemporary Educational Psychology*, 8(3), 317–344. https://doi.org/10.1016/0361-476X(83)90019-X

Peters, M. L. & Smith, B. (1993). *Spelling in Context: Strategies for Teachers and Learners*. Windsor, Berks: NFER-Nelson.

Roth, K. & Guinee, K. (2011). Ten minutes a day: The impact of interactive writing instruction on first graders' independent writing. *Journal of Early Childhood Literacy*, *11*(3), 331–361.

Tardy, C. M., Sommer-Farias, B., & Gevers, J. (2020). Teaching and researching genre knowledge: Toward an enhanced theoretical framework. *Written Communication*, *37*(3), 287–321. https://doi.org/10.1177/0741088320916554

Wells, G. (1991). Talk about texts: Where literacy is learned and taught. In D. Booth & C. Thornley-Hall (Eds.), *The Talk Curriculum*. Carlton, VIC: Australian Reading Association.

Williams, C. (2017). Learning to write with interactive writing instruction. *The Reading Teacher*, *71*(5), 523–532.

Draw, Talk, Write, and Share (DTWS)

Noella M. Mackenzie

Introduction

"To become truly literate, children need to learn to create, comprehend and use single mode (written, visual or spoken) and multimodal texts" (Mackenzie, 2022a, p. 9). This chapter will focus specifically on one pedagogical approach to the teaching and learning of writing in the early years of school: *Draw, Talk, Write, and Share* (DTWS). The approach is supported by considerable research that has explored the relationship between talking, drawing, and early writing conducted by the author (see for example, Guo & Mackenzie, 2015; Mackenzie, 2011, 2014; Mackenzie & Hemmings, 2014; Mackenzie & Veresov, 2013). The chapter builds on some of the groundwork provided in Chapters 2 and 9. A short background to DTWS is provided before explicit instructions for how to use this approach are provided. Prompts to aid reflection are embedded throughout the chapter. Suggestions for how parents may support young children as they learn about text creation are included and recommended readings complete the chapter.

Background

DTWS is the outcome of a number of research projects conducted by the author (Mackenzie, 2011) in early years classrooms and preschools. Mackenzie was influenced by the plethora of research that demonstrated the relationship between drawing and writing. Research from the 1980s and 1990s reports a strong relationship between early writing and drawing (for example, Caldwell & Moore, 1991; DuCharme, 1991 and Kress, 1997). More recent research has come to similar conclusions (for example, Brooks, 2017; Dyson, 2009; Friedrich, Portier & Peterson, 2021; Genishi & Dyson, 2009; Kress & Bezemer, 2009; Mills, 2011; Neumann, 2023; Pinto & Incognito, 2022; Shagoury, 2009). Caldwell and Moore described drawing as a flexible, invented, personal symbol

DOI: 10.4324/9781003439264-10

or sign system that is unconstrained and does not require learned interpretation (1991). In contrast, "writing systems are closed systems determined by cultural context and constrained by rules" (Mackenzie & Veresov, 2013, p. 23). When drawing and talking are valued, texts created by young writers are longer and more complex than when conventional writing is introduced without the supports of drawing and talking (Mackenzie, 2011). "There is also a strong relationship between children creating texts which incorporate both visual and written elements and their ongoing ability to create and interpret multimodal texts" (Mackenzie & Veresov, 2013, p. 23). An earlier study conducted by Caldwell and Moore also concluded that drawing was a viable form of rehearsal for narrative writing in the second and third grade (1991), although teachers using DTWS have demonstrated that drawing also supports information texts and poetry. However, despite the research evidence, many teachers continue to restrict young learners' opportunities to draw and talk, focusing on conventional written language from the very start of the first year of school. Likewise, in some preschools, drawing remains an option or choice. As a consequence, some children can miss the opportunity to explore mark-making at preschool. This creative process provides many informal learning opportunities including, but not limited to, creative expression and fine motor skill development.

Draw, Talk, Write, and Share (DTWS)

The DTWS process is now recognised in many Australian schools as a supportive and flexible pedagogical approach to writing, that allows teachers to cater for a range of learners in early years classrooms. Some Grade 2 and 3 teachers have also utilised the approach as a way of introducing multimodal text creation and as a support for their more reluctant writers. DTWS has also been successfully utilised by preschool teachers with children who are showing an interest in writing in their final year of preschool. (N.B. Australian children between the ages of 4½ and 6 years may be at school or preschool).

   When an educator utilises the DTWS approach, young writers draw and talk about their ideas first, adding writing when they are ready to do so. They may move through the DTWS cycle (see Figure 10.1) a number of times throughout a writing lesson, across a few days or even a week (Mackenzie, 2022a). Children are encouraged to build on what they already "know and can do," thus providing "a powerful connection between home and school [and preschool] and offering both motivation and scaffolding for early writing" (Mackenzie, 2011, p. 323). The teacher acts as a model and facilitator of the drawing and talking and can take advantage of opportunities for teaching about writing, offering appropriate input to meet group or individual needs. The process looks a little different in each of the settings where it is used: preschool, early years of school, and in grades 2 and 3. The DTWS approach has also been adapted for use as an observation

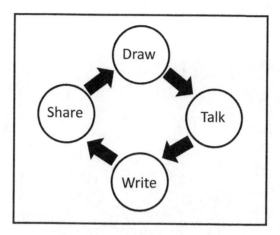

Figure 10.1   DTWS in the early years' classroom, Mackenzie ©

process. I will explain each of these adaptations starting with DTWS in the early years' classroom and then move to DTWS at preschool.

Draw, Talk, Write, and Share in the early years' classroom

DTWS involves three elements (or modes of communication), which have equal weight (see Figure 10.7) along with sharing. The order of implementation is flexible for those who know how to draw and write. However, I encourage young children to start by drawing and talking at the same time – and add writing when they wish. Sharing can be informal as children spontaneously talk as they work, as well as formalised sharing where they learn to listen to others and ask and respond to questions. Some days a child may like to start with writing and other days start with drawing.

Reflection prompt

As children's understanding of written language increases, they will add written texts to their drawings (three modes: draw + talk + write). *In Figure 10.2 Lachlan has started his text using written text: My FAM (family) is a SPRhRO [superhero] [family]. Mum dad Talia Ellen and me lv [live] hR [here]. Mum and dad shr [share] a rm [room].* He then added his drawing and then added names and arrows to show where people sleep. When he was asked about his text he elaborated on the superhero theme, adding richness and complexity to the text. As children add words to their drawings, they will also read these and may add details to their drawing or writing as a result of this extra attention to their written text.

209

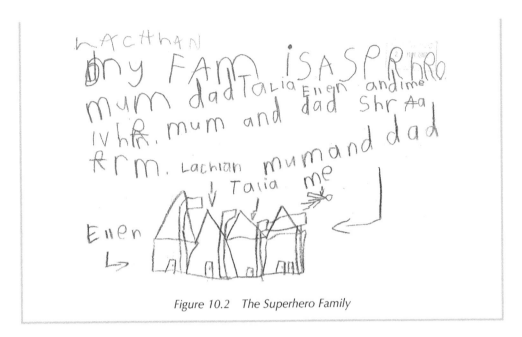

Figure 10.2 The Superhero Family

Getting started with DTWS in the first year of school

For young children who are new to writing and possibly even new to drawing, careful modelling and a clear scaffold seem to help get things going. DTWS can be conducted across several days or even a week. To get all elements operating, we start with discrete steps. Each step involves an initial teacher-led discussion of the topic (5–10 minutes on day 1, less on following days) and teacher modelling (2–3 minutes) followed by 10–15 minutes of the children working individually and talking as they work. Organised sharing happens whenever the teacher feels it will be helpful. The children are given scrapbooks with large, blank pages (without lines) for this process. Some teachers call these "Free Drawing and Writing Books".

In these books children can draw and write freely and creatively. If you prefer you could use individual pieces of blank paper.

Step 1: Participation in a shared experience (Day 1)

DTWS begins with a short discussion of a shared experience relating to a curriculum area (e.g., Science), a visitor, excursion, or even a favourite mentor text. It is easier for all children to participate and for the teacher to build background knowledge including vocabulary and language if the topic is shared. In the example which follows, the shared experience was of gardening in the shared school garden. This experience was the start of the class Science topic. (The use of short videos or digital photos recorded by the children themselves on tablets can also act as the visual stimulus for talking and writing, although in the very beginning, children's personal drawings are safest, and for some children, remain the most powerful).

Step 2: Teacher modelling drawing and talking (Day 1)

Teachers need to create their own drawings on a large surface visible to all children, (e.g., interactive board, whiteboard, chart paper) so children can clearly see the drawing process in action. The teacher should talk/think aloud as they draw – explaining to the children what they are thinking as they draw (See Figure 10.3). This process should be quick (2–3 minutes) and the drawing should not be too complex. Some teachers worry that they aren't good enough at drawing, but the author's experience suggests it is better to keep it simple and not try to be too clever or too artistic.

> The teacher started step two as a natural extension of the discussion of the gardening experience – *Yesterday we planted flowers in our garden. I am going to draw a flower. Here is the stem and the flower on the top and of course it needs roots to get the nutrients and water from the soil.* Children commented, and the teacher interacted with them while she talked and drew her simple drawing of a flower.

Figure 10.3   The teacher's first attempt at drawing and thinking aloud

Step 3: Teacher scaffolding small groups as they draw and talk (Day 1)

The next step is to move to small groups and have the children draw and talk about the same experience. Some teachers worry that the children will just copy their drawing. However, children with little experience of drawing sometimes don't know where to start. If you are worried, you can cover or remove your drawing before going into small groups. It is great if you can have an adult (e.g., teacher's aide, volunteer) with each table of children – someone who can prompt talk and help those who have had little experience of drawing before coming to school. Don't be afraid to "co-draw" with the most reluctant, but keep your contributions simple. Spend between 10 and 20 minutes at this step. You can adjust the time according to the needs of your students.

Step 4: Teacher revisits original drawing (Day 2)

The teacher goes back to her own drawing and adds further details (see Figure 10.4) – again thinking aloud and explaining her thinking about the need for further details to help her audience get more information from her drawing. This "thinking aloud" helps reinforce the power of revisiting texts to develop our ideas, as we draw and or write.

Figure 10.4   The teacher adds details to drawing and thinks aloud

Teacher: *"Yesterday I drew a picture of a flower, but when I was looking at my flower … I realised … that I hadn't added a couple of things that I now think are important. I need to add some soil and a bud. A bud is like a baby flower that hasn't opened yet. I also noticed that the leaves had little veins on them"* (see Figure 10.4).

Step 5: Scaffolding small groups as children draw and talk (Day 2)

As per step 3, but this time encourage the children to now add further details to their original drawings.

Step 6: Adding labels to drawings (Day 3)

In step 6, the teacher demonstrates how to add written text (labels) to drawing (see Figure 10.5). For most children, the first label they will add will be their name (see discussion below for DTWS in preschool), but with modelling by the teacher, children will

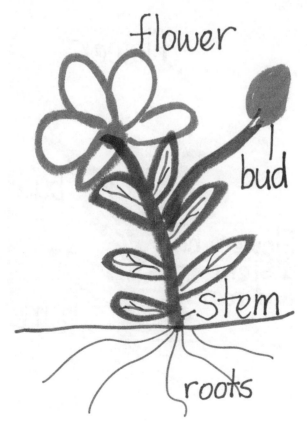

Figure 10.5   Teacher models how to add labels to a drawing

learn to add simple labels to their drawings. This step is further supported by the shared experience that allows the teacher to build relevant knowledge, including vocabulary. In Figure 10.5 you can see how the teacher has added some labels to her drawing, explaining why she has chosen the particular elements to label. Keep these to a minimum to begin with – I like to stay with three or four labels.

Step 7: Scaffolding small groups as they add labels to their drawings (Day 3)

This step happens as per Steps 3 and 5, although the teacher is helping children add labels. The teacher's example should be visible, so that some of these labels can be used by children. Although children should be encouraged to also add their own labels, it is safe for them to start with the teacher's labels. This is another reason for keeping the teacher's labels to a minimum. Children may use invented spelling for their labels or copy conventional spelling from words located in the room. The idea is to bring this new mode of writing into the text which now has a mix of two modes (drawing and writing).

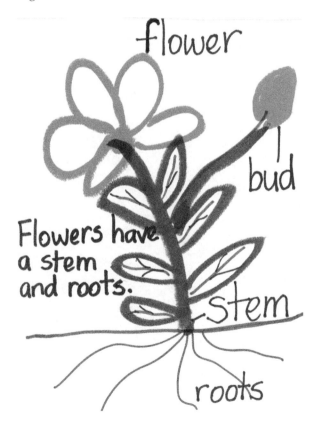

Figure 10.6   Teacher uses labels to construct a sentence

Step 8: Expanding the written text (Day 4)

When Steps 1–7 are working well and children are more confident with written text, the teacher can demonstrate how to take labels and create some simple phrases or sentences. In our current example, the text is quite simple – (see Figure 10.6). This would then carry over into the small groups as per Steps 3, 5, and 7 as children learn to use their own labels to create sentences.

Sharing

Sharing should take place informally any time children are working on their own texts in small groups. More organised sharing can take place at any stage of the process when the teacher feels the need. Some teachers like an initial sharing after the first drawing step (so that ideas can be shared for adding details to the drawing), and again after the text has been completed. The children's texts are central to the conversation during the *Sharing* stage of DTWS. Some children will need considerable scaffolding to learn how to listen, make eye contact, and respond (ask or answer questions, make suggestions, or make comments). This *"serve and return"* process often needs modelling at the start of the first year of school.

"Serve and return" works a bit like a game of tennis. Eye contact and body language are important to this process. One person "serves" by making a comment or asking a question about their colleague's text. The listener then responds (*returns*), with an answer, comment, or suggestion before asking their own question. The number of serves and returns changes as children become more comfortable with the process. I start with pairs, but three and four children can learn to take turns once the routines are established. I like to bring in another teacher to model this process with me.

Reflection prompt

Are you nervous about drawing in front of your class? Don't be. I am not very good at drawing, but I find young children do not mind. In fact, I think it helps them to take risks with their own drawing. Keep your drawings simple. I sometimes ask children to help me with my drawing and they love it.

DTWS at Preschool

In the preschool context all four elements of DTWS are present, but the emphasis should be on drawing, talking, and sharing. Children will start by drawing, independently or with support from an Early Childhood Educator (ECE). Sharing provides an opportunity for conversation – allowing ECEs to prompt children to talk with each other, listen, and take turns. This also helps children share their mark-making with families as they will have rehearsed what to talk about, when they take their drawings home. At an appropriate time, an ECE will teach a child how to add their name to their drawing. This may not happen until towards the end of the final year of preschool, although some children may ask to learn how to write their name sooner. Learning to write their name brings in the Write element of DTWS (see Figure 10.7).

Some children come to preschool with extensive experience of writing and drawing in their home context. They may have older siblings or parents who are very aware of the connections between drawing and early writing. Other children may have little awareness of drawing and writing from their home situation. If this is the case, the preschool environment needs to provide catch up opportunities for these children. How competent a child will be with early mark-making is determined by opportunity, access to models, access to tools, encouragement, feedback, and the value placed upon the artifacts that they produce (Mackenzie & Scull, 2015). DTWS can provide the structure to support this learning.

In the preschool context, DTWS would be evident if there were a number of the following happening:

1   Evidence of a variety of drawing and writing tools available for children to explore by themselves or with other children. These would not just be available for children who already know how to engage with these tools. The sizes of pencils, crayons, and markers would be appropriate for small hands – short and thick is better than long and thin. Providing the tools and spaces may be enough for children who already know what drawing and writing are all about, for example, those with older siblings

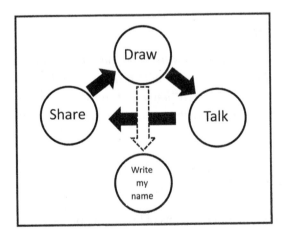

Figure 10.7   Draw, Talk, Write and Share (DTWS) in the preschool context, Mackenzie ©

or parents who encourage and model drawing and writing at home. However, children from homes where they have little exposure to drawing and writing may not spontaneously engage in what to them is a foreign process.

Reflection prompt

Did you know that some preschool children will not know how to draw? If they haven't seen others draw or been provided with the resources and encouragement to draw, they may avoid this activity which seems foreign to them. Some children have no older siblings to copy, and their parents may not understand the importance of drawing to learning. ECEs need to be prepared to sit with children and show them how to engage with this process. They may even need to draw with them as they develop the skills and confidence to engage. Do not be afraid to do this. Do not leave drawing as an optional activity or some children may avoid drawing at preschool.

---

2   Early Childhood Educators (ECEs) would actively encourage children to sit and draw and they may choose to draw with them. They would encourage children to talk as they explore mark-making at whatever developmental stage they may be. They would also share and talk about their own drawings, which would be quite simple. The ECE would write their name on their own drawing and offer to write children's names on their drawings. [Caution: If you are writing a child's name on their artefacts, please orient the child and their work so that they can watch you write from the correct orientation. You are modelling the writing process – we don't want them watching you write in what for them would be upside down. It can lead to children writing their names upside down and in reverse.]

3   Children's labelled artifacts would be displayed for the children and for families to see. Do not send all artefacts home on the same day unless you copy or photograph the work for your displays.

4   Mark-making and play: "One way to invite the whole child to learn is through free play and playful learning" (Hirsh-Pasek, Golinkoff, Berk, & Singer, 2009, p. 65). Therefore, there would be evidence of paper and writing implements alongside role play activities, play environments, and resources. For example, the preschool pretend "restaurant" would have paper for children to create menus and for taking orders; the building corner would have paper and pens for children to draw plans

before building; the hospital corner would have paper and pencils for prescriptions. An ECE will need to play with children to model how the "writing" can be part of the play.

5 Monitoring learning: In the final six months of preschool, an ECE would closely monitor children to see which may need further encouragement to engage in drawing and writing. They may use the DTWS Observation Protocol* to help them with their observations. They would actively engage these particular children in drawing and talking, providing clear modelling of the process and drawing with those children who need extra help. *This free resource can be found at https://noellamackenzie. com/the-draw-talk-write-dtws-observation-protocol/

6 ECEs should also monitor children's interest and ability to write their own name in the last few months before children move from preschool into school. They should have already responded to those children who have asked to learn to write their names, but now they should check on those who may need some extra modelling, encouragement, and support. Name writing is an important step towards engaging in conventional print and is discussed in Chapter 2. It is a big advantage to be able to read and write your name when you start school. Name writing is the Writing component of DTWS in the preschool context.

Reflection prompt

Did you know that learning to write their name is an important rite of passage for all young children? Names are linked to identity. Names are often the first word that children pay close attention to, and it is common for children to use the letters from their name to experiment with letters and words. See Chapter 2 for more on name writing.

7 Children would also be encouraged to share their drawings with other children – to talk about their drawings and to read their name for other children. Sharing promotes both listening and talking.

8 Early drawing and writing milestones were introduced in Chapter 2 (see Chapter 2 appendix for full descriptions of each milestone). Those that are particularly relevant in the preschool context are Milestones 4, 5, 6, and 7 which are achieved by many children between the ages of 3 and 5 years. In the following figures (10.8, 10.9, 10.10, 10.11) you will see illustrations of these milestones.

Figure 10.8   Milestone 4

Figure 10.9   Milestone 5

Figure 10.10   Milestone 6

NIA DUD
MUM LIM DALe

TIereSarPeoPle

Figure 10.11   Milestone 7

Reflection prompt

Have you ever thought about how drawing supports early writing? How much advantage do children who have been given lots of drawing opportunities take into writing? Think about creativity, concentration, self-expression, fine motor skill development, pencil grasp and control. All these skills support early writing.

DTWS with children who can already draw and write

In Figure 10.12 you will note the addition of the four-way arrows in the middle. This is to demonstrate that when children are comfortable with the three modes of communication used in DTWS, the modelling by the teacher may no longer be necessary. Children should be given the option to start their text with drawing or with writing. They may move back and forth between these modes. Talking and sharing can happen at any stage. I would continue to encourage children to add drawings as they need to – particularly in information text writing. Some children like to go back and forth between the two modes creating quite complex multimodal texts. Other children have told the author that when they don't know how to write something, they just draw it instead. This flexibility is very powerful.

Teachers can engage individual children in dialogue to extend their thinking, vocabulary, and sentence structures. Teachers may also act as scribes for children who have at this stage little or no experience of written text creation. Children are also

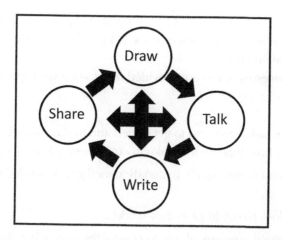

Figure 10.12   Draw, Talk, Write, and Share, Mackenzie ©

encouraged to work collaboratively, sharing ideas and solving problems together. As they begin to master some of the secretarial aspects of writing, they might write first and then draw. They may also go back and forth between the written text and drawing (Mackenzie, 2011). Draw, Talk, Write, Share will get you started and can be used as the strategy for independent writing at preschool and during the first two years of school, but you will also begin to teach children the processes involved in text construction from the very beginning. You will use strategies to teach children what they need to know to become competent writers. Some of these strategies are explained in Chapter 9.

Finding out what they know and can do using the DTWS Observation Protocols

The observation protocols shared here have been developed from protocols originally developed by the author for research purposes (Mackenzie, 2022b). However, teachers who use DTWS as a pedagogical approach have reported how much they learn about their children's knowledge and skills when they stop teaching and take the time to observe children as they draw, talk, and explore early writing. These teachers asked for something to support their observations in a systematic way. Consequently, the protocol you now have, grew from the author and classroom teachers working together to better understand what young children know and can do at any particular time and how they develop a repertoire of text creation processes.

The DTWS Observation Protocol allows an observer to understand what a young child knows, and can do, in terms of text creation from an early age. This observation process values three modes of expression: drawing, talking, and early writing. Importantly, the observer witnesses the process, not just the final product. You may record the session for transcription at a later date – noting that this will only give you the talk mode. I prefer to observe the processes and jot down notes as I go. You can download the protocols from my webpage at no cost.

(**Observation processes** (these are provided in a format with space for comments at the website provided above)

1 Approach to the task: eagerness to get started and to stay focused – staying on task – concentration – how long do they take to complete the task all up?

2 Comfort with, and control of the materials: pencil grasp, handedness, control of the paper.

3 Posture: how does the child sit as they work?

4 Pencil grasp, pencil pressure, ability to control the page while drawing or writing

5 If two or three children – how do they interact with the others? If one child, do they talk to you without prompting as they work or do they need to be prompted? How do they respond to your prompts?

6 If they are talking, try to note down what each child contributes to the talk – is it their work they are talking about or are they noticing other people's texts and commenting – or are they talking about things that are removed from the task altogether?

7 If a child does not interact with other children – or you – it will be important to note this down.

8 Do they make additions or changes to their own drawings as a result of their comments about others? (e.g., "You have drawn a dog; we don't have a dog – I am going to add my cat").

9 Are any children more dominant in terms of talk? Are any children particularly noticeable because they are non-verbal? Or just very limited in their language use?

10 Do any of the children go back and forth between drawing and writing?

11 How does the child respond when you invite them to tell you about their work?

12 If they have added words, can they read these?

Analysis of the text created (these are provided in a format with space for analysis at the website provided above)

1 Did the child talk about the text that they had created in ways that:

   a) explained what they had drawn and written about?

   b) added further meaning?

   c) explained and added to the meaning?

   d) was unrelated to the task?

2 Are the drawings detailed? Describe.

3 Have they written their name (prompted or unprompted)? Is it clear and legible?
or
Have they used a mix of letters/symbols but told you that it is their name?
Did they write their name in upper-case letters or with a capital letter and the rest in lower-case?
Did they add a second name?

4 Did they add text? Is the text in the form of scribble? Random letters/symbols? Individual words? Labels? Sentences?

5 Are there noticeable connections between the drawing and any written words?

6 If the child has written more than one sentence, use the Writing Analysis Tool (Mackenzie & Veresov, 2013; Mackenzie & Scull, 2015) to analyse in terms of text structure, sentence structure, vocabulary use, spelling, punctuation, and handwriting. (the Writing Analysis Tool is available for free at https://noellamackenzie.com/writing-analysis-tool/)

Working with families

Often families have a clear understanding of the importance of reading to their children and perhaps even singing and nursery rhymes, but I find that the message about scribbling and drawing is not as well understood. It is important to share this message. Encourage families to provide a safe space to draw that won't cause too much drama if the pens go through the paper or they go off the edge of the page. Resources are readily available that are suitable for different ages and are non-toxic and washable. Small hands need short, thicker pencils. (See Chapter 7 for more ideas for resources and for other fine motor activities that support drawing and writing.) Encourage families to draw with their children and to be sure that their children see them writing. Ensure that you value children's drawings by displaying and sharing with families. They will value what they see you value and praise. If you only ever praise writing, families will think that is the most important thing.

Glossary of terms

Terminology: Meaning

Constrained skills: Constrained skills are learned quickly, mastered entirely, and should not be conceptualized as enduring individual difference variables (Paris, 2005).

Unconstrained skills: Unconstrained skills develop continuously, or at least for many more years than constrained skills, and they may vary in proficiency (i.e., intercept measures) across people. For example., vocabulary (Paris, 2005).

Recommended readings

Mackenzie, N. M. (2022). Finding out what they know and can do with DTWS. *Practical Literacy: the early and primary years, 27*(1), 23–25.
Mackenzie, N. M. (2011). From drawing to writing: What happens when you shift teaching priorities in the first six months of school? *Australian Journal of Language & Literacy, 34*(3), 322–340.
Mackenzie, N. M., & Veresov, N. (2013). How drawing can support writing acquisition: text construction in early writing from a Vygotskian perspective. *Australasian Journal of Early Childhood, 38*(4), 22–29.

References

Brooks, M. L. (2017). Drawing to learn. In M. Narey (Ed.), *Multimodal Perspectives of Language, Literacy, and Learning in Early Childhood. Educating the Young Child (Advances in Theory and Research, Implications for Practice)*. Springer.
Caldwell, H., & Moore, B. H. (1991). The art of writing: Drawing as preparation for narrative writing in the primary grades. *Studies in Art Education, 32*(4), 207–219.
DuCharme, C. C. (1991). "Pictures make me know more ideas": Lessons from three young writers. *Early Childhood Education Journal, 19*(1), 4–10.
Dyson, A. H. (2009). Writing in childhood worlds. In R. Beard, D. Myhill, J. Riley, & M. Nystrand (Eds.), *The SAGE handbook of writing development* (pp. 232–245). SAGE.
Friedrich, N., Portier, C., & Stagg Peterson, S. (2021). Investigating the transition from the personal signs of drawing to the social signs of writing. *International Journal of Early Years Education, 29*(1), 56–74. https://doi.org/10.1080/09669760.2020.1778450
Genishi, C., & Dyson, A. H. (2009). *Children, language and literacy: Diverse learners in diverse times*. Teachers College Press.
Guo, K., & Mackenzie, N. M. (2015). Signs and codes in early childhood settings: an investigation of children's drawing and second language learning. *Australasian Journal of Early Childhood, 40*(2), 78–86.
Hirsh-Pasek, K., Golinkoff, R. M., Berk, L. E., & Singer, D. G. (2009). *A mandate for playful learning in preschool: Presenting the evidence*. Oxford University Press.
Kress, G. (1997). *Before writing: Rethinking the paths to literacy*. Routledge.
Kress, G., & Bezemer, J. (2009). Writing in a multimodal world of representation. In R. Beard, D. Myhill, J. Riley, & M. Nystrand (Eds.), *The SAGE handbook of writing development* (pp. 167–181). SAGE.
Mackenzie, N. (2022a). Multimodal text creation from day 1 with Draw, Talk, Write, *Share. The California Reader 55*(1), 9–14.
Mackenzie, N. M. (2011). From drawing to writing: What happens when you shift teaching priorities in the first six months of school? *Australian Journal of Language & Literacy, 34*(3), 322–340.
Mackenzie, N. M. (2014). Teaching early writers: Teachers' responses to a young child's writing sample. *Australian Journal of Language and Literacy, 37*(3), 182–191.
Mackenzie, N. M. (2022b). Finding out what they know and can do with DTWS. *Practical Literacy: the early and primary years, 27*(1).
Mackenzie, N. M., & Hemmings, B. (2014). Predictors of success with writing in the first year of school. *Issues in Educational Research, 24*(1), 41–54.

Mackenzie, N. M., & Scull, J. A. (2015). Literacy: Writing. In S. McLeod & J. McCormack (Eds), *Introduction to speech, language and literacy*, (pp. 398–445). Oxford.

Mackenzie, N. M., & Veresov, N. (2013). How drawing can support writing acquisition: text construction in early writing from a Vygotskian perspective. *Australasian Journal of Early Childhood, 38*(4), 22–29.

Mills, K. (2011). 'I'm making it different to the book': Trans-mediation in young children's multimodal and digital texts. *Australasian Journal of Early Childhood, 36*, 56–65.

Neumann, M. M. (2023). Drawing and writing together: Using iPads to support children's language, literacy, and social learning. *YC Young Children, 78*(1), 78–83.

Pinto, G., & Incognito, O. (2022). The relationship between emergent drawing, emergent writing, and visual-motor integration in preschool children. *Infant and child development, 31*(2). https://doi.org/10.1002/icd.2284

Shagoury, R. E. (2009). *Raising writers: Understanding and nurturing young children's writing development*. Pearson Education.

Young children creating multimodal stories in their home, school, and digital spaces

Lisa Kervin and Jessica Mantei

Introduction

The sharing of story is consistent across time, cultures, and communities. Through stories, people share experiences, knowledge, and values and beliefs important in their world. Traditionally, the stories communicated to younger generations express the collective wisdom and understandings valued within a group. Evidence of these traditions endures in the cave paintings and the oral storytelling traditions of ancient cultures. As such, children have traditionally been exposed to storytelling from an early age, where they come to understand what it is to be part of their families, communities, and the world more broadly (Arizpe, Farrell & McAdam, 2013). Stories connect us to people, places, and moments of time. Furthermore, McLachlan (2012) observes, engagement with stories allows children to develop important knowledge about language, vocabulary, and story schemas that will inform their own storytelling and literacy futures. As this knowledge and these understandings develop, children will share stories of their own and pass on their interpretations of their families and community.

In contemporary settings, children continue to be surrounded by opportunities to hear and share stories in their worlds. Modern manifestations of stories appear in visual, photographic, film, and digital media forms. Interactions with others, storybooks, movies and television, toys, digital applications, and important places in their community are fertile ground for story ideas. Opportunities to share a variety of stories, created by those with diverse backgrounds, values different cultural expressions and privileges all voices (Tomsic & Zbaracki, 2022). While children are regularly engaged as participants in story, they too can be powerful story authors.

In this chapter we draw upon three research projects to explore cases of young children using digital technologies to plan, create, and share stories. In each case, the children used digital technologies to express personal understandings about themselves as members of a range of communities such as home, school, and the digital world. What

DOI: 10.4324/9781003439264-11

is clear across the cases is the important role technology played in affording not only the creation of the children's stories, but also the opportunity to share those stories with others.

Reflection prompt

What are the storytelling opportunities children engage with at school and at home? How can you find out about and build these into interactions with children?

Children as storytellers

From a young age, children delight in looking at, listening to, and participating in storytelling activities. Most young children find pleasure in storytelling as they share their experiences, knowledge, values, and beliefs. Hill (2014) observes that the sharing of story engages children emotionally and builds relationships between the teller and the listener. For example, the re-creation of memorable experiences that are funny, embarrassing, thrilling, or even sad connect children with the lives and experiences of others within their family and community. And it is through the connections children make to the stories, real, and imagined, shared by significant members of their lives that their identities continue to develop.

Storytelling is a powerful tool for communication, collaboration, and creativity that not only enables participation within society, but that also builds literacy competency (Engel, 1999). As stories are shared, children develop deepened understandings about language and literacy. They learn about multimodalities through the power of pace, intonation, and volume, about gesture, expression, and body language, and about language choices and precise vocabulary in the creation of a wonderful story. And they learn about the power of the storyteller in using these skills and understandings to represent particular perspectives of themselves and the places with which they engage.

Through storytelling, children can express their present sense of self or "place" in the world (Comber, 2016). They can also explore alternative or future versions as they project to future aspirations – "a life not yet imagined" (Farmer, 2004, p. 155). As authorities on their own lives (Theobald, Danby & Ailwood, 2011), children are well equipped to share their unique perspectives about what they know and to create new stories from their imaginations and aspirations about new topics and new perspectives on the world, both spontaneous and planned. In this chapter we examine the spaces children engage with – home, school, and the digital world – and the stories that emerge when these spaces are used as stimulus.

Technology and storytelling

Storytelling in any form is a multimodal activity. The traditional storyteller relates their tale using voice, sound and silence, movement, gesture and stillness, and even images or props. However, technology offers new opportunities for planning, creating, capturing, and particularly sharing stories with a broadened audience. A review of research focused on digital technologies and storytelling from the period 2010 to 2020 found that increased motivation and confidence and social-emotional competencies were key benefits for digital storytellers alongside digital skill development and opportunities for language and literacy learning (Quah & Ng, 2022).

Increasingly affordable, usable, and portable technologies provide access to engaging, simple, easy-to-use devices and applications for the creation and capture of multimodal digital stories. Digital technologies offer the teller opportunities to draw on the affordances of the linguistic, audio, visual, spatial, and gestural modes in the creation of a story. The ability to capture an oral narrative offers clear opportunities to preserve the stories young children tell, and the capacity to capture and manipulate photographs and images, as well as sound and sound effects, means young children can express concepts and ideas that may be beyond their current language abilities. Further, they are provided with opportunities for review and development.

Children's enthusiasm to engage with the creation of digital multimodal stories presents opportunities for language and literacy learning. As a story grows, the teller may rehearse, revise and make modifications until they are satisfied, or their story may be a spontaneous sharing triggered by something they see or do. The process of retelling the same story helps the story evolve as the teller deepens their connection with its content. It is during this text creation process that educators can engage children in experiences to build not only confidence but also vocabulary and expression, and to consider the ways their message is conveyed across modes. For example, a child and educator may discuss the ways they could connect the oral and visual modes to ensure the viewer of the story will understand the teller's meaning once the story is shared.

Finally, the potential for immediate and wide sharing has significant implications for the process of storytelling. Traditional storytelling offers single, unique performances, but with the creation and capture of stories using technology, a story can be replayed and revisited for a range of purposes and audiences. An obvious benefit is the capacity to share stories with family and friends who do not live near or have regular contact with the storyteller and are therefore not part of this sharing process. Through social media, a story can be shared with established networks for feedback and response along with opportunities to view and respond to the stories posted by others. This broadening of audience may impact decisions made about the stories shared and potentially present the need for increased awareness about the content and intention of a story.

Children telling stories with digital technologies

In this section, we draw from three research projects where children used digital technology to create stories. Each project is described and opportunities for multimodal text creation are explicated through discussion of cases focused on child-created artefacts.

Digital storytelling: Looking to everyday spaces and experiences for stories

In this project, we visited community-based preschool centres to work with children making the transition from preschool to kindergarten (the first year of formal schooling in New South Wales). We supported children aged 4–5 years as they created digital stories in response to activities they like to engage with in their centre. Children created an individual digital story with a researcher as they:

1 Photographed ten events and/or activities they identified they enjoyed at the centre.

2 Individually talked with a researcher about each photograph, explaining why they took it, what happens in that location and any special memories. This conversation was recorded.

3 Worked with a researcher to edit the images and audio into a multimedia presentation.

It is interesting to note though that while each child was invited to take their own photographs, the children mostly wanted to stage a photograph with themselves in it. These images proved to be an important stimulus for the annotation the child provided. We worked with each child to sequence the photographs for the digital story and assisted them with using software to record their annotation, attach the recording to an image, and export it as a QuickTime movie. While we have talked about this project elsewhere (e.g., Kervin & Mantei, 2016) the "stories" that appeared in the children's digital stories are of interest to this chapter. In what follows, we have extracted four scenes from four individual digital stories as examples of the ways children naturally moved into story-like annotations as they responded to the image.

Figure 11.1   Making pancakes

Figure 11.1 illustrates Josh playing in the sandpit at his centre. In his annotation he describes himself making pancakes. It is the connection of the visual with the annotation that builds the meaning Josh attaches to this scene. Neither the image nor script in isolation would make sense nor would it build the sense of his space that Josh is demonstrating. He is able to recount important information about the need for batter and the process of cooking it to make pancakes. His language use represents both the act of playing in the sandpit and making pancakes.

Figure 11.2 depicts Jill at the frog pond with her accompanying annotation. Jill uses the frog pond as a stimulus to talk about her knowledge of the life cycle of frogs while also considering the safety considerations for this space. This mix of information provides the context for Jill to further elaborate on the story of what might (or perhaps even has!) happened in this space.

Figure 11.3 shows Emily standing by a tank housing a yabbie in her preschool classroom. Emily's annotation provides an imaginative account of the possibilities for the yabbie; while the yabbie might indeed climb on the rock, it is not able to climb out of the tank. This annotation provides evidence of Emily imagining possible scenarios demonstrating a sense of story.

Figure 11.4 provides an image and annotation provided by Conor that in isolation appear unrelated. Conor has staged a photograph in the outdoor space and through his annotation connects to a lizard he once saw there, which then leads him to a story of a similar encounter at his home.

Figure 11.2   The frog pond

Figure 11.3   The yabbie tank

Figure 11.4   The blue tongue lizard

Each scene showcases a space and associated experience within the preschool environment that is important for these children. The process of selecting and capturing experiences through digital photographs, talking about them with the researchers, and then sequencing and recording annotations seemed to provide an important scaffold to the process of text creation.

Each of these digital story excerpts shows the potential for story when young children merge image and oral annotation. While the specific focus of the digital story experience was not to tell a story, but rather to provide an account for their interaction with space, this experience led to the children naturally wanting to provide elements of "story" within their creations.

The audience for these stories was defined. The final version of a child's digital story was made available to the educators at the preschool, the future kindergarten teacher, and the child's family. However, while these were the intended (and approved audiences), we acknowledge that the audience for each child's story may have moved beyond this as families used private networks to share their child's story.

Classroom applications: encourage children to collect digital images; these serve as valuable prompts for storytelling as children orally annotate their image(s).

Digital puppet plays: Known environments as a stimulus for story

In this second project, we worked with one class of children in their first year of formal school (aged 5–6 years) in their second term of school. The purpose of this task was for the children to express their understanding of the known environment of their primary school through stories. They initially worked in pairs to draw a bird's-eye map of their school. On smaller, separate pieces of paper, each child drew and cut out an image of themselves to use as characters in their digital puppet plays. We have reported on this storytelling strategy elsewhere (e.g., Kervin & Mantei, 2017), emphasising that these concrete materials were important resources for the children in supporting them to imagine a story they could tell.

The children photographed and imported their map and each character into the *Puppet Pals Director's Cut* app on an iPad in their classroom. Each character was then "cut out" in *Puppet Pals* by tracing the character with their finger on the screen. Following conversations with their partner and the researchers and/or classroom teacher, the children then created and recorded a story about their school using their map as the background and the pictures of themselves as "puppets." Once the stories were made, the children exported the file to the camera roll in preparation for sharing with their audience. In this case, the stories were initially shared on the interactive whiteboard as the children's kindergarten peers and their teachers gathered to celebrate the work. The audience was then broadened when the stories were uploaded to a password protected repository on the school website as kindergarten work samples. Here, family members and other community members who knew the password could access the stories.

To illustrate this process, we draw on work samples from one pair of children from this kindergarten class, Jade and Ella (both aged 5 years), to explore the ways digital technology supported their storytelling process. Jade and Ella's map represented their classroom and the classrooms of their kindergarten cohort, and spaces including the sick bay, canteen, the ladder to their classroom, and even the "chook pen" (chicken coop). A long, winding, blue path along which the puppets travelled to move between the locations connected these spaces. Their character puppets, Jade in blue and Ella in red, were drawn standing on a patch of grass, which moved with the puppets as they travelled over the map. The children spent considerable time playing with their paper map, taking their puppets on an exploration of the space and talking about the possibilities for their story.

Once the map and puppets were imported into the digital space of *Puppet Pals*, the children spent time exploring the affordances of the technology. They explored the way they could move the puppets within the space, the ways they could manipulate the characters' size, position, and proximity in relation to the different locations and to each other.

233

In total, the children made three recordings and deleted two. In their first recording, the children moved their puppets, but they did not speak. On playing it back, Jade observed that "we need to say something," and so they deleted the first recording. In the second, the children moved their puppets and began some dialogue. However, they soon stopped. They realised that they needed to have a plan for the telling of the story so it could be recorded without stopping.

Ella and Jade moved with one of the researchers to a quiet area to record their story. Important at this time was the interaction with each other and the researcher to formulate the plan for the story. Together they discussed and sequenced the events in the story, the opening and closing sections, and the turn-taking that would be required in sharing their story. Finally, the children collaborated to connect their planned oral text with the movements of their puppets.

Jade and Ella's final text shared a story where Ella sustained an injury in the playground and sought help from a friend to report to sick bay. The story is 46 seconds and 104 words long. The transcript from the story and related screen captures are shared in Figure 11.5. Evident in the screen captures is the use of space as the puppets sought each other out, moved between key locations, and supported each other.

As kindergarten children, they saw themselves as the "babies of the school." This became particularly evident through the content of their stories and the ways they represented their characters within this. For example, many of the stories featured characters needing help. Further, many of the oral annotations were completed with the children adopting baby-like tones to their voices.

The task was something the children could all relate to. They all had recent experience of the school context and were able to visually represent and talk about their understandings. Focusing the task on a shared context enabled all children to participate as they brought their knowledge and experiences to the task.

The collaborative nature of the task was important to the final multimodal stories. As the children drew the map and the characters, they spoke about what they were creating. When they developed stories using the map and characters, they negotiated and compromised with each other about what was to be included and excluded. Through talk they were able to make connections to their school and their experiences within this context. This talk was critical to their ability to be able to develop a narrative sequence for their *Puppet Pals* story.

This case illustrates that the process of composing a multimodal story need not be entirely completed on a digital device. The investment of time in the planning and development of concrete storytelling tools (maps and characters) and then playing with and talking about them enabled the children to create their multimodal stories.

Classroom applications: collaborative partners can facilitate storytelling, providing time for children to talk and draw serves as important planning for the creation of multimodal texts with digital resources.

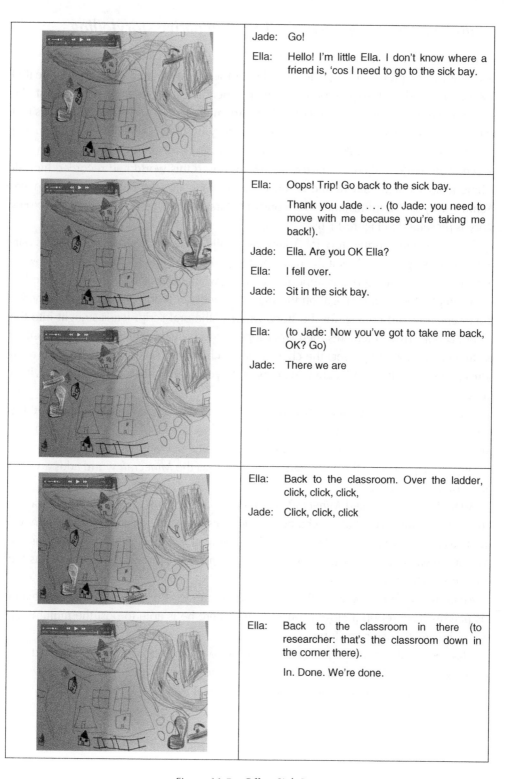

	Jade: Go! Ella: Hello! I'm little Ella. I don't know where a friend is, 'cos I need to go to the sick bay.
	Ella: Oops! Trip! Go back to the sick bay. Thank you Jade . . . (to Jade: you need to move with me because you're taking me back!). Jade: Ella. Are you OK Ella? Ella: I fell over. Jade: Sit in the sick bay.
	Ella: (to Jade: Now you've got to take me back, OK? Go) Jade: There we are
	Ella: Back to the classroom. Over the ladder, click, click, click, Jade: Click, click, click
	Ella: Back to the classroom in there (to researcher: that's the classroom down in the corner there). In. Done. We're done.

Figure 11.5   Off to Sick Bay

Digital games: An opportunity for imaginative storytelling

Our third project focused on the ways early primary children and their teacher engaged with the writing process using iPads. While our focus was on the ways children created text in open-ended classroom-based learning experiences within an area of interest, the example we share was created by one child (Adam, aged 8 years), who created this text external to the classroom as an example of a story he likes to create when producing text at home. He offered this text to our research project. Adam has been working on a *Minecraft* world (called "AdamTown"). He has used this world and recorded himself telling a story (titled "Saving the parents") as he navigates through this virtual space. Adam's story is 2 minutes and 36 seconds in duration and he speaks 217 words. His story is presented in Figure 11.6.

This is an empowering story for Adam. As a child, he identifies the problem (his parents are missing) and solves it (by rescuing the parents). While the story itself follows a typical narrative structure, it is important to acknowledge the role of each of the modes. For example, the visual navigation through the *Minecraft* world "AdamTown" provides the orientation and context for the story, whereas the oral script leads straight into the complication. These elements then work together to provide a resolution. The positive ending of the story empowers the child. It is the child who saves the parents and reassures them – "I will never let anything happen to you again" – before celebrating with a dance.

There is complex interplay between movement through the *Minecraft* world and the accompanying oral story. While either text could exist in isolation, a tour through a *Minecraft* world or an oral story, together they become powerful. The oral text provides a unique perspective to the *Minecraft* world, whereas the *Minecraft* world adds a visual dimension to the story.

Adam has incorporated *Minecraft* "characters" and tools into the story he presents. This is interesting given that the characters and tools play quite a different role in survival mode as a *Minecraft* game is presented. For example, asking characters for help is not part of the game as livestock (such as the sheep) are typically what is protected as the user ensures their safety from the evil zombies.

Adam is a keen follower of other *Minecraft* enthusiasts on YouTube. As such, he and his parents have set up a closed YouTube site where he is able to post the multimodal stories he creates using YouTube.

Classroom applications: Interest and expertise with apps from the home context can serve as powerful stimulus for the construction of text in the classroom. Oral and visual texts can be integrated to create powerful multimodal texts.

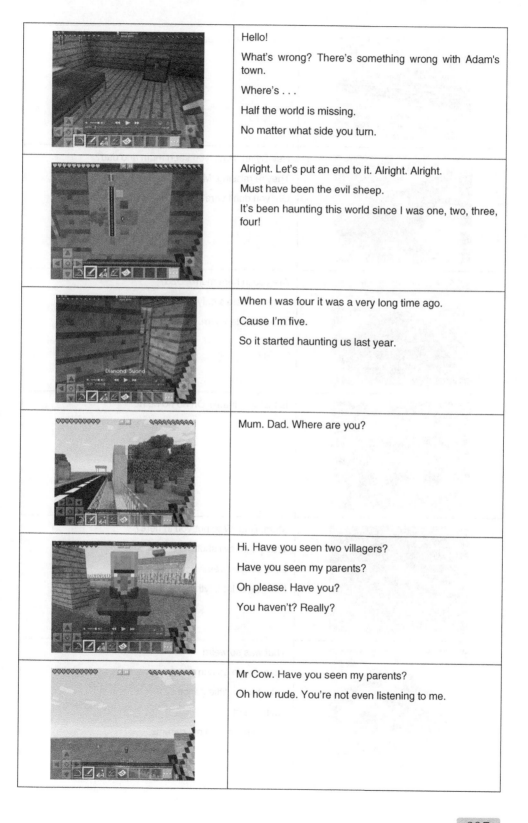

	Hello! What's wrong? There's something wrong with Adam's town. Where's . . . Half the world is missing. No matter what side you turn.
	Alright. Let's put an end to it. Alright. Alright. Must have been the evil sheep. It's been haunting this world since I was one, two, three, four!
	When I was four it was a very long time ago. Cause I'm five. So it started haunting us last year.
	Mum. Dad. Where are you?
	Hi. Have you seen two villagers? Have you seen my parents? Oh please. Have you? You haven't? Really?
	Mr Cow. Have you seen my parents? Oh how rude. You're not even listening to me.

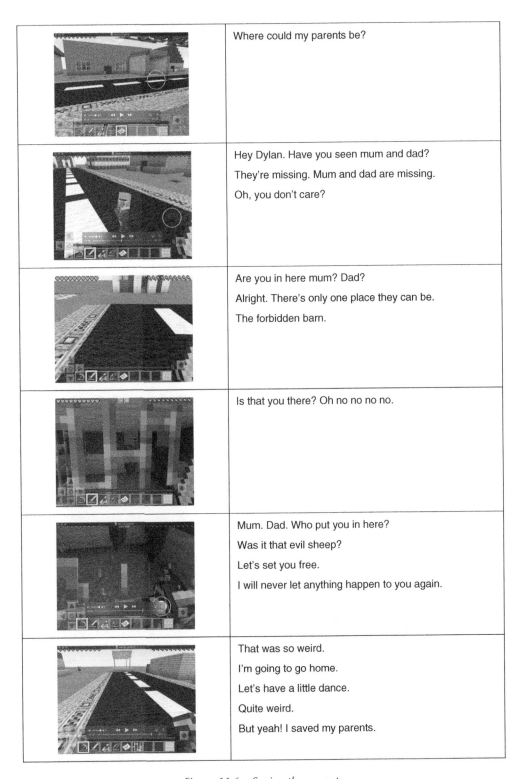

	Where could my parents be?
	Hey Dylan. Have you seen mum and dad? They're missing. Mum and dad are missing. Oh, you don't care?
	Are you in here mum? Dad? Alright. There's only one place they can be. The forbidden barn.
	Is that you there? Oh no no no no.
	Mum. Dad. Who put you in here? Was it that evil sheep? Let's set you free. I will never let anything happen to you again.
	That was so weird. I'm going to go home. Let's have a little dance. Quite weird. But yeah! I saved my parents.

Figure 11.6   Saving the parents

Reflection prompts

What are the possibilities, ethical considerations, and consequences (from the perspective of a young child) for digitally sharing a text? You might consider: What contribution does the text make to the child's digital footprint? Who accesses text in digital environments? How can/might it be used? How might the author respond? What are our responsibilities as the educator?

Lessons learned: Strategies and approaches for teaching and learning

This chapter now moves to deconstruct these three cases of young children creating multimodal stories using digital technologies to offer insights for literacy educators. In each case, the children used digital technologies to express personal narratives and understandings about themselves as members of a range of communities such as home, school, and the digital world (Arizpe et al., 2013). These cases demonstrate the important role technology played in affording not only the creation of the children's stories, but also the opportunity to share those stories with others.

In all cases, the spaces with which children participated offered rich stimulus for stories. Whether it was the everyday prior-to-school or school environment or the fantastic creations of the *Minecraft* world, the children responded to the stimulus in ways that fit the nature of that environment and with stories that connected them to it. The stimulus appeared to prompt the need to talk, to share, to consider, collaborate, and plan the story to be shared.

However, these multimodal texts weren't created without significant preparatory work by each child, often with adult support. Opportunities to gather stimulus by capturing photographs, talking, drawing, and playing a game allowed the children to organise their thoughts as they considered the stories they could tell. There appeared a constant dimension of needing to play throughout this process. In the first case, the child often needed to engage with or complete the activity before moving to the next one to photograph. In the second case, the significant talk surrounding the drawing, cutting out and manipulating characters on the map proved important for testing ideas and for rehearsal for the recording of the story. The third case was the result of sustained development and interaction with a virtual world created by the child. Imaginative tasks such as storytelling appear to be enriched through the imaginative act of play.

Children's use of technology for storytelling can support and encourage their talk and encourage them to explore their language and imagination as they tell their stories. The opportunity for children to engage with technologies that enable them to create their own texts is powerful. Our cases show that children make up stories about spaces and topics that are important to them. Making up characters and telling stories are activities through which children make sense of and test out their understandings about the world and about social roles. Children's everyday storytelling and imaginative exercises are an important part of their literacy development.

Technology enables the utilisation of a range of modalities for the creation of stories. In each case, we saw the children's language and literacy development as they made decisions about language use and image choice. The affordances of the technology to support meaning-making through multiple modes was also evident through the children's experimentation with sizing and placement of those images within the screen as they explored appropriate and powerful ways to use the space. Further, technology allowed the children to review, revise and remake aspects of their story with which they were dissatisfied. This was evident when Jade and Ella moved through three versions of their story until they had combined language, image, sound, and movement in a way they felt properly conveyed their story.

The creation of digital, multimodal texts poses considerations for audience. Each text was disseminated through digital means (for example, access through URL) and, as such, housed in digital environments (for example, web pages, YouTube channels). While these outlets represent exciting opportunities for providing children with an audience for their texts, each poses ethical considerations too as we consider the ability to control the responses and activity of secondary audiences and possible implications related to these actions.

Conclusion

Storytelling is essential for literacy learning progression. Children's enthusiasm to participate with multimodal text creation presents opportunities to engage them in literacy learning as they create, share, and view stories. Storytelling is acknowledged as a precursor to later success in reading and writing. Children's ability to represent thoughts both symbolically and multimodally and to then share these with an audience presents important literacy opportunities. As children tell stories, they learn and practise essential language skills. The opportunity to share these with audiences who may not necessarily share the same temporal and spatial context is valuable.

Working with families

Storytelling is a powerful way to share family experiences. Through story children can be connected to older family members, events of the past, and dreams for the future. Family stories are often multimodal – as words, gestures, props, and even audience participation are combined. There are multiple times to share stories: during mealtimes, before sleep times, driving in the car, walking in nature. Digital technologies can be used to record favourite stories (capturing the voice of significant others), taking photographs of experiences to revisit later, creating digital texts (for example, edited video) to share time and time again.

Glossary of terms

Terminology: Meaning

Multimodal: The interplay between different modes – images, written and spoken words, movement, gestures – within a text.

Text: An expanded definition of text looks to include audio, visual, and multimodal texts produced through digital technologies (Johnston, Kervin & Wyeth, 2022).

Digital technologies: Tools, systems and devices that can generate, create, store, or process data.

Preschool: The year before formal school in the Australian state where the data was collected. This is not a compulsory year of education.

Kindergarten: The first year of formal and compulsory schooling in the Australian state where the data was collected.

Recommended reading

Kervin, L., Danby, S., & Mantei, J. (2019). A cautionary tale: digital resources in literacy classrooms. *Learning, Media and Technology*, 44(4), 443–456. Doi: 10.1080/17439884.2019.1620769

Kervin, L. & Mantei, J. (2015). Drawing + Talk = Powerful insights for teachers of writing. In J. Turbill, G. Barton & C. Brock (Eds.), *Teaching Writing in Today's Classrooms: Looking Back to Looking Forward* (pp. 87–103). Norwood, Australia: Australian Literacy Educators' Association.

Kervin, L. & Mantei, J. (2016). Digital storytelling: Capturing children's participation in preschool activities. *Issues in Educational Research*, 26(2), 225–240. www.iier.org.au/iier26/kervin.html

Kervin, L. K. & Mantei, J. (2016). Digital writing practices: A close look at one grade three author. *Literacy*, 50(3), 133–140.

References

Arizpe, E., Farrell, M. & McAdam, J. (2013). Opening the classroom door to children's literature: A review of the research. In K. Hall, T. Cremin, B. Comber & L. C. Moll (Eds.), *International Handbook of Research on Children's Literacy, Learning and Culture* (pp. 241–257). London: John Wiley & Sons.

Comber, B. (2016). *Literacy, Place and Pedagogies of Possibility*. New York: Routledge.

Engel, S. (1999). *The Stories Children Tell: Making Sense of the Narratives of Childhood*. New York: Freeman.

Farmer, L. (2004). Using technology for storytelling: Tools for children. *New Review of Children's Literature and Librarianship, 10*(2), 155–168.

Hill, S. (2014). *Developing Early Literacy: Assessment and Teaching* (2nd ed.). South Yarra, VIC: Eleanor Curtain Publishing.

Johnston, K., Kervin, L. & Wyeth, P. (2022). Defining digital technology. ARC Centre of Excellence for the Digital Child. https://www.digitalchild.org.au/blog/defining-digital-technology/

Kervin, L. & Mantei, J. (2016). Digital storytelling: Capturing children's participation in preschool activities. *Issues in Educational Research, 26*(2), 225–240. www.iier.org.au/iier26/kervin.html

Kervin, L. & Mantei, J. (2017). Children creating mulitimodal stories about a familiar environment. *The Reading Teacher, 70*(6), 721–728.

McLachlan, C. (2012). Emergent literacy. In L. Makin, C. Jones Diaz & C. McLachlan, *Literacies in Childhood: Changing Views, Challenging Practice* (2nd ed., pp. 15–30). Marrickville, NSW: Elsevier.

Quah, C. Y. & Ng, K. H. (2022). A systematic literature review on digital storytelling authoring tool in education: January 2010 to January 2020. *International Journal of Human–Computer Interaction, 38*(9), 851–867.

Theobald, M. A., Danby, S. J. & Ailwood, J. (2011). Child participation in the early years: Challenges for education. *Australasian Journal of Early Childhood, 36*(3), 19–26.

Tomsic, M. & Zbaracki, M. D. (2022). It's all about the story: Personal narratives in children's literature about refugees. *British Educational Research Journal, 48*(5), 859–877.

Supporting plurilingualism in young writers

Paul Molyneux

In recent years, there has been increased recognition of the existence and potential for "plurilingualism" within the individual and "multilingualism" in society. These concepts dominate and stimulate academic discourse (see Cummins, 2021 and Ollerhead, Choi & French, 2018, for example) and are prominent in enactments of language policy, such as that adopted by the European Union (Council of Europe, 2023). In English-dominant societies like Australia, Canada, the United Kingdom, and the United States of America, viewing students learning English as an additional language as in any way deficient is an incorrect and unhelpful way to address their learning needs. Rather, all children, particularly plurilingual students still building early understandings of English, need to be understood as "multicompetent individuals who draw on the breadth of their meaning-making resources to engage in complex and dynamic communicative practices" (Choi & Slaughter, 2021, p. 82).

So, when these students' existing literacy and cultural resources are understood, affirmed, and extended, they provide a foundation upon which English language and literacy skills can be developed. This chapter discusses frameworks and strategies for understanding young children's plurilingual knowledge and skills and supporting them as writers – in both English and their home languages. Learning to write in a second or additional language takes a different pathway to that of one's first. As such, scaffolding approaches for supporting students' writing (across languages) are needed. Drawing on current research, an explicit focus on *meaning, language,* and *use* is advocated. In addition, the use of rich model or mentor texts and *teaching for transfer* are argued for as a means of supporting young plurilingual learners in English and in other languages. Case studies linking theory and research to exemplary practice are provided throughout this chapter to support the teaching of writing to students of diverse linguistic and cultural backgrounds.

DOI: 10.4324/9781003439264-12

Considering plurilingual pathways and English as an additional language or dialect

Cultural and linguistic diversity is a welcome reality and a rich resource, particularly in countries whose populations and economies have expanded over time through immigration, family reunion, skilled migration, and refugee resettlement. Typically, a multitude of languages *other than English* are spoken in families, the community, childcare settings, preschools, and schools. In Australia, for example, linguistic diversity takes the form of English existing alongside the continued use of Indigenous languages (such as Pitjantjatjara, Woiwurrung, Gumbaynggirr) and international languages of well-established and recently arrived communities (from Dutch to Dinka, Spanish to Sinhalese, Mandarin to Malayalam). The acronym EAL/D is sometimes used to refer to those students learning English as an additional language or dialect. This acronym takes heed of the plurilingualism of Aboriginal and Torres Strait Islander children, whose first language is an Indigenous language, including traditional languages, creoles, and related varieties, or Aboriginal English (Australian Curriculum Assessment and Reporting Authority, 2014, p. 7).

The idea of "translanguaging" (a term coined in the 1980s but revisited and extended by García & Li Wei, 2014) refers to a lived reality and an intentional pedagogy whereby students "draw on and mingle all elements in their linguistic repertoire in all modes" (Feez & Harper, 2021, p. 12). Translanguaging is a helpful construct for teachers to bear in mind as they support students' writing. It recognises a fluidity and dynamism at play as students acquiring English draw on all available resources to communicate. An example of a child deploying or experimenting with different modes of communication can be seen in Figure 12.1, wherein a 5-year-old boy growing up in a Farsi and English-speaking household is using drawing and texting to explore possible ways to express ideas, interests, and feelings.

It needs to be remembered that children developing plurilingual skills while learning English as an additional language are as diverse a group as those learning English as their native language. The child who has attended preschool and primary school in Hong Kong – learning in Cantonese and Mandarin – before migrating to an English-dominant country, the child born in a Vietnamese-speaking household and beginning preschool or school with rich reserves of that language (but little English), and the refugee-background child with little experience of formal schooling and minimal understandings around literacy in the first language are all plurilingual learners of English as an additional language. As the Department of Education and Training, Victoria (2015, p. 5), makes clear, at the time of their initial exposure to learning in English, EAL/D learners might:

1   be at any year level in the school system;

2   have been born overseas or in their country of schooling;

Figure 12.1   Drawing and texting: A 5-year-old's deployment of different communicative modes

3   have had little or no exposure to English;

4   have received formal education equivalent to that of their chronological peers;

5   have had little or no previous formal schooling in any country or may have experi-
    enced a severely interrupted education in their first language.

As such, teaching needs to take heed of the existing skills, knowledge, and experiences
of EAL/D learners and tailor appropriate instructional responses. While there can be no
"one size fits all" approach, there are some common principles and practices that will
support EAL/D learners, and these are the focus of this chapter.

In this chapter, I urge educators and teachers to pay attention to the language origins of
EAL/D children while supporting their acquisition of English. Teachers also need to find out
about the skills, interests, knowledge, and experiences of their EAL/D learners. These should
be seen as *resources* to support learning, rather than impediments or barriers. Languages
other than English are all too often seen as sources of *interference* in learning English.
Research has shown that the opposite is the case (see Cummins, 2000, 2003). As well as
being valuable personal resources with strong emotional connections to family and community, languages other than English provide a foundation and pathway to learning English,
learning about English, and learning through English. All too often, the linguistic and cultural knowledge EAL/D learners bring to the classroom is overlooked, even dismissed.

But – when recognised and affirmed – it can be a powerful way to enhance the child's multi-faceted identity, maximise plurilingual potential, and support learning in English.

> ### Reflection prompt
>
> *Reflect on your own classroom. What skills, interests, knowledge, and experiences do your students bring and what place do they have in the classroom? What evidence of plurilingualism do you observe in your students?*

Finding out about our plurilingual learners

In supporting the early writing of students with emerging understandings of English, it can be a real advantage to know something of their first language and how it works. Understanding that Arabic script is read from right to left, that there are no verb tenses in Khmer, that nouns do not carry plural markers in Vietnamese, or that preposition use in Turkish is very different to English can help us anticipate the challenges learners from those language groups might experience when attempting to apply first language knowledge to English. "Teaching for transfer" has been suggested by Cummins (2008, 2021) as a means of making children explicitly aware of similarities and differences between first and additional languages. If children are able to say, "In English, adding -s or -es usually makes a word plural. In Turkish, we add -ler or -lar," they are articulating sophisticated awareness around how each language works. There are very helpful resources that assist teachers to learn about the languages of their EAL/D students (see Department of Education and Early Childhood Development, 2015; Swan & Smith, 2001).

We should also learn as much as we can about children's language use outside the classroom. Sociolinguistic profiles, often completed by preschools and schools as plurilingual children are enrolled, assist us to understand the degree to which a child has been exposed to English and other languages. These profiles or surveys (see Hertzberg, 2012, for an excellent example) help build an understanding of the cultural and linguistic knowledge children possess, when (and to whom) they communicate in English or other languages, and what educational and other experiences the child has had. Often interpreters, bilingual assistants, or multicultural education aides employed by preschools and schools assist in the collection of this information. It can provide valuable insights into appropriate starting points for instruction.

Similarly, research by D'Warte (2013) and Dutton, D'Warte, Rossbridge, and Rushton (2018) explored innovative ways involving linguistic mapping and language portraits whereby teachers can learn about the linguistic repertoires of their students. Taken up at different levels and ages of language learning (Choi & Slaughter, 2021; Choi, 2022), such approaches have yielded valuable insights even with younger children. In her doctoral research, Rose Iser (2022) collected language portraits from 12 second-generation

Figure 12.2   Language portrait of a second-generation African Australian boy

African Australian students which pictorially revealed the sophisticated ways children construct the plurilingual and multimodal competencies they possess. Figure 12.2, a language portrait completed by one of the students, de-identified as Birhan, reveals how he sees multiple languages, including Arabic, English, and Tigrinya as part of his toolkit. He illustrates where he uses English alone (school, community, world) and where multiple languages and translanguaging occur (with friends, within the family).

Supporting writing in English: Important considerations for plurilingual learners

It is important that we take heed of some key considerations when supporting EAL/D learners and their writing. These are briefly discussed here before a more fulsome discussion of teaching practice is outlined. Essentially, we need to recognise:

- The relationships between spoken and written language and the reciprocity between reading and writing;

- The differences between learners' attainment of conversational fluency and academic language proficiency;

- The need to think about writing in terms of *meaning, language,* and *use*;

- The importance of scaffolding writing through a gradual release of responsibility from teacher to child.

247

While these considerations apply equally to all children learning to write, they are vital to learners challenged by adding English to their existing linguistic repertoire.

While written language builds on the children's skills and understandings around spoken language, more sophisticated understandings around language are required when writing. Richgels (2004) reminds us that "written language must stand alone" (p. 474) given the distance between the writer and the reader, as opposed to the face-to-face interaction communicated through speaking. This is important when planning for EAL/D learners and their writing. Their early writing in English will very strongly reflect oral language, more conversational registers. This is recognition of the fact that conversational fluency (proficiency in the language required for everyday, repeated, or informal interactions) is typically mastered by EAL/D learners as early as six months after beginning schooling in English (Cummins, 2000). Yet, as Raban (2014) notes, conversational language alone will not lead to success in school. Decontextualised language and extended discourse – the literate language of books – are central to children's progress through the school curriculum (Raban, 2014, p. 11) and this academic language proficiency (Cummins, 2000; Gibbons, 2009, 2015) can take five to seven years for EAL/D learners to develop to levels that approach native-like competence (Cummins, 2001).

As such, rich conversations around rich texts – picture books, junior novels, non-fiction texts – provide the foundations around which EAL/D learners can build an understanding of the language they, in time, will incorporate into their own writing. Gibbons (2009) stresses that engaging EAL/D learners in substantive conversations builds both content knowledge and an understanding of how to articulate that knowledge. The development of a vocabulary for speaking and writing results, to a large degree, from book reading and book discussion (Dickinson, Griffith, Golinkoff & Hirsh-Pasek, 2012). Patterns of teacher–child book discussion that prompt, evaluate, expand, and repeat (Raban, 2014) support children's language understandings that can then be deployed in speaking and writing.

Making writing relevant to all students is essential – especially for EAL/D learners who are striving to make connections in their learning in the additional language. Cummins (2000, 2021) suggests teachers of EAL/D learners should adopt a framework that will build academic language learning. This framework adopts a strong:

- *Focus on meaning*: ensuring that teacher talk and language is comprehensible and that children's spoken and written output is as well;

- *Focus on language*: that teachers actively support EAL/D learners' awareness of language forms and uses; and

- *Focus on use*: that children are given the support and opportunity to use language appropriately to reflect their knowledge, communicate through art and literature, and act on social realities.

This framework requires teaching that – in order to achieve literacy engagement and attainment – activates the children's prior knowledge, scaffolds meaning (both input and output), affirms identity (recognising and building on the existing linguistic and cultural knowledge the child possesses) and extends language (Cummins, 2009). Such teaching is consistent with Pearson and Gallagher's (1983) ideas of a gradual release of responsibility (from teacher to child), as well as the scaffolded structure of the genre curriculum cycle (Christie, 2005) – also referred to as the teaching and learning cycle (Gibbons, 2015). A modified version of these cycles is included in Chapter 9. Over the rest of this chapter, what this can look like in practice is outlined – with explicit attention to effective strategies for scaffolding EAL/D learners' writing.

Building on oral language foundations

Language experience (see Wilson, 1979 for seminal work in this area) is a teaching approach that connects direct experience to spoken and written language. In this approach, a shared class experience (in or out of the school; planned or unplanned) could become a vehicle for reflection, talk, and writing. A sudden hailstorm, author study celebrations, or a visit to the zoo are just a few of the many possibilities for a language experience focus. Essentially, in language experience:

- The children actively participate in a shared experience;

- Individual, paired, small-group, and whole-class opportunities are created to talk about the experience. Photographs passed around or distributed to small groups – like those taken during the preparation of sticky rice at a preschool (Figure 12.3) – present a way to stimulate recall of an experience and facilitate focused talk.

Figure 12.3   Photographic sequence: Cooking sticky rice

- A written text (often scribed by the teacher) is constructed around the experience. Here, the children's ideas can be incorporated into a written text that draws on their oral language abilities and models more decontextualised and extended language. Typical teacher prompts at this point can be:
  - *How can we explain this to people who were not there?*
  - *How can we put that in writing? It needs to be different from how we speak.*
  - *Will that make sense to anyone not in our class? What extra details could we add?*

The classroom text in Figure 12.4 emerged from my classroom. After a class excursion to an airport, this photograph, along with others, prompted the children to revisit the experience, identify the key elements, discuss them in conversational registers, and then suggest how those ideas could be conveyed in writing. It allowed for vocabulary building as new specific terms like "terminal," "tarmac," and "hangars" could be revisited and reinforced. This provided the focus on meaning, language, and use that Cummins (2000, 2021) advocates.

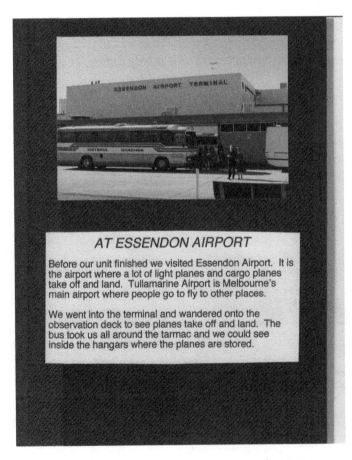

Figure 12.4   Language experience text: At the airport

Reflection prompt

What other classroom experiences might serve as opportunities for language experience teaching? How might you facilitate student talk and build from there to a focus on written language?

A project undertaken by social enterprise and centre for young writers, *100 Story Building* in the early years classrooms at a Melbourne Metropolitan Primary School, centred on supporting children to construct personal stories that they could orally recount through the use of a series of self-drawn pictures. This project (see Macintyre, Sallis, Brown & Molyneux, 2017) honoured and drew on the lived experiences of the children (most were EAL/D learners) and their families. Over a period of weeks, with rich storytelling input by teachers and guests in the classroom, the children decided on their focus, created a series of illustrations, rehearsed their presentations, and then recounted their stories while being filmed (see Figure 12.5). A film premiere night at the school celebrated the children's successes. This method of oral and visual storytelling served as a powerful form of language use and communication in its own right, as well as laying powerful foundations for future writing.

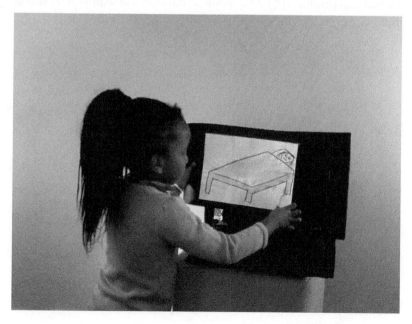

Figure 12.5   Oral storytelling in an early years classroom

Contexts for writing: We all have stories to tell

All too often, little classroom space or time is made for recognising the linguistic and cultural knowledge of our diverse, plurilingual learners. These have been referred to as the "funds of knowledge" (González, Moll & Amanti, 2005; Zipin, 2009) that children and communities possess or the "virtual school bags" (Thomson, 2002; McGregor & Mills, 2017) that children transport to school, the contents of which may be welcomed in the classroom or disregarded. As the *100 Story Building* project highlights, individual interests, family experiences, and cultural knowledge (celebrating Chinese-Vietnamese New Year, fasting during Ramadan, etc.) are fertile potential sources for talk and writing. Unlocking these ideas needs only a little coaxing, as pivotal early work by Calkins and Harwayne (1991) also recounted, detailing how the provision of a notepad and suggestions to closely observe the birds on his rooftop allowed a reluctant student to create a poem of rich detail and emotion.

Classrooms where the varied experiences and backgrounds of the children are valued and talked about provide a stimulating context for children to write. Whether it be interests like collecting basketball cards, a family holiday, or the details of arriving in Australia, plurilingual learners have much to draw on in their writing. For refugee-background children, some memories might be painful or complex to deal with, so the need for teacher sensitivity and empathy is paramount. The two examples below, Figures 12.6 and 12.7, are classroom artefacts of children's writing that drew on their personal experiences. The first was produced by a Vietnamese-background learner who was supported by me as her classroom teacher to:

Figure 12.6   Cover of Vietnamese-background student's classroom published book

We came to Australia on an aeroplane.

4

Figure 12.7   Page from story of travelling to Australia

- Brainstorm the key aspects of her family's trip to Vietnam;

- Decide which events to include and emphasise;

- Draw on her knowledge of the structure and features of a recount;

- Consider what words or phrases she might need to include;

- Draft a written text in chronological order;

- Revise and edit the text to add clarity, remove repetition, and conform with conventions of English grammar;

- Publish the text in book form, organising illustrations and design features.

The second example – Figure 12.7 – captures a page of text that was narrated to me by a newly arrived student with very little English. Acting as his scribe, I recorded simple sentences around the family's flight to Australia from East Timor. This became the child's first published classroom book and the first he could read independently. While still very nervous as a newly arrived, refugee-background learner, it was an enormous confidence boost to his very early English attempts.

Supporting writing and literacy in the first and additional languages

"Identity texts" is the term Cummins (2006, 2021) coined to describe classroom texts that provide children with the opportunity to draw on their cultural and linguistic knowledge in their writing. They affirm children as they "hold a mirror up to students in which their identities are reflected back in a positive light … [and] can be written, spoken, signed, visual, musical, dramatic or combinations in multimodal form" (Cummins & Early, 2001, p. 3). They can also be bilingual or multilingual. A plurilingual learner might be more confident writing in a language other than English before receiving assistance in communicating the same ideas in English. Alternatively, a language experience text, composed first in English, might be translated into another language. Figure 12.8 shows a short text produced in an early years class I taught. Each day, something of significance was talked about and recorded in writing. On this day, it was decided that a child's imminent departure for an overseas trip was important. With assistance from a Turkish speaker, the text was recorded in both English and Turkish.

Making room for other languages in the early years classroom sends a powerful message that proficiency in more than one language is an asset. It also provides an opportunity for children to make meaning in two languages and transfer both content and language knowledge between the two. The most powerful pedagogical arrangement to foster two languages occurs in additive bilingual programs, where two languages are taught for significant parts of the school week and learning takes place about and through both languages. A longitudinal study I was involved in documenting and evaluating (see Molyneux, Scull & Aliani, 2016a, 2016b) created many opportunities for children – from a range of backgrounds – to become literate in English and the Karen language from the Thai/Myanmar region. Rich examples of the children's writing provide evidence of the deep learning that took place across languages, as can be seen in Figure 12.9, a Karen-background child's recounting of a trip to the mountains.

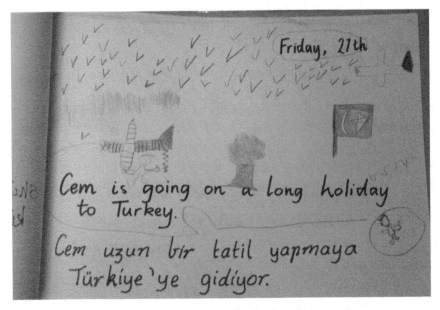

Figure 12.8   Classroom text presented in both English and Turkish

ဘၣ်တၢ်ကွဲးအီၤလၢ ရှံယံလၤမူ

ယလဲၤလၢကစၢၣ်ခိၣ်

လၢနံၤသဘျ့ယလဲၤလၢကစၢၣ်ခိၣ်လီၤ.ယ
ထံၣ်ကစၢၣ်ဒီးသ့ၣ်ထူၣ်လီၤ.ဒီးပအီၣ်တၢ်လၢက
စၢၣ်ခိၣ်ဒီးပဟံၣ်ဖိဃီဖိလီၤ. ဒီးယက့ၤလၢဟံၣ်
လီၤ. ဒီးယကွၢ်တၢ်ဂီၤမူဝံၤယကူၤမံလီၤ.

Figure 12.9   Student recount in the Karen language

   English translation: "I Went to the Mountain": In holiday, I went to the mountain. I saw mountain and trees. Then I had lunch with my family. Then I went home. I watched TV and went to bed.

Reading–writing connections

The close connections and inter-relationships between reading and writing are well recognised, with Clay noting that "establishing reciprocity between those two ways of learning about the printed word" (Clay, 2001, p. 136) expands the child's literacy repertoire. Askew (2009), reflecting on the significance of Clay's body of research, finds that in Clay's view of literacy processing, writing plays a significant role in early reading progress and vice versa. Therefore, in supporting plurilingual learners and their writing, the importance of picture books and reading aloud should not be underestimated. A study undertaken in New Zealand by Dix and Amoore (2010) highlighted the "linguistic spillover" (p. 140) that took place when rich picture books and poetry were used as sources of both pleasure and instruction in writing. Their study found that the children's uptake of vocabulary, semantic and syntactic structures, and other elements of various authors' crafting of narratives were profound and, in turn, transformed their own writing.

Model or mentor texts like those used in Dix and Amoore's (2010) study need to have a prominent place in the classroom. They provide rich models for what Spandel (2009) and Tompkins (2010) refer to as the six traits of powerful writing: ideas, mechanics, organisation, sentence fluency, voice, and word choice. At first, the learners unfamiliar with English will borrow heavily on the scaffolds these rich texts provide. In my teaching experience, as these learners make their first attempts at longer pieces of writing, they often write retellings of well-known stories like *Goldilocks* or *The Three Little Pigs*. In these texts, the ideas are already formed, allowing the children to concentrate on the mechanics of organising and recording the story. In an analysis of writing at one school at which I both taught and conducted research, the school's teacher-librarian could immediately see the way one child, from a Vietnamese family background, had drawn on a narrative text she had introduced in constructing an impressive written piece of his own, as evidenced in the reproduction of his writing below (see Figure 12.10).

Reflection prompt

In the example of student writing below, what features or expressions might indicate the student has drawn from the narrative texts he has encountered?

"Once upon a time, Triceratops was busy looking for leaves to eat when T-Rex bit Triceratops. After a while, they both looked at each other seriously. Then, Triceratops used its three horns to suck up Tyrannosaurus's blood. The dust was everywhere when they were some surrounded by trees and a big mountain."

Figure 12.10   First section of a student narrative, reflecting linguistic spillover from a narrative encountered in the school library

As foregrounded earlier in the chapter, a framework that can make use of model or mentor texts and provide explicit instruction for EAL/D writers is the genre curriculum cycle (Christie, 2005), the teaching and learning cycle (Gibbons, 2015), or the shifting levels of support cycle provided in Chapter 9, this text. Using one of the cycle approaches, children are supported to:

- build knowledge of a topic (ensuring they have content to write about);
- focus on a specific genre or text type as it is modelled and deconstructed for them (enabling them to understand the language structures and features of the genre);
- observe an experienced writer create a text of the type modelled in the earlier step;
- jointly construct a text with the teacher (or other children); then
- independently construct a written text of their own.

The genre curriculum cycle – while it was first developed with the intention of supporting marginalised learners to engage with powerful forms of literacy – is a commonly used framework to support all children to write for different purposes and audiences. Tailoring it for plurilingual learners requires an understanding of their current literacy strengths and needs (built up through collection and analysis of their writing attempts) and the deployment of both macro and micro scaffolding (Parkin & Harper, 2018) to support students' writing and learning.

Here, for example, the focus on "building the field" or topic knowledge development would need to be sufficiently expansive for children to have a very clear body of information to draw into a report. Figure 12.11 below provides an example of a template I have used in my classroom teaching to ensure plurilingual learners have sufficient information to write a report about, in this case about an animal of their choice.

Such templates, accompanied with explicit instruction – using modelled and shared writing to demonstrate the text type, along with published texts to deconstruct the genre – can support children to gain the necessary knowledge to attempt writing of their own. At this stage, contingent scaffolding (Hammond, 2021) is essential, whereby teachers closely observe children as they write and, when necessary, intervene, conference, revisit, and restate knowledge the child needs to overcome obstacles to writing.

Support for authorial and secretarial writing

A teacher's mindfulness of authorial and secretarial aspects of early writing (Peters & Smith, 1993; Mackenzie, Scull & Munsie, 2013) will certainly support students learning to write in English and other languages. Authorial aspects of writing typically refer to the organisation of ideas and information to communicate to an audience, while secretarial aspects refer more to the mechanics: "the surface features of writing, with close attention to spelling, handwriting and punctuation" (Mackenzie et al., 2013, p. 378). For students unfamiliar

Animal Nonfiction Report

The animal I would like to write about is

_____

Here is its picture:

This is what I already know about it:

_____

_____

_____

_____

_____

_____

_____

_____

_____

PLANNING MY REPORT ON _____

What sort of animal?

Body covering: what does it look like?

What does it eat?

Where does it live?

What dangers does it face?

How does it protect itself?

Anything else ...

Figure 12.11   Planning proformas and graphic organisers to assist writing

with the English script and written conventions, explicit attention to the secretarial elements of writing is essential. It has been noted that these learners, in order to move from conversational fluency to academic language proficiency, need to be taught the secretarial understandings or "discrete language skills" as Cummins (2001, p. 65) refers to the grammatical, phonological, spelling, and punctuation conventions of English.

Importantly, this explicit attention to the secretarial aspects of writing can be (and needs to be) embedded in meaningful reading and writing focuses. Shared reading with an enlarged text supports awareness of print directionality and the differences between letters and words, modelled writing supports their understandings of how writers strategise around word choice, use punctuation, and leave spaces between words. Interactive writing – where the teacher and children share the pen or writing implement – allows children to be scaffolded in both authorial and secretarial dimensions of writing (see Chapter 9). Revisiting texts written or read earlier provides an opportunity to pay explicit attention to secretarial skills around spelling, phonology, and syntax. Word families or groupings (built around common onsets or rimes, spelling patterns, morphemes, etc.) can be generated from texts previously read or written. Conventions and understandings around punctuation and paragraphing can be generated by analysing language use in texts shared or created. Such embedded, in-context teaching ensures the children see immediate relevance to the skills, strategies, and understandings under focus. As such, the likelihood of student uptake of the skills and strategies is maximised. Teacher–child conferences, common in all classrooms, provide an ideal opportunity for teachers to strategically address issues that emerge in children's writing: both authorial and secretarial (Figure 12.12).

Figure 12.12   Writing sample of a six-year-old plurilingual boy (first year of school)

Reflection prompt

If conferencing the plurilingual learner above, what features of his writing would you commend him on? What aspects of the writing – assuming this is a typical example – might become focuses for your teaching?

Conclusion

It is often remarked that good teaching strategies designed to support students learning English as an additional language or dialect will support everyone. While this might be the case, the language and literacy needs of children new to English need specific and explicit attention. The acquisition of an additional language should not come at the expense or loss of the first language. As such, educators and teachers need to find ways to value the cultural and linguistic knowledge plurilingual learners bring to the classroom and see it as powerful to acquisition of English. As Hammond and Miller (2015) remind us, EAL/D instruction that both scaffolds and challenges the additional language learner is not only an educational necessity; it is a matter of supporting the welfare and well-being of these children. Cummins (2021) differentiates between school and classroom contexts that are *collaborative* and inclusive of child and community languages and knowledge and those that are *coercive* and devalue the diversity of our communities. As early years educators, we have a moral and ethical obligation to affirm diverse forms of cultural and linguistic knowledge, advancing students' literacy in English and other languages – communicative skills that will empower them at school, in the home, and in the community, now and in the future.

Working with families

The families of plurilingual students are vital resources with whom teachers can work in developing understanding of their children's existing linguistic repertoires. As this chapter has emphasised, sociolinguistic profiles and language portraits help teachers gain powerful insights into children's linguistic and cultural knowledge, as starting points for instruction and support. The collection of this information often draws on family input and, from here, the role of parents and caregivers can be harnessed to support children's plurilingual writing (and literacy more broadly). As classroom helpers, families and their linguistic repertoires can assist in making plurilingualism a daily reality, whether it be through storytelling in home languages, translating writing into English or other languages, and supporting teachers' awareness of aspects of other languages that will enable them to assist their students to make stronger connections between the languages they deploy as plurilingual communicators.

Glossary of Terms

Terminology: Meaning

EAL/D: Referring to students whose first language is a language or dialect other than English and who require additional support to assist them to develop proficiency in English.

Decontextualised language: Language, usually written that conveys sophisticated meanings outside the immediate, informal, and everyday.

Plurilingualism: The dynamic use of multiple languages/varieties and cultural knowledge, awareness, and/or experience in social situations.

Translanguaging: The ability to move fluidly between languages and a pedagogical approach to teaching in which teachers support this ability.

Recommended reading

Baker, C. & Wright, W. E. (2021). *Foundations of Bilingual Education and Bilingualism* (7th ed.). Bristol, UK: Multilingual Matters.

Cummins, J. (2021). *Rethinking the Education of Multilingual Learners: A Critical Analysis of Theoretical Concepts*. Bristol, UK: Multilingual Matters.

Gibbons, P. (2015). *Scaffolding Language, Scaffolding Learning: Teaching English Language Learners in the Mainstream Classroom* (2nd ed.). Portsmouth, NH: Heinemann.

Hammond, J. & Miller, J. (Eds.) (2015). *Classrooms of Possibility: Supporting At-Risk EAL Students*. Newtown, NSW: Primary English Teaching Association of Australia (PETAA).

Hertzberg, M. (2012). *Teaching English Language Learners in Mainstream Classes*. Newtown, NSW: Primary English Teaching Association of Australia (PETAA).

References

Askew, B. (2009). Using an unusual lens. In B. Askew & B. Watson (Eds.), *Boundless Horizons: Marie Clay's Search for the Possible in Children's Literacy* (pp. 101–130). North Shore, NZ: Heinemann.

Australian Curriculum Assessment and Reporting Authority. (2014). *English as an Additional Language or Dialect Teacher Resource: EAL/D Overview and Advice*. Retrieved from www.acara.edu.au/verve/_resources/EALD_Overview_and_Advice_revised_February_2014.pdf

Calkins, L. M. & Harwayne, S. (1991). *Living Between the Lines*. Portsmouth, NH: Heinemann.

Choi, J. (2022). Learning about multilingual language learning experiences through language trajectory grids. In J. Purkarthofer & M-C. Flubacher (Eds.), *Speaking Subjects in Multilingualism Research: Biographical and Speaker-centred Approaches*. Bristol: Multilingual Matters.

Choi, J. & Slaughter, Y. (2021). Challenging discourses of deficit: Understanding the vibrancy and complexity of multilingualism through language trajectory grids. *Language Teaching Research*, 25(1), 80–104.

Christie, F. (2005). *Language Education in the Primary Years*. Sydney: UNSW Press.

Clay, M. M. (2001). *Change over Time in Children's Literacy Development*. Auckland: Heinemann.

Council of Europe (2023). *Plurilingual and Intercultural Education*. Retrieved from https://www.coe.int/en/web/language-policy/plurilingual-education

Cummins, J. (2000). *Language, Power and Pedagogy: Bilingual Children in the Crossfire*. Clevedon, UK: Multilingual Matters.

Cummins, J. (2001). *Negotiating Identities: Education for Empowerment in a Diverse Society* (2nd ed.). Los Angeles: California Association for Bilingual Education.

Cummins, J. (2003). Bilingual education: Basic principles. In J. Dewaele, A. Housen & L. Wei (Eds.), *Bilingualism: Beyond Basic Principles* (pp. 56–66). Clevedon, UK: Multilingual Matters.

Cummins, J. (2006). Identity texts: The imaginative construction of self through multiliteracies pedagogy. In O. Garcia, T. Skutnabb-Kangas & M. E. Torres-Guzman (Eds.), *Imagining Multilingual Schools: Languages in Education and Glocalization* (pp. 51–68). Clevedon, UK: Multilingual Matters.

Cummins, J. (2008). Teaching for transfer: Challenging the two solitudes assumption in bilingual education. In J. Cummins & N. Hornberger (Eds.), *Encyclopedia of Language and Education: Bilingual Education*, Vol. 5, 2nd ed. (pp. 65–75). New York: Springer.

Cummins, J. (2009). Fundamental psycholinguistic and sociological principles underlying educational success for linguistic minority students. In T. Skutnabb-Kangas, R. Phillipson, A. Mohanty & M. Panda (Eds.), *Social Justice through Multilingual Education* (pp. 19–35). Bristol, UK: Multilingual Matters.

Cummins, J. (2021). *Rethinking the Education of Multilingual Learners: A Critical Analysis of Theoretical Concepts*. Bristol, UK: Multilingual Matters.

Cummins, J. & Early, M. (Eds.) (2001). *Identity Texts: The Collaborative Creation of Power in Multilingual Schools*. Stoke on Trent, UK; Trentham Books.

Department of Education and Early Childhood Development (Victoria). (2015). *First Language Assessment Materials*. Retrieved from https://fuse.education.vic.gov.au/pages/View.aspx?id=3c872b8a-d24e-475d-b000-b1fb30b2f561&Source=%252fpages%252fResults.aspx%253fs%253dLanguage

Department of Education and Training (Victoria). (2015). *The EAL Handbook: Advice to Schools on Programs for Supporting English as an Additional Language*. Melbourne, VIC: Department of Education and Training.

Dickinson, D. K., Griffith, J. A., Golinkoff, R. M. & Hirsh-Pasek, K. (2012). How reading books fosters language development around the world. *Child Development Research*, 1–15. doi:10.1155/2012/602807

Dix, S. & Amoore, L. (2010). Becoming curious about cats: A collaborative writing project. *Australian Journal of Language and Literacy*, 33(2), 134–150.

Dutton, J., D'Warte, J., Rossbridge, J. & Rushton, K. (2018). *Tell Me Your Story: Confirming Identity and Engaging Writers in the Middle Years*. Newton, NSW: Primary English Teaching Association of Australia.

D'Warte, J. (2013). *Pilot Project: Reconceptualising English Learners' Language and Literacy Skills, Practices and Experiences*. Sydney, NSW: Department of Education and Training, NSW and The University of Western Sydney. Retrieved from http://www.uws.edu.au/__data/assets/pdf_file/0007/714391/Pilot_Project_Jacqueline_Dwarte.pdf

Feez, S., & Harper, J. (2021). Learning and teaching english as an additional language or dialect in mainstream classrooms. In H. Harper, & S. Feez (Eds.), *An EAL/D handbook* (pp. 1–16). Newton, NSW: Primary English Teaching Association of Australia.

García, O., & Li Wei (2014). *Translanguaging: Language, bilingualism and education*. New York: Palgrave Macmillan.

Gibbons, P. (2009). *English Learners, Academic Literacy and Thinking: Learning in the Challenge Zone*. Portsmouth, NH: Heinemann.

Gibbons, P. (2015). *Scaffolding Language, Scaffolding Learning: Teaching English Language Learners in the Mainstream Classroom* (2nd ed.). Portsmouth, NH: Heinemann.

González, N., Moll, L. C. & Amanti, C. (Eds.) (2005). *Funds of Knowledge: Theorizing Practices in Households, Communities and Classrooms*. Mahwah, NJ: Lawrence Erlbaum.

Hammond, J. (2021). Scaffolding in EAL/D Education. In H. Harper & S. Feez (Eds.). *An EAL/D Handbook*. (pp. 16–18). Newton, NSW: Primary English Teaching Association of Australia.

Hammond, J. & Miller, J. (Eds.) (2015). *Classrooms of Possibility: Supporting At-Risk EAL Students*. Newtown, NSW: Primary English Teaching Association of Australia (PETAA).

Hertzberg, M. (2012). *Teaching English Language Learners in Mainstream Classes*. Newtown, NSW: Primary English Teaching Association of Australia (PETAA).

Iser, R. (2022). *Stories of Language, Culture and Race from African Australian Children, Their Caregivers, and Educators*. Melbourne: University of Melbourne Unpublished thesis.

Macintyre, P., Sallis, R., Brown, R. & Molyneux, P. (2017). Learning and teaching through the arts and storytelling. Language and literacy acquisition. In C. Sinclair, N. Jeanneret, J. O'Toole & M. Hunter (Eds.), *Education in the Arts* (3rd ed., pp. 187–201). South Melbourne: Oxford University Press.

Mackenzie, N. M., Scull, J. & Munsie, L. (2013). Analysing writing: The development of a tool for use in the early years of schooling. *Issues in Educational Research, 23*(3), 375–393.

McGregor, G. & Mills, M. (2017) The virtual schoolbag and pedagogies of engagement. In B. Gobby & R. Walker (Eds.), *Powers of Curriculum: Sociological Perspectives on Education*. (pp. 373–392). South Melbourne: Oxford University Press.

Molyneux, P., Scull, J. & Aliani, R. (2016a). Bilingual education in a community language: Lessons from a longitudinal study. *Language and Education, 30*(4), 337–360.

Molyneux, P., Scull, J. & Aliani, R. (2016b). Catering for diversity through bilingual education: A longitudinal case study. In J. Scull & B. Raban (Eds.), *Growing Up Literate: Australian Literacy Research for Practice* (pp. 213–237). South Yarra, VIC: Eleanor Curtain.

Ollerhead, S., Choi, J. & French, M. (2018). Introduction. In J. Choi & S. Ollerhead (Eds.), *Plurilingualism in Teaching and Learning: Complexities Across Contexts*. (pp. 1–17). New York: Routledge.

Parkin, B. & Harper, H. (2018). *Teaching with Intent: Scaffolding Academic Language with Marginalised Students*. Newton, NSW: Primary English Teaching Association of Australia.

Pearson, P. D. & Gallagher, M. (1983). The instruction of reading comprehension. *Contemporary Educational Psychology, 8*(3), 317–344.

Peters, M. L. & Smith, B. (1993). *Spelling in Context: Strategies for Teachers and Learners*. Windsor, Berks: NFER-Nelson.

Raban, B. (2014). TALK to think, learn and teach. *Journal of Reading Recovery*, Spring, 5–15.

Richgels, D. J. (2004). Paying attention to language. *Reading Research Quarterly, 39*(4), 470–477.

Spandel, V. (2009). *Creating Writers through 6-Trait Writing Assessment and Instruction*. Boston, MA: Allyn & Bacon/Pearson.

Swan, M. & Smith, B. (Eds.) (2001). *Learner English: A Teacher's Guide to Interference and Other Problems*. (2nd ed.). Cambridge, UK: Cambridge University Press.

Thomson, P. (2002). *Schooling the Rustbelt Kids: Making a Difference in Changing Times*. Stoke-on-Trent, UK: Trentham Books.

Tompkins, G. (2010). *Literacy in the Middle Grades: Teaching Reading and Writing to Fourth through Eighth Graders*. Boston, MA: Pearson.

Wilson, L. (1979). *Write Me a Sign: About Language Experience*. West Melbourne, VIC: Thomas Nelson.

Zipin, L. (2009). Dark funds of knowledge, deep funds of pedagogy: exploring boundaries between lifeworlds and schools. *Discourse: Studies in the Cultural Politics of Education, 30*(3), 317–331.

13 When learning to write isn't easy

Natalie Thompson and Janet Scull

Introduction

When learning to write, children need to learn to plan, compose, and record their ideas. The ease with which many children appear to do this often masks the complexities of writing. Each aspect of the process requires deliberate attention and draws across discrete skill sets. Planning and composing are associated with children's developing language skills as they draw on their knowledge of the world, their oral language structures, and vocabulary. Recording requires increasing control over the conventions necessary to convey messages for a given audience. In all, producing a written text involves an understanding of how to apply authorial skills (text structure selection, sentence structure, and vocabulary choices) and secretarial or editorial skills (spelling, punctuation use, and handwriting/keyboarding). To write well, children need to have knowledge and understanding of all these elements.

In this chapter, challenges in writing are considered along with suggestions for how teaching might be adjusted to meet the specific needs of learners who are finding learning to write difficult. There are a range of reasons why children may experience extra challenges with one or more of the dimensions of writing. When this happens, it is important that teachers offer additional support to these children. This might involve the allocation of more time for these students, along with explicit, intentional, and timely instruction and extra practise opportunities. Sometimes approaches to teaching children facing extra challenges are grounded in deficit-models of teaching and learning that focus on what children *cannot do*. While the intention is well meaning, these approaches can become disconnected from the purposeful task of writing for meaning and enjoyment. Instead, we focus on what children *can do*, from a strengths-based approach, building on children's skills to enhance learning (Galloway et al., 2020). This chapter includes the unique story of Eden (not her real name) told through a series of vignettes

DOI: 10.4324/9781003439264-13

that capture the interactions between Eden and one of the chapter authors. Eden's story is used throughout to demonstrate the real-life application of a strengths-based approach and how this supported her learning journey towards success.

Challenges and complexities of the writing process

In Chapter 2, Mackenzie described the drawing and writing journey as a form of spontaneous, simultaneous, and non-linear development. Learning to write is a dynamic journey that is influenced "by normal variation in the pacing and sequence of learning" (Bazerman et al., 2017, p. 355), and while we recognise that children will take various paths to common outcomes, for many different reasons, some children experience extra challenges along the way (Clay, 2014).

First and foremost, we acknowledge the complexity of learning to write (Graham et al., 2019). Learning to write involves the child in an intricate orchestration of making connections between oral and written language forms to construct meaning. The integration of skills related to the composition of messages and the recording of ideas draws on a range of conventions, including phonology, phonics, spelling, grammar, punctuation, and form (Scull et al., 2020). Children also need to learn repair strategies to address problems as they arise including actions such as rereading, pausing, and self-correction (Harmey & Rodgers, 2017). Complexity is also inherent in the move from simply recording speech to engaging with more literate forms of language. While we appreciate the varied communication ecologies of our students, and the diverse forms of language and English that young learners bring to school, we also recognise more advanced forms of writing require children to develop control over particular language registers associated with literacy (Christie, 2005). As a literate form of speech which is quite different from spoken language, writing requires a developing control over vocabulary choices and syntactic competence that permits effective written self-expression (see Chapter 6). Children's early exposure to written text forms, elaborated sentence structures, uncommon vocabulary, and literary language lays a valuable foundation for literacy development in the early years of primary school.

Recent research findings reflect a broadening of understanding about writing to include not only skills but also processes and writing knowledge. Processes that have recently been studied in relationship to writing difficulties include self-regulation, working memory, attention, and executive control (for example see Graham, 2022; Limpo & Alves, 2018; Rosenblum, 2016). For instance, Limpo and Alves (2018) found that targeted teaching in transcription and self-regulation in the early years lessened the severity of difficulties that at-risk students experienced with writing. These researchers defined self-regulation as the ability to "monitor and strategically adjust all components involved in writing" while also managing the "social and physical setting where writing takes place" (p. 391). Instruction was centred around three phases of self-regulation: the fore-thought, the performance, and the self-reflection stage, and strategies included goal setting, planning, self-efficacy, interests, expectations, self-monitoring, and goal flexibility. Teaching specifically about these elements resulted in more complex plans as well as longer and more clearly structured texts and provided evidence for the efficacy of a broadened understanding of the writing process for designing writing programs for struggling writers.

In addition, new understandings about the ways writing knowledge might contribute to difficulties have extended to thinking about the purpose and function of different texts. These new understandings include knowledge about planning and drafting, knowledge about different tools for writing, knowledge about what good writing looks like, as well as knowledge about the topic being written about (for example, see Benjamin & Wagner, 2021; Graham et al., 2015; Graham, 2022). Each of these different types of writing knowledges and processes may need to be considered in detail, assessed and, if needed, incorporated into programs of teaching for students experiencing difficulties.

Another component of writing instruction that has attracted significant research in recent years is the role that knowledge about grapheme phoneme correspondences (GPCs) plays in learning to write, particularly for students with ongoing difficulties. As explained by Ehri (2014), knowledge about GPCs develops through a process of orthographic mapping, whereby connections between graphemes, either single graphemes or groups of graphemes, and phonemes, syllables, or morphemes, are retained in memory. This is argued to be important for writing as the process of orthographic mapping allows for the spelling of words to be written with a level of automaticity. Research continues to confirm that orthographic mapping is essential for proficient reading and writing, and that GPCs need to be explicitly taught (Hiebert, 2023). Recent research (for example, see Elleman et al., 2019; Seidenberg, 2017) suggests that orthographic mapping is enhanced when students are taught about the connections between graphemes and phonemes in words by recognising and analysing the patterns of letters most frequently encountered through reading and writing. This has significant implications for designing instruction for students who experience difficulties with spelling in relation to both their textual diet and the order of instruction of GPCs, a sequence that is determined by what they already know and can do.

The different educational journeys that children experience also contribute to development in writing and include patterns of attendance, school relationships, and instructional histories. There are many reasons why a child's attendance at school might be poor or inconsistent: illness, misadventure, family holidays, and a child's, or a family's, perceived connectedness to school (Mackie & MacLennan, 2015). Missed class time, either due to incidental or long-term absence or changing schools, can contribute to gaps in expected knowledge. Sometimes even the different ways that teachers use instructional language in their teaching can lead to confusions for some children. If these confusions are not untangled quickly, they can cause major misunderstandings that become a barrier to the child's learning.

For some children there may be underlying cognitive, behavioural, or physical impairments that contribute to the challenges they are experiencing. These children might need specialised instruction by expert teachers and/or non-education professionals (such as speech therapists and occupational therapists) who work with teachers, families, and individual children. This group of children is diverse, and their own unique sociocultural backgrounds and educational histories also contribute to their experience of learning to write. Although some children will need specialised adjustments and expert support, they will also need to belong to an inclusive writing community that values purposeful writing and the pleasures of composition.

Yet all children come to school with different understandings and experiences and will need different approaches for them to reach common, expected outcomes. Children learn about literacy depending on what is valued by their families and their communities (Llopart & Esteban-Guitart, 2018). They also learn in different ways according to the abilities, resources and customs of their family. At school, children continue down different paths on their way to becoming literate. Focusing on what children have achieved along their journeys positions them as active participants in their learning and allows for the development of agency and confidence. By acknowledging the multiple pathways to writing and starting with what a child knows, we provide an opportunity for a fresh start with writing.

The view taken in this chapter is supported by sociocultural theory (Vygotsky, 1978), whereby learning is understood to be affected by social experiences and literacy is understood as a repertoire of practices embedded within everyday lives and events. The ways that children learn about literacy, and the types of writing they experience, depend on the social and cultural communities they belong to (Heath, 1983; Graham, 2018). Dyson (2016) suggests that all children bring to school important writing resources including "their language(s), their knowledge of their home places – their markets, their churches, their physical surroundings, their daily rituals – and the images, songs, and stories important to them" (p. 168). Consequently, learning – and in this case learning about writing – is impacted by the larger social structures that exist beyond the classroom. Well before children arrive at school, they have already learned a lot about the literacy experienced in their community. For many children, writing – as it is presented at school – will resemble these experiences. However, for others, that will not be the case. For some children *school writing* might be foreign and new, with little connection to the writing they experience or observe at home or in their community. With limited opportunity to draw on their knowledge of past experiences or make clear connections between *school writing* and the ways texts are composed in life outside school, confusions may develop in the child's understanding of what writing is all about.

Getting to know what the child knows and can do

Teaching is about helping children "to understand and to do what they cannot yet do on their own" (Wilhelm, 2012, p. 50). To establish what a child can already do, and determine precisely what they need to learn to write more efficiently, teachers will need to draw on a range of assessment practices including those intended to screen for students needing extra support, diagnostic approaches designed to identify specific teaching priorities, and assessments that allow the teacher to monitor the progress of learning so that decisions can be made about the efficacy of instruction (Deane, 2023). In Chapter 8, Scull described a range of strategies for assessing writing. The skilful interpretation of this data is an important part of the process of getting to know what the child knows but can only provide a picture based on what was tested. Formal assessments sometimes work from narrow definitions of literacy and are unable to report on the "multiplicity of factors identified in research that are involved in language learning" (Mills, 2008, p. 212), in this case, writing. Getting to know what a child *knows and can do* requires us to go beyond formal assessment data.

Engaging with children's families is critical at this point as the role of parents/caregivers in supporting children's literacy learning has been well documented (Swain & Cara, 2019). First and foremost, parents/caregivers can provide valuable insight into children's learning progressions and their interests and abilities as young writers. We suggest alongside conversations where information about the child is shared, parents are asked to document children's writing at home, through photographs and the collection of artefacts. As González (2005) states, households are "repositories of knowledge," so it is important that educators recognise and use this information when designing teaching interventions.

Knowing children and recognising the rich and diverse language background of students, is particularly important given the number of plurilingual students in our early years classrooms (Australian Bureau of Statistics, 2023). In Chapter 12 Molyneux describes the complex and dynamic language and literacy resources of Indigenous children and children newly arrived from non-English-speaking communities, with children's language repertoires positioned as a foundation for learning (Choi & Slaughter, 2021). Educators need to take account of students' cultural and linguistic backgrounds, and tools such as socio-linguistic profiles can be useful to identify children's current levels of language proficiency and learning pathways. Teaching approaches and strategies for writing that can be planned to support children from diverse language backgrounds are also detailed in Chapter 12.

In the classroom, time must be allocated for open-ended, unrushed, playful activities that will allow for relationship building but will also allow the child to demonstrate to the teacher what it is that s/he knows. Sometimes the teacher will need to withdraw the child from the class for a short amount of time for one-on-one teaching. Activities that support this process include, but are not limited to: drawing-talking-writing (initially the teacher may be the one to do the writing); conversations about topics the child is interested in;

reading to the child; going to the library together to choose books; completing jig-saws together; playing card and board games; doing some art/craft together; teaching the child how to use modelling clay or weaving; perhaps taking photos or videos of the child in the playground, doing things they like to do. During this time, the teacher will be listening and observing, noting down all the things the child can do and what s/he is interested in. This process often leads to the teacher discovering that the child knows more than she originally thought, and the child also learns more about what they know.

Reflection prompt

If you are an early years (EC) educator, how will you collect details of children's early writing experiences to inform your teaching?

If you teach in a school, how will you support the continuity of learning from home and preschool to school to avoid confusions?

What assessment data will inform your practice?

Data gathering and analysis processes build understanding of what is known in both the child and the teacher. The teacher will be more confident in decisions about teaching priorities once time has been spent in this manner, and the child will be more likely to take risks in this safe relationship. Within the current accountability climate, where teachers are under increasing pressure to fit more instruction into class time, making the decision to stop teaching and prioritise getting to know more about the child, and what s/he knows and can do, is becoming increasingly important. As can be seen in the following vignette, this process can uncover unexpected strengths and create opportunities for children to connect the interests and texts of their everyday lives to the teaching contexts in the classroom.

Getting to know Eden

I met Eden when she was in Year 1. She had been identified as having ongoing challenges with literacy and her teacher was worried that she had made little progress with writing since starting school. Her teacher provided assessment data in the form of a letter-sound knowledge profile and a phonological knowledge profile (both assessment tools commonly used in Victoria, Australia). These both showed that Eden was working well below the expected level for Year 1. I worked with Eden two mornings each week for two school terms. In our first meeting, Eden took me on a tour of her school, showing me the important features: the playground, sports shed, and bike track. Eden took photos of these places – to be used in the future for a piece of writing. During our walking and talking I discovered that Eden enjoyed making bracelets out of "loom bands" and had three best friends at school.

Eden chose some books and we read together, talking about the books, books she has at home, and then other things she enjoys doing. I learnt that Eden enjoyed watching "Saddle Club" – she loved going to Scouts, where her Dad was a leader – and that she was going camping with her family on the weekend. I asked Eden if she would like to draw a picture of her family, which she did (see Figure 13.1).

The next week I brought in "loom bands" and Eden taught me how to make a simple bracelet. We looked at the pictures that we had taken the week before and talked about what she liked about school, which was playing outside. I was able to ask about the camping trip she had mentioned and invited her to draw a picture about it (see Figure 13.2).

While she drew this picture, Eden talked about her tent and the step-ladder her brother used to tie the top of the tent closed. I was confused about what was going on in the picture, so Eden added the letters to help me identify each person. I asked Eden if she would like to write about the camping trip. She was reluctant to have a go at writing, explaining that she couldn't write. With some encouragement and reassurance that it didn't matter if she got some of the words wrong, she turned to the lined side of the book and wrote the text you can see in Figure 13.3.

Figure 13.1   Eden's family

Figure 13.2   Eden draws about camping

Figure 13.3   Eden writes about camping

I spent the first four weeks getting to know Eden. We made "loom bands" and I taught her how to add charms onto them. Eden brought in her "Saddle Club" DVDs to show me, and we talked about the show. We organised the pictures we had taken into a book titled "Eden's School" – Eden talked about the pictures, and I typed. We used the Draw, Talk, Write, and Share approach (Mackenzie, 2022), also described by Mackenzie in Chapter 10, often starting with the activities that Eden enjoyed doing outside school, but sometimes with the stories we read. Eden enjoyed reading books about animals, particularly if they made her laugh. I invited her to bring in some of her favourite books from home. Sometimes Eden had a go at writing, often adding initials to her drawings *and occasionally her full name. Sometimes I wrote alongside her as she dictated a story. During this time, I was able to form a detailed picture of what Eden knew about language and writing. I was comfortable I knew some of what she could do and felt I had a starting point to think about where Eden needed to go next in her writing journey.*

Reflection prompt

What might Eden know about writing?

Being clear about teaching priorities

Decisions about instruction and teaching priorities for children experiencing extra challenges with writing must continue to be grounded in an informed model of writing development. Research that contributes to complex and multi-dimensional models of writing emphasises the importance of authentic text creation (Bazerman et al., 2017). From this perspective, meaning-making and authorial skills, while supporting children to also learn the necessary secretarial and editorial skills, are valued.

It may be useful to consider that the principal purpose of writing is "not to produce writing, but to produce reading" (Walshe, 2015, p. 23) – that when you ask any child to write, you are asking them to produce something that will, and can, be read by someone else. Of course, it may be argued that there are other purposes of writing that include organisation, personal reflection and thinking, but in the context of the beginning writer it is useful to frame the purpose, and motivation for writing, in terms of the authentic reader (Camping et al., 2023). From this stance, an important teaching priority is for them to create a text that can be read by the intended audience. This priority might be something that has been planned or one that has arisen directly from an instance of writing. Teaching priorities may have been identified from recent writing assessments or reflections made during a recent writing conference. The purpose of the lesson and the relationship between the teacher and the child will contribute to the decision regarding the teaching priority and the way the teaching is approached. The teacher who knows her child well knows the level of support required. She also knows when to modify goals and accordingly adjust her plans.

While carefully planned teaching priorities are important, so are the unplanned occasions that capitalise on the conditions of a particular writing experience. These are often described as a "teachable moment," a term that refers to the authentic opportunities that arise to teach something that needs to be taught "right then" (Glasswell & Parr, 2009, p. 354). Teachable moments occur as a teacher uses the teaching and learning interaction and the child's text as a type of formative assessment. Teachable moments are reliant on a teacher's knowledge of the child and the writing process and, as documented in the following vignette, require the teacher to be confident to make quick and spontaneous teaching decisions in response to the student's needs.

A teachable moment with Eden

Through my careful interactions and observations, I knew that Eden enjoyed talking and drawing about familiar events, particularly activities she has done with her family. She could structure a recount verbally and possessed a range of topic-specific vocabulary about camping and horse riding, both interests of her's. Eden independently added the initial letters of names to her drawings to help me interpret them. This showed me that Eden had an understanding of audience and the purposeful creation of texts. She could also successfully use the initial letters of familiar names to label her drawings, despite getting some of these letters incorrect on her letter identification assessment.

Drawing became a regular starting point for our writing lessons, and Eden regularly composed detailed and animated texts about her adventures. In Figure 13.4, Eden had drawn about a scout camp that she went on with other scout groups from the region. She told me that they camped next to the lake in tents, and she independently started writing about this. To help me read her text, Eden drew a line between the words and her drawing (tents). Remembering they had read a book about Lake Jindabyne in class, she rushed off to find it to help her write the word "lake."

Figure 13.4   Eden draws and writes about camping by the lake

> *Eden was combining her drawing and writing as she developed her understanding of audience and the purpose of texts. I was beginning to see some recognisable words in her writing and some evidence of both invented and semi-phonetic spelling. In this piece of writing, it was apparent to me that sentence structure and spacing between words was making it difficult for me to read the text and I decided that I would focus on these as an immediate teaching priority.*

As argued by Mackenzie (2011, p. 324), "what teachers prioritise demonstrates to children what they see as important." Teaching priorities which are just beyond what children *know and can do*, understood through a complex and multi-dimensional model of writing development that contributes to the readability of the text, tell the child that writing for meaning is important. Sometimes it helps to tell the child specifically what they are working on, and why, to make sure that what the teacher sees as important is clear to the child. When a teaching priority is formed, the teacher must then decide on the most appropriate teaching strategy. To manage the time, support and attention needed for all children in a class, teaching strategies need to be short, effective, focused, and able to fit in with the whole class organisation. In the section below, a range of strategies that allow for extra support with the different dimensions of writing are considered.

Strategies that allow for extra support with authorial dimensions

Text structure

In the early years, children must learn to coordinate and organise ideas as they write for different purposes and audiences. Working first with single clauses and sentences, children's texts then need to expand to include simply stated ideas in clearly connected sentences, ordered to signal the staging of their texts. As students begin to craft longer texts, and with appropriate teaching and support, they develop control and flexibility over the structure of written texts, moving to the use of paragraphs to effectively sequence and communicate ideas (Scull & Nicolazzo, 2022).

Interactive writing, as described in Chapter 9, allows teachers and students to "share the pen" (or keyboard) as texts are co-constructed, with opportunity for rich conversations and explicit teaching. This process of collaborative authorship allows for differentiated levels of support – as the teacher makes decisions about what children need to be able to actively contribute to the text (Hall et al., 2014; Mackenzie, 2015). Working with individual students or small groups, Interactive Writing can be particularly helpful in providing opportunities for additional support around understanding text structures.

Through processes of co-construction, students' knowledge about text types or genres (such as narrative or information report) can be supported (Wing Jan & Taylor, 2020).

Working with students as co-authors, teachers find Interactive Writing provides time for repeated modelling of the types of decisions writers make in relation to text structure (such as the sequencing of ideas, the purpose of the text and genre-specific elements such as introductions, lists, etc.). Interactive Writing can be combined with drawing and other multimodal text construction, depending on the individual needs, teaching priorities, and instructional context. If the writing was done on an interactive whiteboard (or other digital device), there is also the opportunity to publish the text at the end of the week so the co-constructed text can be re-read, either in class or at home – for further reinforcement.

Sentence structure

Structuring a sentence requires the use of appropriate word and phrase order consistent with standard usage patterns. This involves students in developing a growing awareness of sentence grammar and a variety of sentence types (i.e., simple, compound, and complex structures) (Scull & Nicolazzo, 2022). Sometimes a child experiencing challenges with sentence grammar will be asked to copy a sentence from a text or one that the teacher has written for them. However, this does not allow them an opportunity to practise the composition of texts mentioned above. When children are learning about sentence writing, they will need to be supported with both sentence composition and sentence construction. Children can do this orally using the Draw, Talk, Write, Share approach (Mackenzie, 2022; see also Chapter 10), which allows an adult to provide appropriate scaffolds around vocabulary and sentence structure. At this point, the use of sentence-building activities (see Chapter 5) and mentor texts (see Chapter 9) may also be helpful. Teachers can encourage students to "borrow a line of text," using the grammar of a given sentence to craft their own, gradually adding complexity and challenge to the task (Dorfman & Cappelli, 2007).

The cut-up story (Clay, 2016) strategy might also be useful. This strategy starts with a child's recorded text. The teacher writes the sentence onto a strip of cardboard. As soon as the child has finished writing, the teacher shows them the sentence written on the card and asks them to read it. The teacher then asks the child to say each word as she cuts the sentence up (word by word). Having the child's original model of the sentence in front of them, the teacher asks if the child can put the sentence back together, with instructional focus on the specific teaching priority. At the end of the lesson the words are put into an envelope – with the correct sentence written on the front. This provides opportunities for the child to reassemble the sentence either at another time in class, with the teacher, student mentors, or another adult at school, or at home. As demonstrated in the following vignette, cut-up stories offer an immediate opportunity for focused and timely instruction that can fit within the everyday classroom writing routine.

Cutting up Eden's story

After explaining to Eden that I was having a little difficulty reading her writing because I couldn't see the different words that made up her sentence (Figure 13.4), I asked her if she would like me to help her have another go at writing her sentence. I explained how writers write more than one draft of their writing and get help from other writers. I wrote the sentence as Eden "read" (remembered) her sentence out loud and we had a go at reading it together. I then asked Eden to read each word as I cut them out.

I displayed her original writing sample and the cut-up words in front of Eden and asked her if she would like to have a go at putting her sentence back together. Sometimes Eden needed some prompting to find the word she was looking for. We played around with the different order of words before Eden decided on the order shown in the image below. With some prompting, Eden arranged the words with a finger-width space between them as shown in Figure 13.5. We finished the lesson by reading over the sentence as Eden pointed to each of the words – with some assistance. I put the words in an envelope, with the correct sentence written on the front, and gave these to her classroom teacher for repeated practise throughout the week.

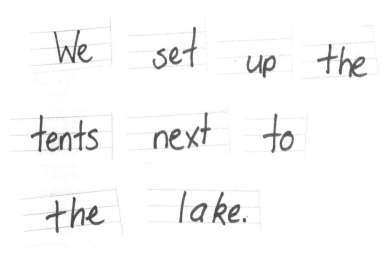

Figure 13.5   Eden's cut-up story

Vocabulary

When students' vocabularies are not large, their prospect for literacy success is dependent on rich classroom language experiences (Hiebert, 2020). This is true for early reading and writing. In order to write a text, an author needs to connect with their experiences and access their knowledge and vocabulary about a topic. Some children will need extra support with this element, particularly if their unique life encounters are very different to the types of topics valued, and written about, in school. Support for vocabulary development is discussed in Chapters 5 and 10 in this text.

Creating opportunities for children to read and write about something they are an expert on is one approach to support vocabulary learning (Donovan, 2016). A way to do this is through the use of personalised texts.

Personalised texts are written about something the child is familiar with and interested in. These texts start with conversations – getting to know what the child knows, valuing his knowledge and expertise. This offers an opportunity to build vocabulary around what the child knows and with help, form these ideas into a story. While the child dictates, the teacher can record the text, providing timely scaffolds around vocabulary choices and sentence structure. Photographs or drawings can also be used in the creation of a published text as shown in Figure 13.6. Working within familiar territory allows the child to feel in control of the writing experience. Re-reading this text to the child, and providing opportunities for the child to read it too, demonstrates that ideas or stories can be written and read, thus promoting the reciprocity of early reading and early writing that is often undervalued in early literacy instruction (Clay, 2016).

Figure 13.6 Peter's personalised text

Strategies that allow for extra support with secretarial dimensions

Handwriting

Despite the prevalence of digital devices, handwriting is still highly valued, and often preferred in early years classroom for learning to write. Handwriting is recognised as a complex skill, as the fine motor demands of handwriting are mapped to orthographic information about how letters are formed and sequenced to record words (Limpo & Graham, 2020). Not all children will come to school with enough drawing experience to develop efficient pencil grasp, posture, and control over different writing tools. To support writing fluency, it may be useful to provide extra opportunities, such as drawing and painting, to support the development of these foundational skills, alongside explicit instruction and practise specific to letter formation (see Chapter 7).

In addition, when handwriting is not easy, the task of writing strictly within lined paper may be overwhelming. Clay (2016) suggests that children continue to be offered opportunities to write without the restrictions of lines and the added pressure of print size, direction, straight lines and page layout. One way to do this is to offer a blank page for writing. This allows for the intentional teaching of specific handwriting needs, within the context of meaningful writing, without the need for the child to attend to all of the required elements of spatial layout.

Spelling

Learning to write with efficiency and automaticity requires the development and accurate application of culturally determined spelling systems or conventions (Wulff et al., 2008). Correct spelling begins to develop through exposure to print and experimentation with different word forms. Daffern (2015) argues that, at school, spelling is further progressed through "contextualised, explicit and reflective instruction in phonology, orthography and morphology" (p. 33). Children experiencing challenges with spelling will need extra support, with repeated and explicit instruction, beginning with common letter patterns and the writing of single syllable words with regular, and easy to hear, Consonant-Vowel-Consonant (CVC) patterns to more complex phonic sequences and the use of visual memory to write high frequency words and apply morphemes appropriately (Mackenzie et al., 2015).

The use of Elkonin Boxes is a teaching strategy that allows for extra support with the phonological dimensions of spelling. Originally developed by a Russian psychologist (Elkonin, 1973), this technique has been adapted for use in reading and writing programs in classrooms all over the world.

For writing, Elkonin Boxes can be used in the context of an authentic writing experience when a child comes to a word they are unsure of how to write. Designed to scaffold spelling, this approach helps a child to hear the separate sounds (phonemes), in the correct sequence, in a word (McCarthy, 2008). As shown in Figure 13.7, Elkonin Boxes are joined squares, drawn by the teacher, that represent the number of phonemes in a word. A counter is placed below each box. The teacher begins by modelling the procedure by saying the word slowly (but naturally), pushing the counter into the first, second, and so forth, box as she says the corresponding phoneme. Moving the counters back to below the boxes, the child has an attempt at saying the word slowly and pushing the counters into the box at the right time. After doing this, the child can attempt to record the symbols that represent the phonemes they hear in each box, as shown in Figure 13.8. The first time a child pushes up the counters, they may hear a dominant sound (e.g., the first or last phoneme). Once a letter has been recorded in the appropriate box, the process is repeated, as the child listens for other sounds. Depending on what the child knows and can do, the teacher may need to assist with this, particularly where there are two letters that represent a single phoneme, silent letters, or where a sound could be represented by several letters or letter combinations. When all boxes are filled, the child can write the word into their text. Elkonin Boxes are a strategy used at the point of need to help a child record their text. Many teachers who use this strategy find it useful to draw the squares on a blank page so that the *working out* doesn't impact the readability of the composition. Having a working out or practise page available when writing is useful for

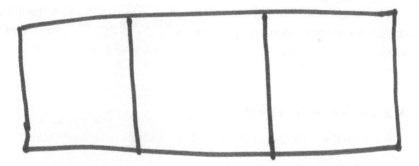

Figure 13.7   A teacher draws Elkonin Boxes on a blank page

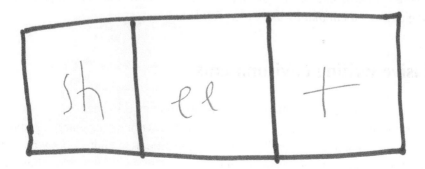

Figure 13.8   A child uses Elkonin Boxes to write the word "sheet"

279

this, and other teaching strategies – particularly for children experiencing ongoing challenges who may be used to seeing messy corrections in their writing. This also demonstrates that working out or having a go are normal elements of learning to write and that writing does not have to be correct in the first, or even subsequent, attempts.

Punctuation

In their study of change over time in writing samples of students in Year 1, Mackenzie et al. (2015) show that secretarial and editorial elements of writing, such as punctuation, support authorial aspects and that some of these secretarial elements may require explicit instruction. Explicit instruction is described by Luke (2014, p. 1) as "teacher-centred" instruction with clear goals and outcomes. In this approach, instruction is highly structured as teachers provide explicit explanations followed by "modelling and guided practice" (Blair, et al., 2007, p. 435).

Explicit instruction regarding punctuation, for students experiencing difficulty in this area of writing, requires a teacher to be clear about the specific rule that needs to be learnt, how it is applied, and how to clearly communicate this to the child along with offering appropriate examples and opportunities to practise. One way to do this is to use a think-aloud strategy (Blair, Rupley & Nichols, 2007) during modelled or shared writing. The teacher might use these experiences to notice, name, and justify the use of different punctuation markers, develop generalisations about their functions, and apply this knowledge to enhance students' own writing (Scull & Nicolazzo, 2022).

Think-aloud for punctuation

During an interactive writing session, the children and teacher have co-constructed the sentence, Jackson flew to Sydney.

At this point in time, the teacher has the pen and has written the first three words "Jackson flew to…"

Stopping before writing the word Sydney, the teacher thinks-aloud, "I am about to write the name of a place. I want my reader to know that this is a place. I am going to show them that by using a capital letter."

Inclusive writing environments

There is a range of evidence-based models and frameworks that teachers can draw on to support them in designing inclusive learning environments that offer opportunities for targeted teaching for small groups and individuals. Multitiered systems of support is a framework of three levels of increasingly scaffolded instruction that includes high-quality, universal teaching to the whole class (tier 1), small group teaching targeted to the needs of a few (tier 2), and individualised teaching (tier 3). That is, students at tier 2 have already received high quality universal instruction in tier 1, and on top of this the extra scaffolding offered at tier 2. Tier 3 students receive individualised instruction in addition to that offered in the first two tiers. Multitiered systems of support have a significant research base (see, for example, Peterson et al., 2022) and is a model that teachers find valuable and easy to implement (Stuart et al., 2011). Another model that focuses on flexibility in teaching methods, materials, and assessment is Universal Design for Learning (UDL). UDL is premised on the argument that learner diversity is expected and that adopting just one approach to teaching results in barriers to learning for some students. Using UDL, teachers are guided to plan for multiple means of representation, expression, and engagement (Rose & Meyer, 2002) in order to remove potential barriers students might experience. UDL also has a growing evidence-base (for example see Capp, 2017) and is considered to be effective for enhancing engagement in writing, particularly for struggling writers, through offering students some choice in how they learn, how they engage, and how they express themselves (Hashey et al., 2020).

These models open opportunities to teach to diversity and support children experiencing difficulties with writing within an inclusive classroom. However, in his meta-synthesis of what works in schools, Hattie (2009) identified that the most impactful element of the classroom environment is a teacher who maintains high expectations for all students and creates positive student-teacher relationships. More specifically, in their meta-analysis of research on effective writing practices, Graham et al. (2015, p. 507) found that effective writing environments are motivating and pleasant, where "teachers support students and their writing efforts and students support each other." Similarly, Dyson (2016, p. 170) noted that for children experiencing success in writing despite challenges, there was a sense that their writing mattered in terms of "social recognition and respect from others." The approaches to teaching discussed above provide opportunities to attend to these elements of effective practice to create inclusive writing environments that offer equitable access to "an enabling literacy curriculum" for all children (Comber, 2011, p. 6). They allow students to work within the familiar, provide opportunities for meaningful teacher–student and student–student relationships, and encourage teachers to maintain the expectation that all children will write purposefully, in a range of forms and for a variety of audiences. In her influential book on teaching *hard-to-teach* children, Lyons concluded that "it is not possible to separate emotion and cognition" (2003, p. 107). Learning to write is a complex task, and children need belief in themselves, self-confidence, and the motivation to persist.

Reflection prompt

Can you identify any practices that you do, or would like to do, that show children that their writing matters and is respected?

Conclusion

Eden writing at the end of the year

Eden and I continued to meet each week for two terms. We painted, made more "loom bands," and searched Google for images of Saddle Club characters that we used to write a story. Eden continued to draw and write purposefully, and I continued to read and enjoy her stories. I utilised a number of strategies, such as those mentioned above, to teach Eden both secretarial and authorial elements of writing – always explaining what we were working on and how it would make her text easier, or more meaningful, to read. We continued to share books, with Eden often asking to read Olga the Brolga *by Sheena Knowles. Eden continued to draw first and became more confident and independent in writing simple sentences, using familiar vocabulary, to complement her drawings. In our final week together, Eden chose to write about Olga, shown in the image below (it reads "Olga the Brolga looks like a platypus. She wanted to dance.")*

Eden attended a special development school and had a range of cognitive and communication impairments that contributed to her writing journey. Taking the time to get to know what Eden knew and could do, providing opportunities for her to compose within the known by using the Draw, Talk, Write, Share approach (Mackenzie, 2022, see also Chapter 10), and providing timely and effective scaffolds within the context of purposeful meaning-making worked. Eden made significant progress in learning to write, but her most notable development was in her self-belief as a writer and her inclusion into a community of writers.

Figure 13.9   Eden's final text

In this chapter it has been argued that there is a multiplicity of factors that contribute to writing challenges and that children's diverse sociocultural backgrounds and educational histories impact on learning. Inclusive approaches to teaching that maintain purposeful and authentic contexts for writing can engage (or re-engage) these students and can do much to address the educational trajectories of children impacted by material inequities (Comber & Nixon, 2013) or problematic educational histories. Teachers need to be active problem-solvers who commit to the ongoing process of finding approaches that work for the individuals in their class/care. By starting with what children *know and can do*, teachers can provide opportunities for children to be successful with writing, allow extra time and practice, and design timely instruction that connects writing to a child's lifeworld. In doing so, teachers can offer these children a fresh start with writing.

Working with families

The following list contains suggestions for teachers as they engage with parents and caregivers to support children who find learning to write challenging. Importantly, this positions family members as partners, as teachers value and respect parents'/caregivers' insights and knowledge of the child, building collaborative relationships to support children's learning.

1 Ask parents to share drawings and writing samples that their child has completed at home, to add to the evidence base available to assess students' early writing abilities.

2 Ask parents to discuss their child's interest and preferences, as a starting point for co-constructing meaningful, interest-based texts with the child.

3 When describing writing challenges with parents and caregivers, teachers should be careful and considerate in their explanations. While not talking down to parents, the language used should be clear and accessible, identifying specific concerns, along with details of the areas of learning to write that will be focus of future teaching.

4 Provide a range of everyday writing activities that parents/caregivers can complete with their child at home, such as writing shopping lists, leaving notes for siblings, writing text messages, and making greeting cards for family members.

5 Meet regularly with parents and provide updates on the child's progress.

Recommended reading

Dyson, A. H. (2016). *Child Cultures, Schooling and Literacy: Global Perspectives on Children Composing Their Lives*. New York: Routledge.

Graham, S., & Harris, K. (2016). A path to better writing: Evidence-based practices in the classroom. *The Reading Teacher, 69*(4), 359–365. DOI: 10.1002/trtr.1432

Mackenzie, N.M., & Veresov, N. (2013). How drawing can support writing acquisition: text construction in early writing from a Vygotskian perspective. *Australasian Journal of Early Childhood, 38*(4), 22–29.

References

Australian Bureau of Statistics. (2023). *Standards for Statistics on Cultural and Language Diversity*. ABS. https://www.abs.gov.au/statistics/standards/standards-statistics-cultural-and-language-diversity/latest-release

Bazerman, C., Applebee, A., Berninger, V., Brandt, D., Graham, S., Matsuda, P., Murphy, S., Rowe, D., & Schleppegrell, M. (2017). Taking the long view on writing development. *Research in the Teaching of English, 51*(3), 351–360.

Benjamin, S., & Wagner, M. (2021). Developing accomplished writers: Lessons from recent research. *Phi Delta Kappan, 102*(6), 44–49. DOI:10.1177/0031721721998155

Blair, T. R., Rupley, W. J., & Nichols, W. D. (2007). The effective teacher of reading: Considering the "what" and "how" of instruction. *The Reading Teacher, 60*(5), pp. 432–438. DOI:10.1598/RT.60.5.3

Camping, A., Graham, S., & Harris, K. R. (2023). Writing Motives and writing achievement of elementary school students from diverse language backgrounds. *Journal of Educational Psychology*. Advance online publication. DOI:10.1037/edu0000796

Capp, M. J. (2017). The effectiveness of universal design for learning: A meta-analysis of literature between 2013 and 2016. *International Journal of Inclusive Education, 21*(8), 791–807. DOI:10.1080/13603116.2017.1325074

Cappelli, R. (2007). *Mentor texts: Teaching writing through student's literature, K–6*. Portland, Maine: Stenhouse.

Choi, J, & Slaughter, Y. (2021). Challenging discourses of deficit: Understanding the vibrancy and complexity of multilingualism through language trajectory grids. *Language Teaching Research, 25*(1), 80–104.

Christie, F. (2005). *Language Education in the Primary Years*. Sydney, NSW: University of New South Wales Press.

Clay, M. M. (2014). *By Different Paths to Common Outcomes* (2nd ed.). York, Maine: Stenhouse Publishers.

Clay, M. M. (2016). *Literacy Lessons: Designed for individuals. Part 2*. (2nd ed). North Shore, NZ: Heinemann.

Comber, B. (2011). Changing literacies, changing populations, changing places – English teachers' work in an age of rampant standardisation. *English Teaching, 10*(4), 5–22.

Comber, B., & Nixon, H. (2013). Urban renewal, migration and memories: The affordances of place-based pedagogies for developing immigrant students' literate repertoires. *REMIE: Multidisciplinary Journal of Educational Research, 3*(1), 42–68.

Daffern, T. (2015). Helping students become linguistic inquirers: A focus on spelling. *Literacy Learning: The Middle Years, 23*(1), 33.

Deane, P. D. (2023). Assessment in writing and reading In S. Graham, Z. A. Philippakos, & J. Fitzgerald (Eds.), *Writing and Reading Connections: Bridging Research and Classroom Practice*. New York: The Guilford Press.

Donovan, E. (2016). Learning to embrace our stories: Using place-based education practices to inspire authentic writing. *Middle School Journal, 45*(4), 23–31, DOI: 10.1080/00940771.2016.1202657

Dyson, A. H. (2016). Making space for missing childhoods: Implications for theory, policy, and pedagogy. In A. H. Dyson (Ed.), *Child Cultures, Schooling and Literacy: Global Perspectives on Composing Unique Lives* (pp. 167–178). New York: Routledge.

Ehri, L. C. (2014) Orthographic mapping in the acquisition of sight word reading, spelling memory, and vocabulary learning. *Scientific Studies of Reading, 18*(1), 5–21, DOI: 10.1080/10888438.2013.819356

Elkonin, D. B. (1973). U.S.S.R. In J. Downing (Ed.), *Comparative Reading: Cross-National Studies of Behavior and Processes in Reading and Writing* (pp. 551–579). New York: Macmillan.

Elleman, A. M., Steacy, L. M., & Compton, D. L. (2019). The role of statistical learning in word reading and spelling development: More questions than answers. *Scientific Studies of Reading, 23*(1), 1–7.

Galloway, R., Reynolds, B., & Williamson, J. (2020). Strengths-based teaching and learning approaches for children: Perceptions and practices. *Journal of Pedagogical Research, 4*(1), 31–45.

Glasswell, K., & Parr, J. M. (2009). Teachable moments: Linking assessment and teaching in talk around writing. *Language Arts, 86*(5), 352–361.

González, N. (2005). Beyond culture: The hybridity of funds of knowledge. In N. Gonzalis, L. Moll & C. Amanti (Eds.) *Funds of Knowledge* (pp. 29–46). Mahwah, N.J. : L. Erlbaum Associates.

Graham, S. (2018). A revised writer(s)-within-community model of writing, *Educational Psychologist, 53*(4), 258–279, DOI: 10.1080/00461520.2018.1481406

Graham, S. (2022). A walk through the landscape of writing: Insights from a program of writing research. *Educational Psychologist, 57*(2), 55–72. DOI:10.1080/00461520.2021.1951734

Graham, S., Harris, K. R., Fishman, E., Houston, J., Wijekumar, K., Lei, P.-W., & Ray, A. B. (2019). Writing skills, knowledge, motivation, and strategic behavior predict students' persuasive writing performance in the context of robust writing instruction. *The Elementary School Journal, 119*(3), 487–510. DOI:10.1086/701720

Graham, S., Harris, K. R., & Santangelo, T. (2015). Research-based writing practices and the common core: Meta-analysis and meta-synthesis. *The Elementary School Journal, 115*(4), 498–522. DOI:10.1086/681964

Hall, A. H., Toland, M. D., Grisham-Brown, J., & Graham, S. (2014). Exploring interactive writing as an effective practice for increasing Head Start students' alphabet knowledge skills. *Early Childhood Education Journal, 42*(6), 423–430. DOI: 10.1007/s10643-013-0594-5

Harmey S. J., & Rodgers, E. M. (2017). Differences in the early writing development of struggling children who beat the odds and those who did not. *Journal of Education for Students Placed at Risk (JESPAR), 22*(3), 157–177, DOI:10.1080/10824669.2017.1338140

Hashey, A. I., Miller, K. M., & Foxworth, L. L. (2020). Combining universal design for learning and self-regulated strategy development to bolster writing instruction. *Intervention in School and Clinic, 56*(1), 22–28.

Hattie, J. (2009). *Visible Learning: A Synthesis of over 800 Meta-analyses Relating to Achievement.* Abingdon: Routledge.

Heath, S. B. (1983). *Ways with Words: Language, Life, and Work in Communities and Classrooms.* New York: McGraw-Hill.

Hiebert, E. H. (2020). The core vocabulary: The foundation of proficient comprehension. *The Reading Teacher, 73*(6), 757–768.

Hiebert, E. H. (2023). Thinking through research and the science of reading. *Phi Delta Kappan, 105*(2), 37–41. DOI:10.1177/00317217231205940

Limpo, T., & Alves, R. A. (2018). Tailoring multicomponent writing interventions: Effects of coupling self-regulation and transcription training. *Journal of learning disabilities, 51*(4), 381–398. DOI:10.1177/0022219417708170

Limpo, T., & Graham, S. (2020). The role of handwriting Instruction in writers' education, *British Journal of Educational Studies, 68*(3), 311–329, DOI: 10.1080/00071005.2019.1692127

Llopart, M., & Esteban-Guitart, M. (2018). Funds of knowledge in 21st century societies: Inclusive educational practices for under-represented students. A literature review. *Journal of Curriculum Studies, 50*(2), 145–161. DOI:10.1080/00220272.2016.1247913

Luke, A. (2014). On explicit and direct instruction. *Australian Literacy Association Hot Topics,* May, 1–4.

Lyons, C. A. (2003). *Teaching Struggling Readers.* Portsmouth, NH: Heinemann.

Mackenzie, N. M. (2011). From drawing to writing: What happens when you shift teaching priorities in the first six months of school? *Australian Journal of Language and Literacy, 34*(3), 322.

Mackenzie, N. M. (2015). Interactive writing: A powerful teaching strategy. *Practical Literacy: The Early and Primary Years, 20*(3), 36–38.

Mackenzie, N. M. (2022) Multimodal text creation from day 1 with Draw, Talk, Write, Share. *The California Reader (TCR)* 55(1), 9–14.

Mackenzie, N. M., Scull, J., & Bowles, T. (2015). Writing over time: An analysis of texts created by Year One students. *A Publication of the Australian Association for Research in Education, 42*(5), 567–593. DOI:10.1007/s13384-015-0189-9

Mackie, I., & MacLennan, G. (2015). The crisis in Indigenous school attendance in Australia: Towards a materialist solution. *Journal of Critical Realism, 14*(4), 366–380. DOI:10.1179/1476743015Z.00000000075

McCarthy, P. A. (2008). Using sound boxes systematically to develop phonemic awareness. *The Reading Teacher, 62*(4), 346–349.

Mills, K. (2008). Will large-scale assessments raise literacy standards in Australian schools? *Australian Journal of Language and Literacy, 31*(3), 211–225.

Petersen, D. B., Staskowski, M., Spencer, T. D., Foster, M. E., & Brough, M. P. (2022). The effects of a multitiered system of language support on kindergarten oral and written language: A large-scale randomized controlled trial. *Language, Speech & Hearing Services in Schools (Online), 53*(1), 44–68. DOI:10.1044/2021_LSHSS-20-00162

Rose, D. H., & Meyer, A. (2002). *Teaching every student in the digital age: Universal design for learning.* Association for Supervision and Curriculum Development.

Rosenblum, S. (2016). Handwriting features and executive control among children with developmental dysgraphia. *The American journal of occupational therapy, 70*(4_Supplement_1), 7011500041. DOI:10.5014/ajot.2016.70S1-PO4054

Scull, J., Mackenzie, N.M., & Bowles, T. (2020). Assessing early writing: A six-factor model to inform assessment and teaching, *Educational Research for Policy and Practice.* DOI:10.1007/s10671-020-09257-7

Scull, J., & Nicolazzo, M. (2022). Punctuation, sentence structure and paragraphing. In D. Thomas & A. Thomas (Eds.) *Teaching and Learning Primary English,* (pp 207–225). South Melbourne, Victoria: Oxford University Press.

Seidenberg, M. (2017). *Language at the Speed of Sight: How We Read, Why So Many Can't, and What Can Be Done About It.* New York: Basic Books.

Stuart, S., Rinaldi, C., & Higgins-Averill, O. (2011). Agents of Change: Voices of Teachers on Response to Intervention. *International Journal of Whole Schooling, 7*(2), 53–73.

Swain, J., & Cara, O. (2019). The role of family literacy classes in demystifying school literacies and developing closer parent–school relations. *Cambridge Journal of Education, 49*(1), 111–131. https://doi.org/10.1080/0305764X.2018.1461809

Vygotsky, L. (1978). *Mind in Society: The Development of Higher Psychological Processes.* Cambridge, MA: Harvard University Press.

Walshe, R. D. (2015). Writing as process. In J. Turbill, G. Barton, & C. Brock (Eds.), *Teaching Writing in Today's Classrooms: Looking Back to Look Forward* (pp. 13–25). Adelaide, SA: Australian Literacy Educators' Association Ltd.

Wilhelm, J. D. (2012). What must be taught about writing: Five kinds of knowledge and five kinds of composing. *Voices from the Middle, 19*(3), 50–52.

Wing Jan, L., & Taylor, S. (2020). *Write Ways* (5th ed.). Oxford University Press.

Wulff, K., Kirk, C., & Gillon, G. (2008). The effects of integrated morphological awareness intervention on reading and spelling accuracy and spelling automaticity: A case study. *New Zealand Journal of Speech-Language Therapy, 63*(3), 24–40.

Index

Note: Pages in *italics* refer to figures and pages in **bold** refer to tables.

For Product Safety Concerns and Information please contact our EU
representative GPSR@taylorandfrancis.com Taylor & Francis Verlag GmbH,
Kaufingerstraße 24, 80331 München, Germany

Printed and bound by CPI Group (UK) Ltd, Croydon, CR0 4YY
08/06/2025
01897006-0020